Digital Universe

This book is dedicated to my loving wife and life partner

Nanci Eileen Seel

who endured many hours of separation over several years while I worked on the manuscript. She has accomplished more than she is aware to make our academic and creative endeavors a success, while creating a warm home for our family. This book would not have been possible without her support.

*

The book is also dedicated to two scientists and humanists who intimately understood the digital universe from very different perspectives – and were both visionaries that I wish I could have worked with:

Joseph Carl Robnett Licklider
(1915–1990)
computer scientist and intellect augmentation visionary
and
Neil Postman
(1931–2003)
semanticist and astute critic of technology

Peter B. Seel

Digital Universe
The Global Telecommunication Revolution

A John Wiley & Sons, Ltd., Publication

Registered Office
John Wiley & Sons Ltd, The Atrium, Southern Gate, Chichester, West Sussex, PO19 8SQ, UK

Editorial Offices
350 Main Street, Malden, MA 02148-5020, USA
9600 Garsington Road, Oxford, OX4 2DQ, UK
The Atrium, Southern Gate, Chichester, West Sussex, PO19 8SQ, UK

For details of our global editorial offices, for customer services, and for information about how to apply for permission to reuse the copyright material in this book please see our website at www.wiley.com/wiley-blackwell.

Library of Congress Cataloging-in-Publication data is available for this book.
ISBN 9781405153294 (hardback)
ISBN 9781405153300 (paperback)

A catalogue record for this book is available from the British Library.

Set in 10/12.5 pt Century-Book by Thomson Digital, Noida, India
Printed in Malaysia by Ho Printing (M) Sdn Bhd

1   2012

Contents

Preface

This book is about computer-based information and communication technologies and their substantial effects on contemporary life. In more developed nations, digital displays are found everywhere, from small ones on mobile phones to enormous projected ones in movie theaters. The typical worker in the information age spends her or his day engrossed with digital technology and then goes home to yet another set of digital devices for communication, information-processing, and entertainment. These technologies have given society an unparalleled range of tools for communication and connectivity. Anyone in the world with a mobile telephone – presently five billion people of the earth's population of seven billion – can be reached with a few keystrokes. Increasing proportions of these subscribers will have full Internet access as they upgrade to 3G and 4G services, and their tiny mobile phones may be one key solution to bridging the digital divide between the information "haves" and "have nots" on the planet.

This is an unprecedented era in the evolution of humanity. During the lifetime of those born after 1940 there has been an astonishing augmentation of human intellect by online access to all of the world's collective stored information. The barriers to planetary communication presented by the babel of human languages have been diminished by online translation, and their accuracy will improve in this century. Access to this sea of information is not enough – we as a society must have the intellectual tools to make sense of it all and the individual and societal wisdom to use it wisely. Digital devices have improved our access to knowledge, but cannot yet make us wise.

In my own lifetime, I have witnessed the power of television to telecast events in real time as they occur anywhere on the planet. I started my career in educational technology and media production just as the first personal computers appeared on desktops in the workplace. We connected them to VCRs to deliver computer-based training programs linked to related video programs. While working on my doctorate in the early 1990s, I recall a friend dragging me into a computer lab to see something new online called the World Wide Web. At the time we had no clue that a day would come when anyone could create a personal website in less than 30 minutes using templates available at Weebly, Wix, or Google Sites. The notion that a website dedicated to building social relationships would have over 800 million worldwide subscribers would have been hilarious in 1995 – now I access my Facebook page daily to look for new posts from my friends. We live in an era with access to remarkable information and communication technologies that call to mind Arthur C. Clarke's observation that "any sufficiently advanced technology is indistinguishable from magic."

This book is about the global use of these technologies and their effects on society. Some of these effects are beneficial in enhancing human communication and understanding. Others are less benign as they encourage increasingly sedentary lifestyles and technological dependence. The stories of how information and communication technologies evolved to those that we use daily is a fascinating one and form a significant part of this book. The contemplation of the future of these technologies as we augment our personal and collective intelligence is a compelling topic that we will examine in these chapters. My hope is that the exploration of these themes will encourage you to think critically about the technologies that you use today and how they might enhance or detract from human life in the future.

Acknowledgments

This book would not have been completed without the ongoing support of Elizabeth Swayze, my editor at Wiley-Blackwell. She believed in the importance of the topic and provided ongoing encouragement despite several missed deadlines. Boston project editors Julia Kirk and Allison Kostka advised on image rights and permissions and kept the pressure on to acquire the needed clearances. The text was insightfully edited by Janet Moth in the United Kingdom – her suggested revisions were always an improvement.

Useful comments on the text were provided by my longtime friend and co-author on previous book projects, Dr. August E. "Augie" Grant of the University of South Carolina. Paul Saffo and Helayne Waldman provided early guidance for the project. Amy Reitz and Carol Anderson-Reinhardt assisted in editing chapters and their feedback is gratefully appreciated. Nicole Brush translated the correspondence in French with the Mundaneum staff in Mons, Belgium, concerning the photos of Paul Otlet. Professor Don Zimmerman of Colorado State University was helpful in providing support from CSU's Center for Research on Writing and Communication Technologies. Johannah Racz provided an excellent index. I would also like to thank the Public Communication and Technology graduate students enrolled in my Telecommunication seminar for their insightful comments on the text – especially Lisa Gumerman and Rachel Timmons.

Assistance in locating photographs for inclusion in the book was provided by Marianne Heilig for her father's photos, George Despres at MITRE, Lauren Skrabala at RAND, Angela Alvaro at Banco de España, Leonard Kleinrock at UCLA, Dina Basin at SRI, Christine Engelbart and Mary Coppernoll at the Doug Engelbart Institute, Jayne Burke at NYU,

Jan Walker at DARPA, Eric Mankin and Claude Zachary at USC, Shana Darnell at CNN, Sophie Tesauri at CERN, and by photographers Patrick Troud-Chastenet, Irene Fertik, and Gary MacFadden. Peter J. Seel assisted with the simulated texting-while-driving photo. Many images were provided by photographers via the Creative Commons, and this has become a helpful resource for authors and educators worldwide.

Moral support in the long march to the completion of this book was provided by my family, my sister Deborah Ungerleider, and friends Kevin Nolan, Cindy Christen, and Ken Berry. There have been many helping hands in a project of this magnitude and duration – thank you all.

Some Key Terms

AI	artificial intelligence
AR	augmented reality
BBS	Bulletin Board System
CAD	computer-aided design
CBT	computer-based training
CPU	central processing unit
CRT	cathode ray tube
DBS	direct broadcast satellite
DDoS	distributed denial-of-service
DNS	Domain Name System
GUI	graphical user interface
HCI	human–computer interaction/interface
HMD	head-mounted display
IC	integrated circuit
ICT	information and communication technology
IMP	Interface Message Processor
IP	Internet Protocol
ISPs	Internet Service Providers
LAN	local area network
MRAM	magnetoresistive random-access memory
NCP	Network Control Protocol
OS	operating system
P2P	peer-to-peer
TCP	Transmission Control Protocol
TIPs	Terminal Interface Processors
UDC	Universal Decimal Classification

UGC   user-generated content
VoIP   Voice over Internet Protocol
VR   virtual reality
WAN   wide-area network

Part I

Introduction and Framing

1

The Digital Universe: A "Quick-Start" Introduction

Consumer electronic products have become so complex and feature-rich that it is now commonplace to find a brief "quick-start" guide or poster that accompanies the 100+-page manual for a new digital television set, personal computer, or mobile phone. Manufacturers understand that impatient consumers (and that includes most of us) generally skip reading the manual first – that is, until a non-intuitive feature stumps the user. Then we are likely to call the helpline instead of referring to the manual, much to the exasperation of call center agents around the world. On a positive note, quick-start guides provide enough basic information so that we can successfully install the software or power up the device and quickly begin using it.

This brief introduction serves as the "quick-start" guide for this book, which is *not* a manual or a how-to text for functioning in our digital world. Rather, this book provides a tour of the digital universe, tracing the evolution of the age of information from its inception to the crucial period in which we live today.[1] Digital universe is a term that describes a global human environment saturated with intelligent devices (increasingly, wireless ones) that enhance our ability to collect, process, and distribute information. A key purpose of the book is to stimulate readers to think critically about the pervasiveness of information and communication technologies (ICT) in contemporary societies and how they affect our daily lives. The digital universe that we inhabit is complex and becoming more so as technology evolves and becomes more ubiquitous. "Ubiquity" is a key term that will be used frequently throughout the book – it means to be present in every place, or "omnipresent." It is often used as part of a commonly cited technology term, "ubiquitous computing," that describes an environment where computers and intelligent devices are omnipresent. This describes the future of the human environment in societies around the world.

We live in an interesting period in human evolution due to the diffusion of information and communication technologies. The future of machine-assisted communication and related developments in information-processing and artificial intelligence hold great promise for – as well as potential hazards to – human well-being. Information technologies play a central role in when, where, and how we communicate with each other, and their centrality will increase in the future. These technologies are now pervasive in our lives at work and at home, and have blurred the boundaries between these locations to the point where they are often indistinguishable. Digital citizens are connected and "linked in" 24 hours a day – seven days a week. Lewis Mumford made the observation that any widely adopted technology tends to become "invisible" – not in a literal way, but rather in a figurative sense.[2] Television and computer displays have become so ubiquitous that we don't think twice about seeing them in classrooms, airports, taverns, and certainly in the workplace. At times on a university campus it appears that everyone has a mobile phone and is busy either texting a friend or talking with them. This would have been a remarkable sight in 1995, but today it is so commonplace that few notice. We are surrounded by telematic devices to a degree that would have been unimaginable in the 20th century, and they will become even more pervasive as they become more powerful and useful in the 21st.[3]

My hope is that in the process of reading this book you will become a more critical observer of the social use of ICTs, that you will assess the positive and negative consequences of using them, and that you will gain new perspectives in the process that will add richness and depth to your knowledge of human communication and intelligence.

Three Types of Digital Literacy

Stuart Selber provides a useful model for computer literacy that we might apply to our study of the digital universe. He defines three distinct types of literacy (see Table 1.1).[4] First, people in the teleconnected world

Table 1.1   Three types of computer literacy

Category	Metaphor	Subject position[a]	Objective
Functional literacy	Computers as tools	Individuals as users of technology	Effective employment
Critical literacy	Computers as cultural artifacts	Individuals as questioners of technology	Informed critique
Rhetorical literacy	Computers as hypertextual media	Individuals as producers of online content	Reflective praxis

[a] Note that in Selber's text he refers specifically to users as "students." I prefer the term "individuals" as it describes a much larger group – all of those living in the Digital Universe.
Source: Modified from S. A. Selber, *Multiliteracies for a Digital Age* (Carbondale, IL: Southern Illinois University Press, 2004).

should have a **functional literacy** with computers and software as tools to be used in daily life. In the journalism department at the university where I teach computer-mediated communication, we devote extensive time using expensive hardware (and constantly updated software) to teach prospective journalists and communicators how to use these digital tools. In fact, much of what we term computer education around the world is focused on teaching hardware and software usage. However, Selber makes the astute observation that this type of education provides only one aspect of the literacy that humans need to function in a world filled with digital technologies; digital citizens should also be critically and rhetorically literate.

Becoming Critically Literate

The second category in Selber's model is **critical literacy.** It assumes the social embeddedness of technology in all networked global societies and highlights the cultural, economic, and political implications of its use. Critically literate users are "questioners of technology" and its applications, and they examine both the positive and negative implications of technology adoption. This is a key theme in this book and an essential aspect of becoming an educated user of technology.

Positive affirmations of information and communication technologies are omnipresent. Hardware manufacturers, software producers, consumer electronics retailers, and the marketing infrastructure that promotes these products and services all ensure that we are aware of their positive attributes. When an innovative information or communication technology is introduced, the advantages are widely touted as part of the marketing campaign. The attributes are often focused on improving the speed of telecommunication, making an information-processing task more efficient, or a combination of these two factors. As consumers adopt these products, the negative consequences are often slow to emerge.

Selber's critical-cultural perspectives of ICT are focused on the examination of hegemonic power relations in society. These perspectives are significant, especially in terms of studying the ramifications of the digital divides that exist between those who have access to information and those who do not. Economic and political perspectives are also useful in studying technology standardization decisions, among other key policy issues. However, I encourage readers to expand their critical perspectives beyond the economic and political to examine fundamental issues of human communication and its automation. For example, how does the mediation of communication (putting a machine in the middle) affect human expression and discourse? Are humans losing a key aspect of the oral communication tradition valued by scholars such as Harold Innis – or has it been repurposed by the mobile phone and the video camcorder? How have communication technologies affected human storytelling traditions and the stories we tell? The critical component of digital literacy is thus focused on the social effects of the use of information and communication technology. It is a rich field of study that encompasses consumer behavior, human psychology, political science, language, philosophy, economics, and human – computer interaction. Some of the most interesting questions about the human use of technology are investigated by social and computer scientists in these fields. In this text we examine the perspectives of critical observers of technology including Harold Innis, Lewis Mumford, Jacques Ellul, Marshall McLuhan, and Bill McKibben.

One of the more perceptive critics of the social use of technology is the late Dr. Neil Postman, a New York University professor, semanticist, and widely read social critic. Postman is the author of *Technopoly*, an insightful critique of the role that technology plays in advanced information societies.[5] His critical perspectives will be addressed in subsequent chapters, but a few key points are relevant here. For Postman and his critical colleagues, knowledge of the history of the development of technology is essential. One cannot predict the future development trajectory of any information or communication technology without understanding its evolution to the present. The history of computing technology is filled with fascinating stories of how "computers" evolved over time from what used to be a human profession to chips found in billions of intelligent devices. While this text is not a comprehensive history of the evolution of ICT from the telegraph to the present day, I have provided the necessary background to comprehend the social context of these technologies and their effects. It is not ironic that studying the history of the evolution of information and communication technology is inherently humanistic. Stories about the development of telegraphy, telephony, television, and the Internet are fundamentally about human creativity, altruism, greed, and ambition. This historical background is presented as needed in a non-linear fashion that you are likely familiar with in locating information online.

Rhetorical Literacy

The third type of digital literacy referenced by Selber is **rhetorical literacy.** In this context digital technologies are conduits for "hypertextual media" and individuals are viewed as "producers of technology." This viewpoint describes the world of what is termed Web 2.0 today and Web 3.0 of the near future. We take the power of hypertext and hypermedia for granted in a world where they are found in all online environments. The ability to seamlessly and easily link related content online has transformed the human processing and distribution of information.

The concept of linking information and building webs of knowledge was espoused by Belgian bibliographer Paul Otlet and integrated into his Mundaneum project in Brussels in the early 20th century.[6] Additional detail is provided about Otlet and his ideas in Chapter 6; however, an introduction is appropriate in the context of rhetorical literacy. Otlet's vision was to create a massive catalog of all human knowledge and creative work and then provide access to it using electrical communication. An inquiry from a user on any topic would be directed to the Mundaneum in Brussels by telegraph or telephone, where the staff would access millions of index cards (much like a library card catalog of that era) to locate the answer. The return response to the requester was communicated by telegraph or telephone. Otlet's dream in the 1930s was to use a then-new technology known as television to relay the information (with related visuals) back to the requester. His visionary scheme exists online today in the form of Wikipedia, Google, and the Web.

Vannevar Bush in 1945 expanded on Otlet's Mundaneum concept with an idea for an electromechanical system for linking information (both textual and visual) in his Memex.[7] The Memex would have recorded and stored information on the then-new medium of microfilm, but the unique concept in Bush's device was a system of switches that would record information about the linkages made between various forms of related content. He termed these linkages "associative trails," and the concept was a harbinger of what is known today as online hypertext. The flaw in Bush's concept was the lack of a universal cataloging system similar to Otlet's that would allow random access to the information sought. Bush's "As We May Think" article in *Atlantic Monthly* and *Life* magazines was very influential in shaping the information-access dreams of a generation of computer scientists in the mid-20th century.[8]

Among them was information scientist Ted Nelson, who coined the term "hypertext" in the 1960s as a means of describing "branching and responding" textual links between related information.[9] As part of his Project Xanadu[10] to make all human information accessible to all on Earth, he also described "hypermedia," which is related content not constrained to be text, or what we know at present as "multimedia." In the early 1990s Tim Berners-Lee used the fundamental concepts of hypertext and hypermedia to construct his "Mesh" system of linked documents that evolved into the World Wide Web.[11]

In the era of Web 2.0, citizens of the digital universe are not just passive downloaders of digital online media, but increasingly are active producers of new content. This video, text, music, art, and sound content may be digitized and uploaded to the Web as linked hypermedia. The creation and communication of user-generated content (UGC) online has transformed a digital universe dominated by computer scientists and highly specialized Web developers into a global society where anyone can publish anything – that governments will allow.

Cybernetics

Another key aspect of digital literacy is deciphering the source of key terms related to information and communication technology. The archaic meaning of "communication" was to literally hand a message from person to person, as would a messenger in ancient Greece. One might think that "broadcasting" applies only to radio and television, when its etymology is derived from an agrarian term meaning "to sow." Before the invention of mechanical planting machines, farmers would walk through their fields and "broadcast" the seeds for a new crop by scattering them by hand. Today electronic messages are "scattered" through society through the air by phone, radio, and television and via fiber-optic cables on land and under the sea.

A key term for the digitally literate is "cybernetic." It is derived from the Greek term "kybernetes," meaning a pilot, steersman, or governor.[12] The modern derivation is that cybernetics involves feedback mechanisms providing command-and-control functions in closed systems. Cybernetic perspectives assist in understanding complex systems that include circular causal chains that make up feedback loops that regulate the functioning of a system. The study of cybernetics applies to many diverse disciplines, but the focus in this text is on its relevance to information and communication systems.

The root "cyber" has been embedded into many commonly used terms involving ICTs, such as "cyberspace" (e.g., the digital universe), "cyberpunk" as a style of postmodern literature, and "cyborg" to describe a bionic blend of human and machine. Cybernetics should not be construed as applying only to machine-based systems. All humans rely on cybernetic feedback loops in our bodies to manage vital functions such as respiration and blood circulation – and especially for communication with others.

We learn how to acquire new digital knowledge and skills through elaborate feedback loops with friends and family and with formal instruction. You try your hand at taking digital photos and then sharing them online with friends. You receive useful feedback about your photographs and modify your image acquisition and processing skills accordingly. In a Web 2.0 universe the feedback loops may be immediate and personal ("I don't like my picture taken at the party last weekend – please delete it") or it may be distant and more impersonal (bidding on a digital camera on eBay). These interactive mechanisms are at the heart of related Web 2.0 technologies such as Wikipedia. With social networking and other Web 2.0 tools you can expand your feedback options and use them to acquire new knowledge and skills, especially those concerned with new telecommunication technologies. This text provides the background needed to understand the evolution of these technologies and then encourages you to think critically about how they affect human life today and in the future.

Navigating this Text

This book is divided into five main sections:

Part I. Introduction and Framing – Chapters 1, 2, 3
Part II. Internet and Web History – Chapters 4, 5, 6
Part III. Telecommunication and Media Convergence – Chapters 7 and 8
Part IV. Internet Control, Cyberculture, and Dystopian Views – Chapters 9, 10, 11
Part V. New Communication Technologies and the Future – Chapters 12, 13, 14

As noted above, this text is written for non-linear access so chapters can be read in random order if desired. However, it is probably best to read the Moore's law and critical perspectives chapters (2 and 3) first, since key concepts introduced there are elaborated upon in subsequent chapters. Also, the history chapters (4–6) will be more coherent if read in sequential order.

Chapter 2 defines Moore's law and explains its centrality to technologies in the digital universe. Its implications for telecommunication, ubiquitous computing, and intelligent devices are examined in the context of their effects on daily life. The chapter concludes with thoughts on the sustainability of Moore's law in this century. Chapter 3 provides the critical analysis of the digital universe that was alluded to in Selber's literacy model. The perspectives of critics of technology such as Jacques Ellul and Neil Postman are examined in regard to their application to information and communication technologies. The pro-social and pathological effects of living in the age of information are discussed – with an emphasis on the role that speed and efficiency play in the adoption of new communication technologies.

Part II is focused on the creation of the Internet and the World Wide Web. Chapter 4 reviews the origins of the Internet in the Cold War and the influential role that computer scientist J. C. R. Licklider played in its development. The central role of the US Department of Defense in creating the Advanced Research Projects Agency (ARPA) and its ARPANET highlight the controversy over the motivation for developing the first nationwide data network. Chapter 5 analyzes the evolution of the ARPANET into the Internet between 1980 and 1990. The contributions of key innovators such as Vinton Cerf and Robert Kahn (developing TCP/IP and other key network protocols), Ted Nelson (the concept of hypertext as a linking tool), and Doug Engelbart (creating interface technologies) are discussed in the context of the creation of the global Internet. Chapter 6 introduces Paul Otlet and his creation of the Mundaneum in Belgium between 1910 and 1934 – a precursor of the World Wide Web 60 years before its creation. The role of Tim Berners-Lee is examined in his conceptualization of the merger of hypertext, TCP/IP, and a domain name system into a universal document accession system he called "Mesh" (and the world now knows as the Web). The chapter concludes with an analysis of what we call Web 2.0 and how it might evolve in the coming decade into Web 3.0.

Part III begins with Chapter 7 and a review of the development of telegraphic communication systems in Europe and North America and their linkage via undersea cables. These quickly spanned the globe and led to the concept of a "wired world." As the wires were converted from copper to fiber-optic cables in the past 20 years, these often overlooked connections made possible the global Internet. The "flat world" described by Thomas Friedman is defined by these connections and how they facilitate the role of telecommunication in outsourcing digital work and in the creation of global teams by public and private organizations. Chapter 8 focuses on digital convergence in the shift from analog to digital media. The benefits of media convergence are examined, along with its negative effects on existing media such as newspapers and radio and television broadcasting.

Part IV begins with Chapter 9, on the battles over public and private control of the Internet. The role of e-commerce is studied in the context of this struggle for control over the past 20 years. In Chapter 10 we examine global cyberculture and the role of digital telecommunication in fostering this new culture. The perspectives of media critic Marshall McLuhan are examined in light of what he called the electronically connected "global village." Digital divide issues are studied in terms of disparities in access to these digital services in various parts of the world. The emergence of global social networks is an outgrowth of the bonds formed by early pioneers on the Internet that transcended space and time. However, there are attempts by some governments to limit free access to the Internet, and these are examined in the context of national priorities that promote censorship and the construction of intentional barriers to the free flow of information. Chapter 11 deals with the "dark side" of the Internet. It examines online privacy issues and the threats to personal privacy and data security posed by hackers, viruses, and Webbots. It concludes with an outline of several simple steps that we can take to protect our privacy online and shield personal information from unwanted disclosure.

The final section – Part V – is focused on the evolution of new telecommunication and digital technologies that will affect global societies in coming decades. Chapter 12 examines the blended universe of wired and wireless communication technologies. Television has morphed from a wireless broadcast technology to a wired one via cable services and with online content streamed over the Internet using IPTV. Telephones are now mobile television viewers with content streamed live from the Internet or wirelessly accessed from local broadcasters. Mobile phones provide the always on, always accessible means of staying in contact with family and friends. The mobility of these services means that there will be no "away" from ICTs, and the chapter analyzes the social ramifications of being continuously connected. Chapter 13 explores the creation of virtual worlds that humans can inhabit through participation in online games. Computer games have come of age in the past two decades and have achieved a remarkable level of realism that makes active participation compelling. The chapter will also examine new applications of immersive "augmented realities" that superimpose computer-generated images over related scenes in the material world.

The book concludes with Chapter 14, which provides several perspectives on the future of the digital universe. The immediate future is bright as Moore's law drives down the cost of digital tools while greatly improving their power and our access to them. As the digital divide shrinks, more humans will have access to these tools to connect and work with others. Some future ICT scenarios are utopian – that humans will co-evolve with technology and adopt the best aspects of machine intelligence and memory. Others are dystopian – that machine intelligence will eventually surpass that of humans and our role in the future may be that of maintenance staff for the cybernetic world. The reality will likely be somewhere between these polar visions. Why spend time thinking about these futures? Each of you will spend your lifetime living there, so giving some critical thought to these scenarios may be instructive. I hope you enjoy this journey through the digital universe as a virtual road map for connected life in the decades ahead.

notes

1. By "we," I am referring to citizens of the planet Earth who use information and communication technologies. This would include most of the 90 percent of the world's population that will have mobile phone access (but not necessarily possess one) by 2020.
2. L. Mumford, *Technics and Civilization* (New York: Harcourt, 1934).

3. "Telematics" is another term used to describe information and communication technologies.
4. S. A. Selber, *Multiliteracies for a Digital Age* (Carbondale, IL: Southern Illinois University Press, 2004).
5. N. Postman, *Technopoly: The Surrender of Culture to Technology* (New York: Vintage, 1992). Neil Postman died in 2003 at the age of 72, a loss to his community at New York University and to all who value his perceptive contributions to education, the study of semantics, and critical views of technology.
6. P. Otlet, *International Organisation and Dissemination of Knowledge: Selected Essays of Paul Otlet*, ed. W. B. Rayward (London: Elsevier, 1990).
7. V. Bush, "As We May Think," *Atlantic Monthly* (July 1945), 101–8. "Memex" is a portmanteau of memory and index.
8. Ibid. The article was republished with illustrations in the September 10, 1945 issue of *Life* magazine.
9. T. H. Nelson, *Literary Machines: The Report on, and of, Project Xanadu Concerning Word Processing, Electronic Publishing, Hypertext, Thinkertoys, Tomorrow's Intellectual Revolution, and Certain Other Topics Including Knowledge, Education and Freedom* (Sausalito, CA: Mindful Press, 1981).
10. Ibid.
11. T. Berners-Lee, *Weaving the Web: The Original Design and Ultimate Destiny of the World Wide Web by its Inventor* (New York: HarperOne, 1999).
12. The Greek word *kybernan* is also the source of the English word "govern."

2

Thinking About Moore's Law

Few phenomena in the digital universe have had such a profound effect on information and communication technology as Moore's law. It can be stated succinctly in two different ways:

- "Transistor density on integrated circuits doubles about every two years." – The Intel Corporation[1]
- "The size of each transistor on an integrated circuit chip will be reduced by 50 percent every twenty-four months." – Raymond Kurzweil[2]

The doubling of computer central processing unit (CPU) speed and storage capacity every two years since 1958 has dramatically affected every type of digital technology. This doubling presents an exponential growth rate in computing and storage capacity that is astonishing for its longevity over half a century (see Figure 2.2). Consider any device that you use daily that has a digital processor or storage chip in it – a mobile phone, portable music player, digital camera, tablet computer, television set, or any other device that can process or store digital information. The simultaneous miniaturization and exponential expansion of the processing power of these chips makes it possible for a mobile phone

Digital Universe: The Global Telecommunication Revolution, First Edition. Peter B. Seel.
© 2012 Peter B. Seel. Published 2012 by Blackwell Publishing Ltd.

Figure 2.1   Gordon Moore in front of a projected and greatly enlarged silicon wafer containing many integrated circuits. "Moore once computed that if the automobile industry followed a similar doubling pattern as ICs [integrated circuits], cars today would get 100,000 miles per gallon, travel at speeds of millions of miles per hour, and be so inexpensive that it would cost less to buy a Rolls-Royce than to park it downtown for a day. However, a friend pointed out that the car 'would only be a half-inch long and a quarter-inch high,' and not very useful at those dimensions." (Michael Kannellos, 2005) *Photo*: Copyright © 2005 Intel Corporation.

to include a music player, Internet browser, video camera, and GPS location finder. Next time you use your mobile phone, consider its power as an information-processing device and think about the reaction of Alexander Graham Bell if he could see it demonstrated.

Dr. Yale Patt, a computer scientist at the University of Texas at Austin, addresses Moore's law in his lectures by asking the following question of the audience:

What is Moore's law about?
(a) Physics?
(b) Computer process technology?
(c) Computer micro-architecture?
(d) Psychology?

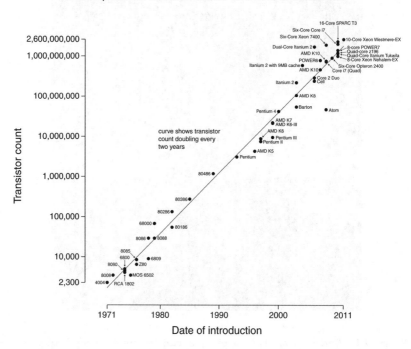

Figure 2.2   Moore's law holding true. *Source*: Moore's law diagram by Wgsimon.

The correct answer, according to Dr. Patt, is (d) – Psychology.[3] His thesis is that Moore's law has become a self-fulfilling prophecy. Designers of integrated circuits (and their managers) at Intel, Hitachi, AMD, and other chip manufacturers have psychologically adapted to the expectation that there will be a new generation of chips every 18–24 months with double the capacity of previous versions. If Intel does not deliver new chips with this improved capacity, its executives know that AMD or other competitors will.

As a pattern of growth, few natural systems can sustain exponential doubling for long. Resource constraints, environmental degradation, or other natural limits inhibit growth. These limitations have long led critics to suggest that Moore's law was unsustainable, but they overlooked that this is a human-created technology based on the fundamental properties of silicon, not an organic phenomenon. The technological implications of Moore's law are not all sweetness and light. The computer you bought two years ago is now worth less than half of what you paid for it – assuming that you can find anyone who would want to buy it in your community. The only real options are to donate it or recycle the components. There is a planned obsolescence associated with Moore's law that is very good news for chip makers, computer manufacturers, and software producers – and not such great news for consumers. We will return to this aspect of Moore's law below, but it is worth contemplating in terms of developing a sense of critical literacy discussed in the introductory chapter.

The Prediction

In 1965, then-Fairchild Semiconductor executive Gordon Moore published a short article in the April issue of *Electronics* magazine entitled "Cramming more components onto integrated circuits."[4] In the article, Moore predicted that within a decade (by 1975), evolving silicon chip technology would permit the fabrication of integrated circuits (ICs) with 65,000 components (transistors) on a single chip. Given the state of IC manufacturing in 1965, his then-startling prediction suggested that the number of transistors on a chip would double each year in the decade between 1965 and 1975. Moore included a table (see Figure 2.3) that featured a logarithmic scale demonstrating this doubling of components

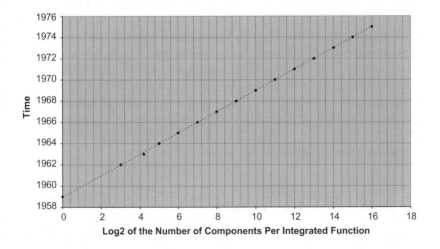

Figure 2.3   Moore's law re-plotted. *Source*: Modified by the author after original in *Electronics*, 38/8 (April 19, 1965).

on a chip from 1962 to 1965 and then extending this plot into the future. I have reversed the X and Y scales in the version in Figure 2.3 (with time on the Y scale) for the sake of clarity. Note that this calculation was based on just four confirmed data points (1962 to 1965), and was quite a bold prognostication given the predicted doubling of components at yearly intervals. Yet Moore's prediction for this remarkable technological feat proved to be prescient, even if the doubling intervals were to be closer to 18 to 24 months.

Three years later, Moore left his position of director of the research and development laboratories at Fairchild to start a new company with partners Robert Noyce and Andrew Grove. Its name was short and memorable – the Intel Corporation. In 1975, Moore revised the time frame for chip evolution from one-year intervals to two years in a speech he gave to the Institute of Electrical and Electronics Engineers (IEEE).[5] For several decades Moore modestly declined the honor of having the law named after him and attributes the name to California Institute of Technology computer scientist Carver Mead.[6] It was to provide a pre-scient method of reference for the exponential growth in the power of integrated circuits over the following 40 years. This doubling phenome-non also applies to memory chips such as in flash drives,[7] and has proved accurate for the microprocessors that are at the heart of all personal computers. Computer users understand and appreciate the improve-ments in processing speed in CPU chips, especially those developed in the last two decades. Other uses of IC technology are less obvious. Today's automobiles, for example, have a number of computer chips that govern critical functions such as fuel injection, safety features, and electronics that can sync to a mobile phone for hands-free use. Many models include a wireless keyless entry and ignition system that uses digital technology to allow access to the vehicle and the ability to start it. In high-theft urban areas this is an important feature to consumers, despite the added cost. If your vehicle is stolen, electronic devices hidden inside can enable police to track and recover your car. At the time of Moore's prediction, this technology was imaginable only in James Bond films.

Implications for Computing and the Digital Universe

Computer scientists commonly refer to "ubiquitous computing" to de-scribe a world that is filled with "intelligent" devices. The increase in integrated circuit speed and power, combined with the dramatic drop in price per transistor, has made it possible to embed powerful chips in almost every device or tool that uses electricity. These embedded devices make it possible to add a remarkable variety of intelligent functions to what were previously "dumb" tools and appliances. The telephone is an ideal example. What was previously a very simple device that could be used intuitively by raising the handset to one's ear and then dialing the number with a rotary wheel or a keypad is now a much more complex instrument. My camera-equipped, quad-mode mobile phone that is also is a digital video player came with a 79-page instruction book. In the future, mobile phone users may have to take a short course in phone feature programming to learn how to use all the functions built into their mobile phone/computer/camera, not to mention the thousands of downloadable apps available.

There was a time when a person could walk into someone's home that they had never visited before and easily make a phone call, turn on the television, or perform a simple task such as boiling a kettle of water. We are confronted today by appliances with astonishing capabilities and with equally complex operational learning curves. I would like to suggest a term that describes this trend in the evolutionary design of previously simple-to-operate appliances – "complexification." The future will see greater applications of artificial intelligence (AI) in product design to ease the stress on users, but as the cliché states, "there is a great future for complexity." The challenge for engineers and product designers in coming decades will be to create devices that have great functional power, but are also easy to operate.

The implications of Moore's law for citizens of nations that use advanced digital technology will be significant in the future. Since Internet access is available to 25 percent of the global population of over seven billion, this includes a significant portion of humanity.[8] Chip performance will increase while device prices will continue to fall. Storage of digital content on chips is now so cheap that electronic devices can have enormous storage capacity, especially phones and cameras. Chips will be embedded in a wide range of products that will have remarkable levels of intelligence. The complexification of the telematic world will increase at a steady pace, with happy consumers if these devices are easy to use and maintain, and not so pleased if they are not.

In addition to complexification, concern over the diminishment of privacy in this digital universe will become a significant issue in many nations of the world. With cameras embedded in every mobile phone and surveillance systems observing almost every commercial transaction, there are already well-publicized concerns about the negative effect on personal privacy. Many health clubs in the United States have banned mobile phones after publicity about cases where less-than-scrupulous club members took photos in locker rooms and then distributed them online. We will examine these and related digital privacy issues in Chapter 11.

Technological Determinism

Technological Determinism is a point of view that a society's technology determines its history, social structure, and cultural values. It is a negative term that has been used to criticize those who credit technology as a central governing force behind social and cultural change as overly "reductionist." Author Thomas Friedman, in his book *The World is Flat* (2005), freely admits to being a technological determinist, stating that "capabilities create intentions" in regard to the role that technology plays in shaping how we live.[9] Examples he cites are the Internet facilitating global e-commerce, and work-flow technologies (and the Internet) making possible the off-shoring and outsourcing of disaggregated tasks around the world. Friedman states:

> The history of economic development teaches this over and over: If you can do it, you must do it, otherwise your competitors will [and] ... there is a whole new universe of things that companies, countries, and individuals can and must do to thrive in a flat world.[10]

It is rare to find an observer of modern life willing to go on record in this regard, and I commend Friedman's courage in doing so. His perspective is worth our critical consideration. While it is clear that a wide range of factors influence social change, including culture, economics, and politics, among many others, Friedman advances technology to a privileged position due to its ubiquity in contemporary life, and he is correct in his assessment that "capabilities create intentions." The development of the MP3 compression format for music files makes a good case study. When recorded music was only available on vinyl records, there were few options available for copying songs. As technology evolved, one could make a cassette tape of a record, but the copy was of poor quality and one had to fast forward and rewind the tape to find a desired song. Once digital technology appeared with the advent of music on compact discs, users could "rip" individual songs onto a computer's hard drive as digital files.

Copyright holders such as record companies weren't immediately concerned since users had to buy the CD to copy the music. However, with the rapid spread of the MP3 file format[11] users of this technology developed large libraries of songs in this format. It wasn't long until a company, Napster, developed a unique technology for users of their service to copy music files to their own computer from another user that had the desired songs. Then another user could copy it to his or her computer, and so on. By the time the recording industry sued to shut down Napster and similar services, the genie – and the music – were out of the bottle. Without the widespread adoption of the MP3 digital file format and the development of successful peer-to-peer (P2P) file-sharing technology, music piracy would not have been as simple and easy to accomplish.

The legal system and related government legislation are almost universally *reactive* to technological innovation. Digital technology industries are developing innovations at speeds linked to Moore's law, and the legal system struggles unsuccessfully to keep pace. Despite court decisions that shut down Napster (until they adopted a fee-for-music model) and similar P2P services, US music industry sales peaked at $14.5 billion in 1999 and declined to $10 billion in 2008.[12] Paid digital downloads have increased since 2005, but part of the overall reduction in revenue to the US music industry can be attributed to continued widespread file-sharing by music fans. Another trend that is negatively affecting music sales is the streaming of music on Internet sites such as Pandora, Spotify, and Imeem.[13] Why buy music if you can listen to hundreds of diverse genres online for free?

Despite the technology-driven patterns in IC manufacturing and music piracy, there are problems with the perspective that technology itself determines adoption. The primary concern with adopting a worldview that a society's technology "determines its cultural values, social structure or history" is that it is inherently reductionistic. Some social scientists would argue that the determinism arrow should flow in the opposite direction – that cultural values, social structures, economics, and history determine which technologies are created and adopted. This view, while more comprehensive, fails to give sufficient weight to the unforeseen consequences of the diffusion of new technologies. These technologies are not created in a social vacuum – many are only introduced after years of research and development driven by detailed economic analysis of potential markets. The complication arises from the unintended consequences of the use of the new tool, product, or service. The irony is that, short of the unlikely near-term development of time travel, we cannot know what these unforeseen consequences might be. Nanotechnology, one of the key technologies that are facilitating the creation of ever more powerful CPUs on a chip, has raised questions about its safety when combined with dramatic advances in genetic engineering and biotechnology.[14] We'll analyze these concerns in Chapter 14 on the future of the digital universe.

The Rise of Nanotechnology and the Future of Moore's Law

What is the future of Moore's law? How much longer can it be sustained in the face of the fundamental laws of physics? Many scientists have predicted the imminent death of Moore's law over the past 20 years, stating that there are fundamental physical limitations to how many small circuits can be compressed on a chip before current leakage (and related heat build-up) cause it to fail to function as designed. Gordon Moore acknowledged these limitations in 2005:

> In terms of size [of transistor] you can see that we're approaching the size of atoms which is a fundamental barrier, but it'll be two or three generations before we get that far – but that's as far out as we've ever been able to see. We have another 10 to 20 years before we reach a fundamental limit. By then they'll be able to make bigger chips and have transistor budgets in the billions.[15]

For now, the development of nanotechnology has extended the life of Moore's law by developing methods for the creation of ever-smaller circuits. Nanotechnology is the design and production of devices (and systems) at a scale that strains human comprehension. Dimensions are measured in nanometers – eight to ten atoms equal one nanometer. At this scale, a human hair is about 70,000 to 80,000 nanometers in width. The National Nanotechnology Initiative in the US defines it as follows: "Nanotechnology is the understanding and control of matter at dimensions of roughly 1 to 100 nanometers, where unique phenomena enable novel applications."[16]

Nanotechnology and creative electrical engineering have enabled the fabrication of ever-smaller electronic circuits. Early in 2007, chip manufacturer Intel announced that it had succeeded in developing an innovative type of integrated circuit that utilized new metallic alloys that facilitated the creation of very tiny circuits on a chip.[17] At the time, the state of the art in chip fabrication defined circuits with a dimension of 90 nanometers (if one is counting, that is equivalent to 900 atoms in width). Intel announced that 22-nanometer circuits would be available in 2011 for their chips for CPUs in desktop, notebook, and tablet computers.[18] Smaller is better, and Toshiba has developed a prototype chip with 15 nanometer circuits. This level of miniaturization would yield low-cost 100 GigaByte portable flash drives. The creation of new IBM-developed technologies for IC design such as one-atom-thick "graphene" carbon lattices and silicon "nanowires" placed vertically on a chip have the potential to significantly expand the number of circuits on a chip in the near future.[19]

Moore's law marches on long after many pundits had predicted its demise. The continued doubling every two years of the number of transistors on a chip indicates that the processing power and storage capacity of these chips will continue to double as well. Chip manufacturers are fabricating CPUs with multiple processors to reduce heat loads and improve processing speeds in computers and other digital devices. Intel chief technical officer Justin Rattner predicts that in the next ten years CPU chips will expand from dual and quad core designs to chips with 100 cores or more.[20] The emerging design challenge for computer scientists and engineers is creating operating systems and programs that can utilize the immense parallel processing power of these powerful chips. As these design and programming challenges are solved, the fundamental components of the tablet computer, the mobile phone/video camera/music player, and the widescreen 3-D digital display will have greatly enhanced digital processing power. In the digital universe of the near future, we will see powerful chips embedded in every conceivable electronic product, and perhaps in ourselves as well.

Notes

1. Intel Corporation, *Moore's Law: Raising the Bar* (2005). Retrieved February 12, 2009, from http://download.intel.com/museum/Moores_Law/Printed_-Materials/Moores_Law_Backgrounder.pdf.
2. R. Kurzweil, *The Age of Spiritual Machines; Glossary* (2009). Retrieved February 13, 2009, from http://www.kurzweilai.net/meme/frame.html?main=/articles/art0273.html.
3. Dr. Yale Patt, personal communication, April 17, 2007.
4. G. E. Moore, "Cramming More Components Onto Integrated Circuits," *Electronics* 38/8 (April 19, 1965). Retrieved February 12, 2009, from http://download.intel.com/research/silicon/moorespaper.pdf.

5. G. E. Moore, "Progress in Digital Integrated Electronics," *Technical Digest*, proceedings from the 1975 International Electron Devices Meeting of the IEEE (1975), 11–13. Retrieved February 12, 2009, from http://download. intel.com/museum/Moores_Law/Articles-Press_Releases/Gordon_Moore_ 1975_Speech.pdf.

6. M. Kanellos, "Moore Says that Nanoelectronics Face Tough Challenges," *CNet News* (March 9, 2005). Retrieved February 10, 2009, from http://news. cnet.com/Moore-says-nanoelectronics-face-tough-challenges/2100-1006_3- 5607422.html).

7. S. Franssila, *Introduction to Microfabrication* (New York: Wiley, 2004).

8. Internet World Stats. Retrieved March 31, 2010, from http://www.internet- worldstats.com/stats.htm.

9. T. E. Friedman, *The World Is Flat: A Brief History of the 21st Century* (New York: Farrar, Straus & Giroux, 2005), 374.

10. Ibid.

11. MP3 is an acronym for the MPEG-1 audio layer 3 compression scheme used to shrink music files by 90 percent.

12. D. MacMillan, "The Music Industry's New Internet Problem," *Business Week* (March 3, 2009). Retrieved September 19, 2009, from http://www.business- week.com/technology/content/mar2009/tc2009035_000194.htm.

13. Ibid.

14. B. Joy, "Why the Future Doesn't Need Us," *Wired* 8/4 (April 2000). Retrieved February 14, 2009, from http://www.wired.com/wired/archive/8.04/joy. html.

15. M. Dubash, "Moore's Law Is Dead, Says Gordon Moore," *Techworld* (April 13, 2005). Retrieved February 12, 2009, from http://www.techworld.com/ opsys/news/index.cfm?NewsID=3477.

16. National Nanotechnology Initiative, *What Is Nanotechnology?* Retrieved February 14, 2009, from http://www.nano.gov/html/facts/whatIsNano.html.

17. J. Markoff, "Intel Says Chips Will Run Faster, Using Less Power," *New York Times* (January 27, 2007). Retrieved February 14, 2009, from http://www. nytimes.com/2007/01/27/technology/27chip.html.

18. N. Patel, "Intel Announces 22 nm Chips for 2011," *Engadget* (September 22, 2009). Retrieved February 6, 2011, from http://www.engadget.com/2009/09/ 22/intel-announces-22nm-chips-for-2011/.

19. K. Bourzac, "Graphene Transistors that Can Work at Blistering Speeds," *Technology Review* (February 5, 2010). Retrieved February 6, 2011, from http://www.technologyreview.com/computing/24482/?a=f.

20. D. Lyons, "Moore's Law Doesn't Matter," *Newsweek* (August 24, 2009), 55.

3

Critical Perspectives

E-mail and the Age of Interruption

The effects of Moore's law in creating ever more powerful information-processing and communication devices over the past half-century has led to a dramatic expansion of the use of these tools in daily life. Few of us living and working in the digital universe could contemplate daily life without our mobile phones, MP3 players, netbooks, and tablet computers. These devices have become ubiquitous and are now so commonplace that we pay little attention to their users – unless they bump into us while composing a text message. We no longer assume that a lone person walking along staring into space and having a loud conversation with an unseen person is mentally ill. He is merely using his mobile phone with a wireless headset. What is remarkable is the relatively rapid diffusion of mobile devices used in public places since 2001, and technology savants predict that the explosion in the number of mobile communication technologies will only increase in this century.

While these mobile telecommunication devices are highly visible, I would argue that other digital communication technologies have had an equal or greater effect on networked societies. Few have evolved as quickly or been as widely adopted in information-oriented societies as e-mail and its cousins texting and twittering.[1] While text messaging used to be the teenage communication medium of choice, adults of all ages are

Digital Universe: The Global Telecommunication Revolution, First Edition. Peter B. Seel.
© 2012 Peter B. Seel. Published 2012 by Blackwell Publishing Ltd.

now texting instead of calling or e-mailing. E-mail is seen by many users (and that includes myself) as both a remarkable communication tool and a daily curse. On the plus side, a single important e-mail message can be sent with a single click to a list of hundreds, thousands, or even millions of people at once. On the negative side, a single spam advertising message can be sent with a single click to lists of hundreds, thousands, or even millions of people at once. Teleconnected people swim daily in an ever-rising sea of relevant messages and irrelevant spam. Software firm Symantec estimated that 80 percent of U.S. e-mail traffic in 2007 was spam.[2] Obviously they have a vested interest in this market since they sell spam-filtering software, but even a conservative estimate would indicate that the use of e-mail has turned into a massive cat-and-mouse game of attempting to outwit global spammers.

Perhaps only a telephone conversation can equal e-mail or a text message in terms of communication speed and efficiency. E-mail is the clear technology of choice when a written record of communication needs to be generated, when there are multiple recipients to a message, or if a digital document needs to be attached to the message. I routinely spend two to three hours every working day writing e-mail messages and replying to them. This includes a significant amount of time deleting spam messages inviting me to make millions of dollars in Nigerian financial dealings, refinance my home, view scandalous photos of celebrities, or contribute to innumerable social causes. All of the unfiltered spam has to be screened and deleted, lest an important message be overlooked. I've stopped looking at the extensive list of filtered messages that is e-mailed to me daily in a form of institutionally supported spam – it is simply too long. I can only hope that some valid messages are not tossed out with the spam.

The widespread adoption of e-mail is part of its accursed blessing. In large organizations such as the university where I teach and conduct research, e-mail is *the* primary means of asynchronous communication. It also means that any unread personal e-mail will pile up in the university's e-mail servers (several powerful computers with significant storage capacity) until it is either read or deleted. One of the major disincentives to taking a long vacation is the mountain of unanswered e-mail that accumulates in one's absence. Dealing with this backlog requires that one return from a vacation a day early to sort through the important messages. Another option is to take along a laptop or netbook so that e-mail can be read and answered while taking time to get away from the office. The faint buzzing sound we hear is back-to-nature philosopher Henry David Thoreau spinning in his grave.

The tradeoff for the speed, convenience, and efficiency of e-mail is the time required each day to read and reply to a long list of messages. It is estimated that professionals in the U.S. spend 40 percent of their time at work reading and sending e-mail[3] – extrapolate this figure to the millions of networked professionals around the world and this global time commitment to computer-mediated communication borders on the astonishing. Another significant downside to e-mail is deciding what to do with all of it. The greater the e-mail volume, the more time-consuming these decisions become. Since I have a packrat tendency to keep almost all non-spam e-mails in the event that I might need to retrieve an essential message in the future, I often need to sort related messages into dedicated storage folders.[4] I doubt that I could do my job efficiently without e-mail as it is so central to fast and efficient communication between faculty, students, staff, and administrators. For students it provides a usually reliable method of reaching faculty with questions about course assignments, deadlines, and grades. One interesting twist to the speed and efficiency of e-mail is that, because it can be used in a synchronous way much like a telephone call, students accustomed to a daily world filled with instant messages sometimes become upset when a reply to their e-mail is not immediate. This is a significant negative aspect of the increasing speed of information-processing and transmission linked to Moore's law – *because a task can be accomplished quickly using digital technology, it becomes an expectation that it always will be.*

Another negative aspect to this always-on networked environment is that of interruption. Author Thomas Friedman calls this era the "Age of Interruption" and cites former Microsoft executive Linda Stone as elaborating that these interruptions create an environment of "continuous partial attention."[5] He had this insight when he was traveling in the Amazon jungle in Brazil in 2006 and was disconnected for four days from both mobile phone and Internet access. As someone who lives his life as a journalist and author typically connected 24/7, he found this period of disconnection strangely refreshing. Habitually multitasking in a communication- and information-saturated working environment in New York, he became aware that he was providing only "continuous partial attention" to his environment. When he was immersed in the jungle – without the media connections – he realized how fragmented his urban attention had become.

It is estimated that a computer programmer in a networked work environment is interrupted every 11 minutes by incoming messages or calls. Once interrupted, it may take 25 minutes to return to the task at hand.[6] It may be argued that these interruptions are part of the modern working world, but one has to wonder how many of the interruptions are work-related. Half of US companies surveyed in 2009 have decided to block Facebook (and similar sites) on company computers due to its attractiveness as a social networking site and its perceived negative effects on workplace productivity.[7] Whenever new content is added to Internet sites that one subscribes to, it generates an e-mail or instant message with the siren song of "check this out."

All this started innocently enough, and provides a classic case study of Merton's law of unintended consequences.[8] In their excellent history of the Internet, Katie Hafner and Matthew Lyon relate that the first e-mails were sent in 1964 as part of the Pentagon's Advanced Research Projects Agency (ARPA) initiative to link mainframe computers at major research universities.[9] This predates by five years the official start of the ARPA-NET network at the University of California, Los Angeles on September 2, 1969 – the date accepted by most historians as the founding of the Internet. The ARPANET was designed for computer time-sharing rather than personal messaging, but users soon discovered that there was plenty of available bandwidth on the system for what we know today as e-mail. By 1971, several ARPANET users, including Richard Watson at Stanford Research Institute (SRI), had started experimenting with sending electronic messages using a "mailbox" protocol.[10]

Computer programmer Ray Tomlinson at ARPANET contractor Bolt, Beranek and Newman (BBN) in Boston is credited with developing the first networked e-mail program in 1971. He developed an e-mail system that could communicate between different types of computers by including the now well-known @ symbol between the user name and the host address.[11] This addressing system allows for the almost infinite expansion of e-mail addresses as it now includes the country code for all host systems outside the United States.[12] After Tomlinson developed this universal addressing system and refined the communication protocols, e-mail quickly became one of the most popular applications on the ARPANET and was a harbinger of the popularity of contemporary social networking technologies such as Facebook and Twitter.

The creation of the Internet will be addressed in Chapters 4 and 5, however it is important to note here that the human desire to electronically communicate to others predates the development of the Internet. The success of the telephone as a communication tool was based on its ability to facilitate real-time voice dialogue. In large organizations in the teleconnected world today, employees typically have little say about which communication modes they will use. E-mail is as a primary tool for intra-organization and external client communication, and ignoring one's messages for any interval beyond one day will lead to irritated phone calls from colleagues and customers. Failure to reply promptly to a client's inquiry could lead to a loss of their business, and possible termination of one's employment. To ensure a speedy response, some companies have set minimum time requirements for employees to reply to client e-mails.

This time pressure (both from within the organization and from one's personal work ethic) to reply to messages, combined with the increasing number of electronic interruptions, adds yet another stress-inducing component to the workday. For many of those employed in the networked world, a central question is how to balance the need to accomplish daily work-related tasks and still allocate the time needed to manage e-mail, voice-mail, web teleconferences, and conventional written communication. The central question to examine is: In this teleconnected world of multiple modes of communication, *do we control these technologies – or do they control us?* Information workers today often feel that they are servants of communication technology rather than the other way around. This perception is not a new one, and it is helpful to review the work of key critics of technology's role in contemporary life to gain useful perspectives that are especially applicable today.

Jacques Ellul's Critique of Technology

French theologian, sociologist, and philosopher Jacques Ellul (1912–94) was a prolific writer and perceptive critic concerning the role that technology plays in modern life. He was the author of several books that dealt with the effects of technology, including *The Technological Society* – one of his most-cited works.[13] First published in France in 1954, the English translation was issued in 1964 at the behest of Aldous Huxley, author of *Brave New World*, who considered Ellul's book a seminal work on the role of technology in society. The French edition of the book was titled *La Technique: L'Enjeu du siècle*, (*Technique: The Stake of the Century*). In the text Ellul defined "La Technique" as "the totality of methods rationally arrived at, and having absolute efficiency (for a given stage of development) in every field of human activity."[14]

This all-encompassing definition moves beyond a simplistic view of technology as strictly tools and hardware to a much broader definition that includes every area of what Ellul terms "rational" human endeavor. From this perspective such diverse activities as cooking, playing basketball, sleeping (influenced by mattress technology and pharmaceutical sleep aids), sending a text message on a mobile phone, teaching a college

Figure 3.1   Jacques Ellul. Photo by Patrick Troud-Chastenet.

course, gardening, and even sex (e.g., the use of contraception or romantic music playing from an MP3 device) would involve the use of "la technique," as defined by Ellul. The rationality aspect was important to Ellul as it reflected his view that technique in any given field of activity evolves over time toward its most efficient use. The evolution of technique toward "absolute efficiency" is a key theme in Ellul's writings on technology, a thread picked up by later critics of the role of technology in contemporary life such as Neil Postman. Ellul scholar Darrell Fasching observed of his worldview:

> Modern technology has become a total phenomenon for civilization, the defining force of a new social order in which efficiency is no longer an option, but a necessity imposed on all human activity.[15]

Figure 3.2   Neil Postman.

While acknowledging the benefits provided by contemporary technologies, Ellul stated that there is always a price to be paid by society in their
adoption. Each innovation, according to Ellul, creates "pernicious effects
that are inseparable from favorable effects."[16] Ellul sees these forces as
"contradictory elements [that] are always indissolubly connected." He
also stated that the adoption of technology by society (in the broad "la
technique" sense that he defined), "raises more problems than it solves"
and that "every technique implies unforeseeable effects." To summarize
these key points:

- The favorable effects of technology are "inseparable" from the negative ones
- These effects have "contradictory elements" that are "indissolubly
  connected"
- The adoption of technology by society "raises more problems than it
  solves"
- Technological adoption creates "unforeseeable effects"[17]

Ellul also viewed the mass media as complicit in the evolution of the technological society:

> It is the emergence of mass media which makes possible the use of propaganda techniques on a societal scale. The orchestration of press, radio and television to create a continuous, lasting and total environment renders the influence of propaganda virtually unnoticed, precisely because it creates a constant environment. Mass media provides the link between the individual and the demands of the technological society.[18]

Ellul wrote extensively about the role of propaganda in perpetuating the modern technological state and viewed mass media as playing a central role in its dissemination. He also alludes in this quote to the ubiquity of communication technology in creating a "constant environment" where we are bombarded daily with media messages. Ellul made these observations about mass media before 1994 (when he died), and we can only imagine his critical assessment of contemporary 24/7 media access via mobile phones and the Internet.

Is Ellul's view of technology too negative – specifically, his assessment that technology "raises more problems than it solves"? On first exposure to Ellul's writings, I thought it was too extreme a stance, especially when considering the specific benefits provided to society by the electrification of home and industry, advances in medical technology, and the creation of new tools for communication at a distance, among others. How can one argue that society has not overwhelmingly benefited from the development and widespread adoption of these technologies?

The availability of electricity in the home and workplace has transformed modern life. Visualize the drudgery required in a home in the days before electrification – my grandmother had to wash the clothing for a family of ten by hand until electric power lines were extended to their Ohio farm in the 1930s. Imagine a modern factory without electric motors or an office tower without elevators or air conditioning. However, recent evidence indicates that world societies may have to pay a very high environmental price in the form of global warming for unprecedented levels of energy usage and the pollution created in generating that energy. Global warming may also be directly related to our level of electronic technology usage, particularly if these technologies are powered by generation facilities that burn coal or other fossil fuels, as is the case in most of China. If we cease any further increases in global levels of carbon dioxide tomorrow, the levels of CO_2 in the atmosphere will be at record levels for another 100 years.[19]

Ellul also provides unique insights as part of his philosophical analysis of the relationship between technology and theology. His perspective is that contemporary society "worships" technology – that technology has been deified, or made godlike, as science collided with religious scriptures. The debate over evolution that began with the publication of Darwin's *The Origin of Species* in 1859, and continues with conflicts over teaching an alternative concept of "intelligent design" in schools, is but one example of this collision. Many technology users today lament the "complexification" of once simple tasks such as using a telephone. Swearing at a complicated "intelligent" appliance is not emblematic of a worshipful act.

In a 2006 survey by the Forum to Advance the Mobile Experience (FAME) of 15,000 mobile phone consumers in 37 countries, the most common complaint of users was "function fatigue."[20] FAME director Dave Murray stated that "There are too many product features that consumers don't use, or don't know how to use, and it frustrates them."[21] Rather than reduce the number of available features to minimize mobile phone complexity, Murray suggested that retailers should do a better job of educating consumers on the myriad features of their phones. The future doesn't hold much hope in this area – there are now thousands of downloadable applications of varying complexity available for 4G mobile phone users.

Ellul's perspectives on awarding godlike status to technology have been cited by other scholars critiquing the role of technology in society, and his philosophy had a direct influence on the thinking of technology critic Neil Postman as expressed in his influential book *Technopoly*.[22] Postman defines a "technopoly" as

> a state of culture. It is also a state of mind. *It consists in the deification of technology, which means that the culture seeks its authorization in technology, finds its satisfactions in technology, and takes its orders from technology.* This requires the development of a new kind of social order, and of necessity leads to the rapid dissolution of much that is associated with traditional beliefs. (emphasis added)[23]

To Postman, computers represent the ideal modern symbol of technopoly, a pervasive use of technology that affects every aspect of contemporary life. Computerization emphasizes *speed* and *efficiency*, elements that Postman considered as hallmarks of technopoly. I would offer computer technology in the form of e-mail as a prime example. Postman extended this line of thought further than Ellul, concluding that the widespread adoption of computer technology would lead to an "information glut, information without meaning, information without control mechanisms."[24] The widespread adoption of e-mail has led to an information glut, one that Postman was able to witness (he died in 2003 at the age of 72).[25] We struggle daily to make sense of all those electronic messages arriving by e-mail, phone, text, and tweet and then spend time sorting and organizing those that we wish to save. We rely on related computer technology in the form of spam filters to spare us from having to sort out legitimate messages from the blizzard of junk mail in daily messages. We will soon have intelligent digital agents that will understand our communication preferences and then sort and perhaps answer our electronic messages.

This phenomenon is related to another of Ellul's criticisms of technology – that as a global society we seek to remedy problems caused by technology with other technical solutions. For Ellul, these technical solutions are often worse than the problem they were designed to solve. Even with well-understood complex systems, technical fixes often fail at critical junctures. As Lewis Thomas notes in regard to complex urban systems in his insightful book *The Medusa and the Snail*: "Whatever you propose to do, based on common sense, will almost inevitably make matters worse rather than better."[26] Spam filters are a good example of a technical solution to a problem caused by technology (universal access to the Internet). Ellul understood this aspect of technology, and it provides a cautionary tale as electronic communication systems become ubiquitous and we become increasingly dependent on them for critical functions throughout the world.

The Tao of Digital Technology – Yin and Yang

Perhaps a Taoist view of digital technology might facilitate a greater understanding of the complex relationships between society and technology. The Taijitu symbol and the yin and yang elements associated with Taoism can be adapted for this purpose. Technology is the lighter, active, yang part of the symbol and in China is symbolized by fire. There is an elegant symmetry, with technology representing the fire element since the discovery of fire was one of the earliest uses of technology by our ancestors. Applied to modern digital telecommunications, the fire of yang represents the pulsing light of lasers as information is circulated over the Internet in millions of fiber-optic cables and as the glow emanating from a telecomputer or phone display. The yin element – the darker, passive half symbolized by water – represents society. In this sense it is helpful to think of society as both active and reactive. Technology evolves to meet human needs – which obviously will vary over time. Antibiotics were developed to deal with the effects of bacteria and infectious diseases that have caused millions of human deaths over the centuries. Medical science has developed treatments for illnesses caused by viruses such as influenza only to discover to our chagrin that bacteria such as those that cause tuberculosis (that we thought were under control) have evolved into drug-resistant strains.

The yin–yang relationship of technology and society is a useful model to temper the worldview of self-admitted technological determinists such as Thomas Friedman while allowing the perspective that techno-logical developments do, in fact, influence society. The converse is also true – that technology is part and parcel of the society created by humankind and is actively influenced by economics, politics, and a host of other human activities and beliefs. The yin–yang relationship of technology and society is a dynamic one with evolving cybernetic feedback loops. This view of the digital universe allows that "technological capabilities do create intentions" as Friedman noted – it also encourages us to simultaneously consider the Ellulian perspective that "technique" is a much broader concept than just tools and machines. Technology is embedded in every aspect of contemporary human life and is a response to our needs, both real and imagined. Digital technology takes the merger of society and "la technique" to the next level of embeddedness, as we create and adopt technologies that are mobile, compact, and can understand and anticipate our needs. The development of artificial intelligence and agent technology has evolved to a nascent stage, but combined they will take the embeddedness of digital technol-ogy in society to a remarkable – and, to some, alarming – new level in this century.

Is the Digital Future One of Doom and Gloom?

In April 2000, *Wired* magazine published an article titled "Why the Future Doesn't Need Us," written by Bill Joy, then the chief scientist of Sun Microsystems.[27] Drawing on dystopian visions of the future of genetics, robotics, and nanotechnology, he concluded that a future is feasible where robotic systems might take over the management of all global systems (whether invited to or not). These networked systems, if given unrestricted opportunity to manage global affairs for the world's human population, might decide that we are expendable competitors for the world's resources, and terminate humanity. If this sounds like the lethal "Skynet" artificial intelligence system of the *Terminator* series of science fiction films, it is not too far off the mark. Bill Joy's *Wired* article was widely read and cited as an example of how advanced technology might evolve in a dystopian manner during the 21st century – without restrictions imposed by world governments.

Joy was attacked after publication of the article as a "neo-Luddite" – one who is opposed to modern technological change. The Luddites were a group of textile workers who attacked the newly installed knitting machines in the Midlands of England in 1811 as a way to forestall mechanization. They were not successful.[28] As one who co-founded Sun Microsystems and helped create TCP/IP, the fundamental communication protocol for the Internet, it is erroneous to cast Bill Joy as a Luddite. In fact, it was due to his reputation as a computer scientist involved in the creation of the Internet that people read and seriously considered his vision of possible dystopian futures. In the 19th century, coal miners in England and Wales carried cages with canaries in them into the deep pits to alert them to dangerous mine gases.[29] Joy provides a similar advance warning about the potential dangers to civilization of these 21st-century technologies.

The digital universe is fundamentally linked to development of nanotechnology (it is essential for the continued extension of Moore's law in the next two decades) and the computer-based analysis of complex genetic sequences. Information technology is also central to the evolution of artificial intelligence in robotic systems. However, I am hopeful that the same digital technologies that are supporting development in these areas will also facilitate the communication of the possible consequences, at least those we can foresee. Joy's *Wired* article was widely disseminated over the Internet (and is easily accessible on their website[30]) and has led to a lively online debate of its premises.

Ironically, the digital universe that could lead to these possible dystopian aspects of the diffusion of information and communication technology is also the same system that can alert humanity to the dangers of unrestricted development. The canary in the modern "mines" of technology is information. The Internet, to no one's surprise, has emerged as a primary medium of communication about the implications of the development of technology. The work of related organizations such as the Long Now Foundation (focused on long-term thinking) and the Lifeboat Foundation (which has an influential board of scientists advising it on nanotechnology and biotechnology) is facilitated by the Internet and, yes, e-mail plays a central role in their communication.

Negotiating the Role of Technology in Modern Life

The role that technology plays in our lives can be negotiated, to a point. People in contemporary networked societies have a great deal of choice concerning their use of technologies to communicate and recreate. We each make daily choices about whether to carry a mobile phone, digital music player, tablet, netbook, or other portable electronic device. When it comes to the working world we may not have as much choice. Increasingly, employers are requiring that employees be electronically connected to the company 24 hours a day, seven days a week. The numerals 24/7 are universally understood by workers in Bangalore, Beijing, Boston, and Berlin. We are losing the clear demarcation line between home and work that has been in place since workers stopped shopping in company stores and living in company houses in 19th-century mining towns. The option of working at home by telecommuting has been a boon to many, especially parents with pre-school children in the house. The downside for telecommuters has been learning where to draw the line between work and home. 24/7 access means that laboring for one's employer can extend far beyond the traditional 40-hour work week.

Aside from work, we do negotiate with ourselves and our families about when to adopt a new technology and how it will be used. Parents fret over whether to give a teenager a mobile phone for safety reasons, knowing that its usage will be predominantly social in sending text messages back and forth. For adults, turning off one's mobile phone can be seen by friends and colleagues as an anti-social act – likewise the failure to answer an e-mail within a day. We can negotiate with the usage of communication technology, up to a point, where social norms have increasing influence. This process of negotiating the use of technology by both individuals and organizations will be explored in subsequent chapters. It is a multifaceted and continually evolving aspect of the digital universe of information and communication technology. However, one has to marvel at the clueless person in a crowded theater who takes a mobile phone call in the middle of the film – and then begins to describe the plot to the person on the other end.

Notes

1. Twitter™ is a registered trademark of Twitter, Inc. of San Francisco, California. Twitter technology is a social networking and micro-blogging service where users can read and post text-based messages (called "tweets") of 140 characters or less. See Twitter.com.
2. J. Hopkins, "How To Avoid Spam Avalanche," *USA Today* (February 21, 2007), 3B.
3. Ibid.
4. An alternative e-mail option is to create and use one of Google's Gmail accounts with a 7.3 GigaByte storage capacity. With this account capacity, one would probably never need to delete or edit received e-mail. The downside is that one's e-mail is stored in a Google server in the Internet "cloud" with attendant privacy and security issues. See Chapter 11, on privacy and security, for further discussion of these topics.
5. T. Friedman, "The Age of Interruption," *New York Times* (July 5, 2006). Retrieved July 16, 2009, from http://query.nytimes.com/gst/fullpage.html?res=9E03EFDA1230F936A35754C0A9609C8B63&sec=&spon=&pagewanted=print.
6. J. Erickson, "Programmer Productivity," *Dr. Dobb's Journal* (September 26, 2009). Retrieved October 5, 2009, from http://www.ddj.com/development-tools/220100341.
7. Associated Press, "Step Away from the Facebook – Is It Clever to Block Websites?" (July 14, 2009). Retrieved July 16, 2009, from http://www.independent.co.uk/life-style/gadgets-and-tech/features/step-away-from-the-facebook–is-it-clever-to-block-websites-1745334.html.
8. R. K. Merton, "The Unanticipated Consequences of Purposive Social Action," *American Sociological Review*, 1/6 (December 1936), 894–904.
9. K. Hafner, and M. Lyon, *Where Wizards Stay Up Late: The Origins of the Internet* (New York: Touchstone, 1996).
10. J. Abbate, *Inventing the Internet* (Cambridge, MA: MIT Press, 1999), 106–7.
11. Ibid.
12. US users of e-mail are the only netizens in the world who do not have a country code at the end of their e-mail addresses.
13. J. Ellul, *The Technological Society* (New York: Alfred A. Knopf, 1964). First published in French in 1954 by Librairie Armand Colin in Paris.
14. Ibid., p. xxv.
15. D. J. Fasching, The Thought of Jacques Ellul: A Systematic Exposition (New York: Edwin Mellen Press, 1981), 17.
16. J. Ellul, "The Technological Order," *Technology and Culture* 3/4 (Fall 1962), 412.
17. Ibid.
18. Ellul, *The Technological Society*, 22.
19. Intergovernmental Panel on Climate Change, *Climate Change 2007: The Physical Science Basis – Summary for Policymakers* (2007). Retrieved on March 6, 2009, from http://www.ipcc.ch/#.

20. FAME, *Global Mobile Technology Users Overwhelmed by Device Features; Under-whelmed by Buying and User Experience* (February 12, 2007). Retrieved February 18, 2007, from: http://www.fameforusers.org/news/pr. html#021207.

21. L. Cauley, "Cellphone Users Complain About 'Function Fatigue'," *USA Today* (February 14, 2007), 5B. Retrieved August 30, 2011, from http://www.usatoday.com/tech/products/2007-02-13-function-fatigue_x.htm.

22. N. Postman, *Technopoly: The Surrender of Culture to Technology* (New York: Vintage, 1992).

23. Ibid., 71.

24. Ibid., 70.

25. Postman lived in an age of computerization, but wrote 18 books by hand in notebooks with a felt-tip pen, did not own a computer, and never used e-mail – a remarkable achievement in this era of almost universal computer use in the academy. Source: J. Rosen, "Neil Postman (1931–2003): Some Recollections," *Press Think* (2003). Retrieved March 6, 2009, from http://journalism.nyu.edu/pubzone/weblogs/pressthink/2003/10/07/postman_life.html.

26. L. Thomas, *The Medusa and the Snail: More Notes of a Biology Watcher* (New York: Viking Press, 1979), 110.

27. B. Joy, "Why the Future Doesn't Need Us," *Wired* (April 2000). Retrieved March 14, 2009, from http://www.wired.com/wired/archive/8.04/joy.html.

28. K. Sale, *Rebels Against the Future: The Luddites and Their War on the Industrial Revolution* (Reading, MA: Addison-Wesley, 1996).

29. If the canary keeled over in its cage due to exposure to poison gasses in the mine shaft, the miners made a hasty retreat until the area could be properly ventilated. The canaries weren't harmed in the process. Their cages contained small bottles of fresh air which were used to revive the tiny birds. They were too valuable to the miners to let them suffer any harm.

30. See n. 27 above.

Part II

Internet and Web History

4

Origins of the Internet

Foundations

The global Internet as we know it today started out with a very different mission and illustrates the law of unintended consequences discussed in Chapter 3. The foundation for its creation was the launch into Earth orbit of the USSR's Sputnik I satellite on October 4, 1957. It is remarkable that a machine the size of a basketball orbiting the Earth every 98 minutes had such a significant effect on the Cold War and the future of telecommunication.[1] One month later, Soviet scientists and engineers launched Sputnik II with a dog aboard as a passenger. At this point the Russians clearly had a major lead in the global race into space.

With the demise of the USSR in 1991, it is difficult for those born after that date to appreciate the fear the Sputnik launch created among American citizens during the 1950s. The Cold War was in deep-freeze mode after the Korean conflict, and the fact that the Russians were orbiting a tiny spacecraft over the United States was an intimidating development to many Americans. The era was characterized by the rapid deployment by the United States and the USSR of intercontinental ballistic missiles (ICBMs) topped with unfathomably powerful thermonuclear weapons. The prospect of war using these doomsday technologies was very troubling to President (and former general) Dwight Eisenhower and the US Congress. The Sputnik launch led to a massive

Digital Universe: The Global Telecommunication Revolution, First Edition. Peter B. Seel.
© 2012 Peter B. Seel. Published 2012 by Blackwell Publishing Ltd.

national effort to improve the state of American science, technology, and education at all levels. One aspect of this national initiative was increased funding for research by universities and national laboratories – much of it sponsored by the Defense Department. The Advanced Research Projects Agency (ARPA),[2] mentioned in Chapter 3, was created by President Eisenhower with the support of Congress in February 1958, less than six months after the launch of Sputnik.[3]

As a former military officer, President Eisenhower understood through life-long personal observation the negative effects of inter-service rivalry. He was also wary of the nation's "military-industrial complex" – a term used in his 1961 presidential farewell address to the nation.[4] The military services had their own research and development arms such as the Office of Naval Research (ONR) that funded the development of the first automatic digital computer, the Mark 1, by Howard Aiken and his research team at Harvard University. It was constructed by IBM and delivered to Harvard in 1944.[5] During World War II, the US Army's Ballistic Research Laboratory funded the development of ENIAC, the world's first programmable electronic computer, at the University of Pennsylvania. It was initially used in 1946 to calculate ballistic trajectories for artillery firing tables.[6] The development of new artillery pieces during the war created a need for gun-specific tables required to accurately place artillery rounds on target. Thus, the first application for the modern electronic computer was to assist in making a relatively old weapon – the cannon – more accurate.

At MIT's newly created Lincoln Laboratory in 1951, the US Navy and then the US Air Force funded the development of the Whirlwind computer for air defense coordination. It later evolved into the SAGE air defense system also developed by the Lincoln Lab (Figure 4.2).[7] While each of these pioneering systems played key roles in the evolution of computer technology, their development was separately funded by the Army, Navy, and Air Force – evidence of the competition for computing resources (and related appropriations) by the main branches of the Department of Defense (DoD). In this environment of intense inter-service competition for weapons systems research funding, ARPA was created to draw upon the nation's scientific expertise (primarily from the academic community) to work on both applied and basic research. The new organization was unusual in that its management was assigned to civilians in the Pentagon who reported directly to the Secretary of Defense, rather than any one military service.[8] President Eisenhower repeatedly emphasized that civilians were at the top of the chain of command at the Pentagon, with himself as commander-in-chief.

DARPA's Information-Processing Technology Office

DARPA's mission statement at present is not far from the original, and it is to:

> maintain the *technological superiority* of the U.S. military and *prevent technological surprise from harming our national security* by sponsoring revolutionary, high-payoff research that bridges the gap between fundamental discoveries and their military use. (*emphasis added*)[9]

While the leadership of the agency and its sponsored programs have evolved since 1958, the mission statement makes clear its intention is to avoid technological surprises (e.g., similar to Sputnik) and to leverage technological innovation to support the military services. The intention is for DARPA to focus on long-range research and development, with the individual services conducting their own research focused on near-term needs. One key focus of DARPA since the 1960s has been information science and technology. Its Information Processing Technology Office (IPTO) was created in 1960 and its research work continues today, including the DARPA Grand Challenge events involving autonomously piloted vehicles.[10] IPTO also funded recent research in magnetoresistive random-access memory (MRAM) that would allow Moore's law to be sustained well into this century.[11]

IPTO projects built upon ground-breaking computer science research that linked widely distributed systems controlling the Semi-Automatic Ground Environment (SAGE) air defense system. Deployed in 1963, the SAGE system used 30 large mainframe computers built by IBM (based on the pioneering Whirlwind computer developed by the Massachusetts Institute of Technology) to coordinate US air defense systems.[12] It was the world's first large-scale, computer-based, command-and-control system that operated in real time. It used telephone lines to connect control centers, radar installations, and air defense bases to intercept and shoot down hostile aircraft that might enter US airspace. It operated over a 20-year period (1963–83) and introduced a number of innovations in computer science that evolved into technologies that are widely used today, especially the use of graphical user interfaces (GUIs) for interaction between humans and computers.

SAGE operators tracked aircraft on large, round cathode ray tubes (CRTs) and used light guns on the screens to call up additional information on hostile aircraft (Figure 4.2).[13] These CRTs evolved into the first graphical display devices for computers and became the model for

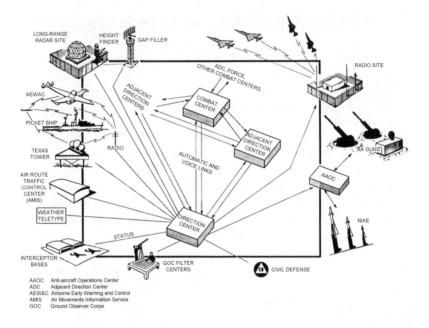

Figure 4.1   The SAGE air defense system. The diagram depicts how a centralized SAGE Direction Center with a massive mainframe computer would track hostile targets and then direct interceptor aircraft, anti-aircraft missiles, and guns against them. The use of telephone lines to link key system elements was an obvious vulnerability in the design. If nuclear strikes disabled parts of the national telephone network, the SAGE air defense system would fail. *Source*: Courtesy of the MITRE Corporation.

aircraft tracking systems used by Federal Aviation Administration (FAA) flight controllers. They are also the antecedents of contemporary desktop and laptop computer displays. The light guns used as a rudimentary Human–Computer Interface (HCI) with SAGE display screens evolved into light pens used by Ivan Sutherland for his groundbreaking Sketchpad computer graphics technology developed at MIT in 1963. Two new professions, software development engineering and computer programming, were created in developing the control programs for the system's Whirlwind II computers. Other breakthroughs in computer engineering, such as magnetic-core storage, modular design, and online databases, can be traced to the development of Whirlwind. In addition, software innovations such as the ability to accommodate multiple, simultaneous users and the use of advanced data system structures grew out of SAGE's development.[14]

Figure 4.2   Operators used light guns on the tactical display systems for the SAGE air defense system. *Source*: Image courtesy of the MITRE Corporation.

Figure 4.3   Mainframe computer supporting the SAGE air defense system. The wide variety of information sources required powerful and enormous computers to quickly sort the incoming data. *Source*: Image courtesy of the MITRE Corporation.

The central point is that the histories of information and communication technology and of US defense research and development have been closely linked since World War II. SAGE provided a platform for combining the national telecommunication network with IBM's Whirlwind computers to provide real-time information-processing power previously unequaled in human history. SAGE demonstrated the power and effectiveness of computer-based systems for military command-and-control purposes on a continent-wide basis. Without large mainframe computers and massive telecommunication systems, this type of real-time, command-and-control function would not have been possible. When linked to remote sensing devices such as radar, computers could process an incoming surge of data at a rate impossible for any human to match. Thus began the human-initiated evolution of ceding information-processing to computers in large-scale systems.

Paul Baran and the Survivable Communications Network

The RAND Corporation[15] was created in 1946 as a research and development organization for the US Air Force and other defense agencies. At RAND, computer engineer Paul Baran focused his research on designing a command-and-control communication network that could survive World War III. Recall that in the post-Sputnik world after 1957, the primary mission of the United States defense establishment was to survive and "win" a nuclear war with the Soviet Union (as if there would be any "winners" after such an apocalypse). Working in RAND's computer science department, Baran proposed the creation of a grid (or web) of interconnected communication nodes with multiple telephone lines connecting them. One of the major flaws in the SAGE system design was the vulnerability of telephone-switching centers located in or near major cities. Baran proposed that the new network's nodes be placed in hardened areas outside of major urban centers to improve their survivability in a nuclear war. He also proposed a new system of "message switching" that divided a message into digital segments, attached an address to each segment, and then sent them by varied routes over the network to their destinations.[16] As Baran stated:

> I found that if a network could be built in the form of a fishnet, then most of the surviving elements would theoretically remain in communication with the other surviving elements. And, to achieve this level of robustness took

only about three times the minimum number of elements needed to build a conventional network.[17]

This was a radical departure from the "circuit-switching" system used by telephone networks in that era. A telephone call of any distance required a central switching point for every call and the maintenance of a complete end-to-end circuit for the duration of the call. The main switching centers for the US telephone network were typically located in the middle of most large cities and were thus highly vulnerable to nuclear attack. As Baran's 1964 diagrams illustrate (Figure 4.4), a distributed network is far less vulnerable to node destruction than a centralized network. AT&T engineers at the time were not supportive of Baran's idea for a distributed network and thought that his message-switching idea would never work. They even refused to provide him with a map of the AT&T network.[18] Baran would get the last laugh today as national telephone networks are converting to packet-switched, Internet-based models that provide greater network efficiency with much lower costs to users.

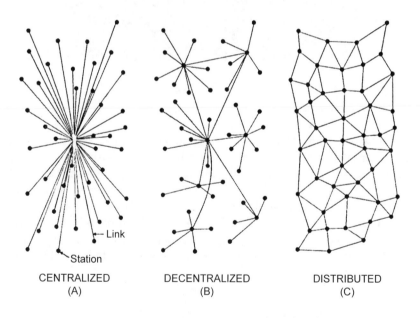

CENTRALIZED   DECENTRALIZED   DISTRIBUTED
(A)   (B)   (C)

Figure 4.4   Baran's comparison of network designs. These 1964 diagrams illustrate the vulnerability of centralized circuit-switched telephone networks (far left) compared with distributed "fishnet" networks (C, at right) that are a glimpse of the future evolution of the Internet. *Source:* P. Baran, "On Distributed Communications Networks," *IEEE Transactions* 19 (1964), 1–9.

Figure 4.5   Paul Baran, photographed at a 1999 CableLabs conference. *Photo*: Cable Television Laboratories.

English physicist Donald Davies developed similar ideas in the United Kingdom at the same time. His motivation for proposing this type of switching network was very different from Baran's. His research group at that time was focused on sharing expensive and scarce computer resources in the UK. They also wanted to develop home-grown computer technology in the UK and not have to rely on US providers for it.[19] He conceived and named the concept of transmitting data "packets" in a packet-switched network that become the model for data transmission in the UK and the ARPANET.

Development of the ARPANET

The purpose of this chapter is not to provide a detailed history of the development of the ARPANET – other authors have documented this story in great detail.[20] To be a critically literate citizen of the digital universe requires a familiarity with the origins of the Internet and some of the conflicts that have evolved with its growth. The Internet as we know it today had its roots in the Cold War, yet it was created by a group of maverick computer scientists, many of whom were part of the counter-culture in the 1960s and 1970s. The clash of cultures between the US government, its agencies (the Departments of Defense and Commerce in particular), and the university-based free spirits of the new network led to conflict as the ARPANET evolved into the Internet. Since 2001, new struggles have emerged over control of the Internet and the dominant role played by US-based agencies.

Any discussion of the evolution of the Internet begs the question of why was it created. In the decades since its inception, the media have reported that the rationale for the creation of the Internet was national defense – that the network was designed to maintain communication linkages across its many nodes even if some of them had been destroyed in a nuclear attack. Given the development of networked computer-based, defense command-and-control systems such as SAGE in the 1950s and early 1960s, this assumption seems logical – especially given the timing of the development of the ARPANET in the late 1960s (at the height of the war in Vietnam). This explanation is only partially true – as with the development of most new technologies, the actual story is more complicated.

Licklider to Taylor to Roberts at ARPA

After ARPA's creation in 1958, it went through a succession of directors and almost folded after NASA diverted much of its funding for space-related programs.[21] ARPA regrouped with a new focus on primary research, much of which had no immediate application in weapons systems.[22] It was in this climate during the Kennedy administration in 1961 that scientist Jack Ruina became ARPA director under Secretary of Defense Robert McNamara. Ruina continued the focus on primary research, and in 1962 hired MIT psychologist Joseph C. R. Licklider to manage a new DoD research program in behavioral sciences.[23] It was another example of the recruitment of the right person, in the right role, at the right time that led to the subsequent development of the Internet.

Licklider was recruited to manage ARPA's Information Processing Techniques Office. Given his new focus on computer networks, Licklider was the ideal person to manage its operations at that time. He worked at

ARPA for just two years, but in retrospect this was a key formative period for the ARPANET. The short term in office was normal for ARPA managers as they typically took a cut in salary for their government service and returned to academic or corporate careers after serving two to four years. The culture of short-term service was unique to ARPA and has lured some of the best minds in technology to the agency since its creation during the Cold War.[24]

In the fall of 1962, Licklider traveled across the US visiting the universities and laboratories that had received IPTO funding for computer facilities. He lobbied actively at MIT in Boston, at Carnegie Tech in Pittsburgh, at Systems Development Corporation (SDC) and RAND in Los Angeles, and at Stanford, SRI, and UC Berkeley in the Bay Area to solicit their participation in time-sharing research. Since ARPA had provided the multimillion-dollar seed funding for many of these labs, he had substantial leverage to invoke in his "request" for participation.[25] It helped that he had the ideal personality for the job – he was a psychologist, and understood the need for each lab to be operated independently. As a former university professor, he understood the academic research environment and the need to provide some latitude in the methods they proposed to use in their computer research. They found Licklider to be a kindred spirit and an unconventional champion for computer research in the Department of Defense.

In April of 1963 he sent his key principal investigators a now-famous memo addressed to the "Members and Affiliates of the Intergalactic Computer Network," and implored them to transcend the boundaries of geography and electronically link their diverse computer systems together.[26] It is a long and detailed memo about computer-based data-processing and its possible applications. He ended the memo with an appeal to balance the needs of the military with those of basic research in computer science:

> I had intended to review ARPA's Command-and-Control interests in improved man–computer interaction, in time-sharing and in computer networks ... The fact is, as I see it, that the military greatly needs solutions to many or most of the problems that will arise if we tried to make good use of the facilities that are coming into existence.
>
> I am hoping that there will be, in our individual efforts, enough evident advantage in cooperative programming and operation to lead us to solve the problems and, thus, to bring into being the technology that the military needs. When problems arise clearly in the military context and seem not to appear in the research context, then ARPA can take steps to handle them on an ad hoc basis. As I say, however, hopefully, many of the problems will

be essentially as important, in the research context as in the military context.[27]

Licklider clearly states in the memo that the purpose of ARPA funding was to support military information-processing needs in command-and-control systems, and that he could foresee that research in this area would advance computer time-sharing technology. He had a substantial budget at ARPA (initially $10 million a year) to construct his vision of a national system of linked time-sharing computer systems.[28] By the time Licklider left ARPA in 1964 to return to MIT, he had laid the foundation for what was to become the ARPANET.

His publications had a profound influence on those working in the nascent field of computer science. Robert Taylor was a research project manager at NASA in 1960 when he read Licklider's "Man–Computer Symbiosis" paper in *IRE Transactions*. His response was, "Yeah! Now we're talking!"[29] At NASA, Taylor had provided essential funding (along with grants from ARPA) to Douglas Engelbart at SRI for his ground-breaking research at Stanford on computer-augmented intelligence and human–computer interface technologies.[30] In 1966, when Taylor moved into the IPTO management position once held by Licklider (Taylor had joined ARPA in 1965), he inherited the ARPA networking project.

Taylor was an ideal successor to Licklider as the head of IPTO, as he shared a similar vision of the potential power of networked systems. There were some practical issues to be addressed. Taylor's ARPA office in the Pentagon contained three computer terminals: a modified IBM Selectric typewriter connected to a computer at MIT in Boston, a teletype machine linked to a computer at UC Berkeley, and a second teletype console which was a remote terminal for the massive IBM Q-32 computer at SDC in Santa Monica, California. Each system had its own unique programming language, operating system, and log-on procedure.[31] The Department of Defense was one of the largest purchasers of computers during the Cold War, and those built by different manufacturers could not communicate with another. Each new IPTO grantee sought ARPA funds to buy additional computers. Taylor sought to resolve this unsustainable Tower of Babel in the academic computer research world. His idea was to concentrate computer resources in centers of excellence (such as with computer graphics at the University of Utah) and then link all ARPA-funded systems together so these resources could be shared. It was an extension of Licklider's ideas about time-sharing, with the added benefit of cost savings and shared expertise among ARPA grantees. ARPA director Charles Herzfeld thought that such a linked system would offer increased reliability provided by the redundant links in the network.[32] As Herzfeld later noted:

> The potential military applications (including the potential for robust communications) were well in our minds, but they were not our primary responsibility. In fact there existed a significant Air Force program devoted to Strategic Command and Control, and related pieces of work were done under that aegis.[33]

Taylor was very assertive in stating to Hafner and Lyon that the ARPANET was *not* built to protect national security. He felt that the media had misinterpreted this aspect of Internet history. He stated that the ARPANET was built for peaceful purposes to link computers across the country for time-sharing purposes.[34] Herzfeld restates this focus as the intention for creating the ARPANET, but confirms that the Defense Department had an interest in building "robust" communication networks. The narrow view is that the ARPANET was built to demonstrate the utility of time-sharing as envisioned by both Licklider and Taylor. The broader perspective is that linked computer systems would be essential for any large-scale, real-time US defense command-and-control system, also envisioned by Licklider in his 1960 article. While ARPA funded (and DARPA continues to fund) many so-called "blue-sky" research projects, the ultimate objective in their mission statement is to sponsor "revolutionary, high-payoff research that bridges the gap between fundamental discoveries and their military use."[35]

This is not a trivial issue. The concept of machine control (using artificial intelligence technology) of key national defense systems is not far-fetched. As Licklider noted, these command-and-control systems must be able to consider multiple threats in real time, and display options for commanders to consider. Taking this concept a step further is the ceding of military decision-making to computers. This is the stuff of science fiction and a theme for films from the 1980s such as *War Games*, where a NORAD[36] computer thinks a simulation game is a real attack on the US. A worst-case scenario was the basis for the *Terminator* films, where Skynet, a US defense system based on artificial intelligence, becomes a sentient network which takes over all military technology and begins to annihilate humanity. The effect of these films on society should not be underemphasized. They paint very negative pictures of the possible evolution of human–computer symbiosis and are retained in the memories of the viewers of these films. They contribute to an innate human suspicion of machine intelligence and the dystopian effects of an artificial intelligence (AI) "singularity" in the future. The theme of an AI singularity will be discussed in greater length in Chapter 14.

Building the ARPANET

In 1966, Taylor received an additional $1 million from ARPA director Charles Herzfeld to extend Licklider's concept of computer time-sharing into a national networked system of computer centers. He needed an astute computer scientist to manage the new networking project, and sought out Larry Roberts, a researcher at MIT's Lincoln Laboratory. Roberts had done pioneering research work linking the TX-0 computer at Lincoln Lab in Boston with the Q-32 computer at SDC in Los Angeles.[37] The person in this key role at ARPA had to be a computer scientist and an expert in electronic communication. It highlights the evolution of the digital computer from a number-crunching calculation device into a powerful tool for communication, a role predicted by Licklider in his 1960 human–computer symbiosis article. Roberts was quite content doing research work at Lincoln Lab and declined the offer from Taylor to move to ARPA in Washington. Taylor was convinced that Roberts was the ideal person to lead the networking project, and in frustration asked Herzfeld to intervene with Lincoln Lab management. ARPA had provided Lincoln Lab with millions of dollars in federal research funds and Herzfeld made a persuasive case to the lab manager that it was in their long-term interest to have Roberts join ARPA for this project. Two weeks later, Roberts accepted the position at ARPA.[38]

Much like Licklider, Roberts combined an inquiring mind with the ability to solve problems in a wide variety of fields. He had great stamina and would work long hours into the night if he had an interesting problem to solve. He was successful in managing the national networking project for ARPA, and after Taylor departed from ARPA in 1967 Roberts became the director of IPTO. He contracted with Bolt, Berenek and Newman (BBN) in Boston to build the network. If these funding relationships appear a bit incestuous (Licklider had come to ARPA from BBN and the company was considered to be a technical "finishing school" for MIT graduates), at the time there was a relatively small group of computer scientists who were in the inner circle of IPTO grantees at MIT, BBN, SRI, Utah, and UCLA.

One member of that inner circle was Wesley Clark, a computer scientist at Washington University in St. Louis (Licklider's alma mater) who contributed one of the key concepts that made the ARPANET technically feasible. At MIT's Lincoln Lab in the late 1950s, Clark taught Licklider the fundamentals of computer programming on the TX-2 system.[39] Clark heard a presentation by Larry Roberts in 1968 about the proposed network that described the fundamental problem of linking computer systems with different operating systems, programming languages, and interface devices (as evidenced by the three unique terminals in the IPTO offices). In retrospect, Clark's suggestion was a brilliant one – rather than deal with the fundamental computer incompatibility problems at the system level, why not create a specialized computer that would manage network communication to and from its paired mainframe? It would be called an Interface Message Processor (with the obligatory acronym, IMP). This solution meant that each of the computers on the network would only need to communicate with its assigned IMP computer. This would simplify the programming needed for network communication. The host computer at each institution would be programmed to communicate with its IMP – rather than every computer on the network. Substantial work was required to connect each host to the

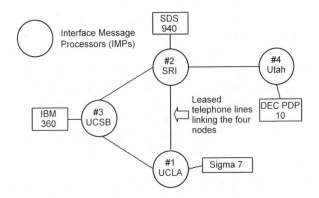

Figure 4.6   The primordial Internet. The diagram is a schematic representation of the first four nodes on the ARPANET in December 1969. The subnet is represented by the Interface Message Processors (IMPs) at each site and the names refer to the type of computers linked to the network: an SDS Sigma 7 at the University of California Los Angeles, an IBM 360 at University of California Santa Barbara, a Scientific Data Systems SDS 940 at the Stanford Research Institute, and a Digital Equipment Corporation PDP 10 at the University of Utah. Part of the fundamental problem was finding a way in which different types of computers could be linked together. The IMPs were a key aspect of the system in that they facilitated data sharing between many diverse types of computers – in essence they were the essential translators in the early Internet. *Source:* Diagram by the author; source Alex McKenzie.

Figure 4.7   Dr. Leonard Kleinrock with a legacy Interface Message Processor at the University of California, Los Angeles, which became node #1 on the ARPANET in 1969. *Photo:* Courtesy of Leonard Kleinrock.

IMP – a process that required both hardware and software solutions and took up to 12 months to implement.[40] The IMPs would form what was to be known as a "subnet" linking all the nodes on the network.

The other key feature of the system is that it would use the packet-switching technology independently developed by Paul Baran at RAND and Donald Davies in the UK. What is remarkable about the ARPANET was that it was a multimillion-dollar calculated risk that it would work effectively. No one knew at the outset if packet switching could be made to work in a very large national network. Recall that engineers at AT&T had said that this technology would never work for a communications network. Bob Taylor made the decision to use packet-switching technology and Larry Roberts signed on to realize this ambitious goal.

Another inner circle member was Leonard Kleinrock, a computer scientist at the University of California Los Angeles. Kleinrock wrote his 1962 doctoral dissertation at MIT on mathematical theories of packet switching in data networks – which he later developed into practical aspects of packet switching for the ARPANET.[41] His pioneering work in the field of data communication led to UCLA receiving substantial ARPA funding and its selection by Larry Roberts as the first institution to receive an IMP computer as node #1 on the embryonic network. On October 29, 1969, Professor Kleinrock supervised the first message sent over the

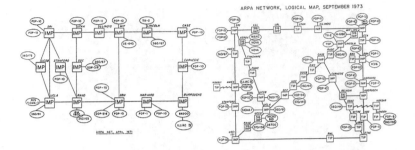

Figures 4.8 and 4.9 Rapid Expansion of the ARPANET. The diagram at left maps the expansion of the ARPANET from 15 participating institutions in April 1971 (by counting the IMPs) to more than 37 in September 1973 in Figure 4.9 at right. Note that by 1973 the use of new Terminal IMPs (listed as "TIP"s in the map at right) allowed institutions without host computers (or with a need for multiple links) to connect to the network. This innovation allowed the network to expand more rapidly. *Source*: DARPA archives.

network from the SDS Sigma 7 computer at UCLA to the SDS 940 computer in Douglas Engelbart's lab at SRI in Palo Alto.[42] The first four nodes were online by December 5, 1969, and the primordial Internet was operational.

Over the next four years the network grew rapidly, with 15 institutions online by 1971 and more than 37 by 1973 (Figures 4.8 and 4.9). Most of these institutions were university computer science departments, but there were also a number of government laboratories involved, such as Lincoln Lab at MIT, and Lawrence Livermore and NASA's Ames research facilities in the Bay Area. The development of Terminal Interface Processors (TIPs) allowed institutions without host computers (or ones that needed multiple connections) to link to the rapidly expanding network. What is interesting to note is that several military installations and contractors appear in the 1973 map, including RAND in California, Fort Belvoir and the MITRE Corporation in Virginia, and the army's Aberdeen post in Maryland. Computing history had come full circle from the commissioning of the ENIAC computer in 1946 by the army's Artillery Command at Aberdeen to the connection of the site to the ARPANET in 1973.

The Father of All Demos[43]

A commonplace event in advanced technology industries is to hold demonstrations of a new software or hardware product for senior company executives who can either green-light or cancel a project. These are high-stakes events, now known by the shorthand term "demo," where a designer's career can hang in the balance. If the demo goes well, the product can be completed and marketed to the public. If the demo goes badly, it places the design team in a virtual purgatory known as "demo hell."[44] Almost all engineers in high-technology companies have experienced "demo hell," and very few of them care to repeat the experience. Demos held for former CEOs Bill Gates of Microsoft and Steve Jobs of Apple have become legendary for the introduction of successful products – and even more so for those engineers who have had to endure the scathing remarks from Jobs or Gates for a product that was not ready to be marketed. The "Mother of All Demos" was the legendary presentation of online information-processing by Douglas Engelbart in San Francisco in 1968, and the splash it created among the ICT elite was not lost on the creators of the ARPANET.

In the fall of 1971, IPTO head Larry Roberts noted that the International Conference on Computer Communications (ICCC) was going to be held in Washington, DC, in October of 1972. As the program chair for the ICCC, Roberts decided that this conference would be an ideal showcase for demonstrating the capabilities of the emergent ARPANET.[45] He enlisted the aid of an engineer at Bolt, Berenek and Newman named Robert Kahn to plan the ICCC demo. Over the following 12 months Kahn and co-planner Albert Vezza of MIT traveled the nation enlisting the support of ARPANET computer scientists and their graduate students for a large hands-on demo of the capabilities of the linked systems on the network. Some argued that the demos should be videotaped in advance for later presentation at the conference just in case the computers on the network should crash in the middle of the presentation.

For the ICCC demo at the Washington Hilton, Kahn and Vezza arranged to have a TIP node on the ARPANET installed by BBN in the hotel meeting room. The TIP could handle up to 63 connected terminals and it was linked to the ARPANET by a special dedicated phone line installed by AT&T. At the time of the demo in October 1972, there was a total of 29 nodes on the ARPANET, so there were many sites and their programs to demo.[46] It was a frantic effort to get dozens of diverse terminals connected to the TIP and debugged in time for a VIP reception on the Sunday before the conference began, but the demo was ready to go on schedule.

The demo was a major success for Roberts, Kahn, Vezza, and ARPA, as over a thousand university computer scientists, graduate students, industry communication engineers, and government officials crowded the room over the following three days. It was a tour de force demonstration that linked diverse computer systems separated by thousands of miles (including a site in Paris). Conference attendees could play interactive chess games, learn about the geography of South America, read the Associated Press news service online (a forerunner of online news access today), and interact with an air traffic control system, among other online experiences.[47] At this point in the early history of information and communication technology, it was a dramatic hands-on demonstration of interactive networked technologies. Using the slang of that era, it could be said that the ARPANET demo was a "mind-blowing experience" for those who participated. It was also a major factor in the adoption of packet switching for telecommunications, silencing the telephone company naysayers who had insisted that the technology would never work.[48] The conference had a major effect on traffic on the ARPANET, which leapt from a slow growth rate of a few percent per month to a 67 percent increase in October 1972. This dramatic growth was sustained in the months afterward.[49] As Larry Roberts had hoped, the demo had put the ARPANET on the map and led to many other institutions signing up to participate in the new network.[50]

The stage was set for the rapid expansion of the ARPANET, with the addition of hundreds of host systems and its gradual evolution into the Internet that we access today. This evolution is the subject of Chapter 5.

Notes

1. P. Harsha, "IT Research and Development Funding," in W. Aspray (ed.), *Chasing Moore's Law: Information Technology Policy in the United States* (Raleigh, NC: Scitech, 2004).

2. Called the Advanced Research Projects Agency (ARPA) by the legislation that created it, it was renamed the Defense Advanced Research Projects Agency (DARPA) in 1972. It was renamed with the ARPA acronym again in 1993 and then changed back to DARPA in 1996. Since this chapter addresses the creation of the Advanced Research Projects Agency, the ARPA acronym is used here.

3. K. Hafner and M. Lyon, *Where Wizards Stay Up Late: The Origins of the Internet* (New York: Touchstone, 1996).

4. Eisenhower did not invent the term. It is first credited to the anti-war platform of the Union of Democratic Control in the United Kingdom at the beginning of World War I. See G. J. DeGroot, *Blighty: British Society in the Era of the Great War* (London: Longman, 1996), 144.

5. Hafner and Lyon, *Where Wizards Stay Up Late*, 24.

6. S. McCartney, *ENIAC: The Triumphs and Tragedies of the World's First Computer* (New York: Walker & Co., 1999).

7. Hafner and Lyon, *Where Wizards Stay Up Late*, 24.
8. J. Abbate, *Inventing the Internet* (Cambridge, MA: MIT Press, 1999), 36. "The director of ARPA reports to the Director of Defense Research and Engineering at the Office of the Secretary of Defense."
9. From the DARPA website at http://www.darpa.mil/body/mission/.
10. See DARPA's Grand Challenge site at http://www.darpa.mil/grandchallenge/index.asp. None of the driverless autonomous vehicles finished the race in 2004, but five cars finished the 150-mile course in 2005.
11. P. Schwartz, C. Taylor, and R. Koselka, "Quantum Leap," *Fortune* (August 1, 2006). Retrieved July 17, 2009, from http://money.cnn.com/magazines/fortune/fortune_archive/2006/08/07/8382582/index.htm. More detail on this technology is included in Chapter 14, on the future of the digital universe.
12. From the MITRE Corporation website at http://www.mitre.org/about/sage/. The Whirlwind II computers developed by MIT for SAGE (and modified by IBM) were created at the cusp of the shift from vacuum tubes to transistors in 1960. Each Whirlwind II computer weighed 250 tons and contained 49,000 vacuum tubes and required a 3,000 kW power supply. The heat load generated by such vast power consumption necessitated special cooling requirements for each site. As a point of reference related to Moore's law, its computing power was less than that of a netbook computer today.
13. Note that the control console contains a built-in cigarette lighter and ashtray at the left of the officer's left hand. Images of the SAGE system are from a fascinating site that the MITRE Corporation has created at http://www.mitre.org/about/photo_archives/sage_photo.html. Pictures used with the permission of the MITRE Corporation. Copyright © the MITRE Corporation. All Rights Reserved.
14. MITRE Corporation, op. cit.
15. RAND is an acronym for Research ANd Development. It was a very influential think tank for American strategy during and after the Cold War. It was satirized as the "BLAND Corporation" in Stanley Kubrick's anti-war film *Dr. Strangelove* in 1964. The not-for-profit company is active today doing consulting work on a wide variety of international issues.
16. P. Baran, "On Distributed Communications Networks," *IEEE Transactions on Communications* 19 (March 1964), 1–9.
17. From the transcript of a speech Baran made in 1999 to a CableLabs conference entitled *Convergence: Past, Present and Future*. Retrieved January 21, 2008, from http://www.cablelabs.com/news/newsletter/SPECS/JanFeb_SPECSTECH/tech.pgs/leadstory.html.
18. See a very interesting interview with Baran conducted by Stewart Brand in the March 2001 issue of *Wired* at http://www.wired.com/wired/archive/9.03/baran.html.
19. Abbate, *Inventing the Internet*, 23–35.
20. See Hafner and Lyon, *Where Wizards Stay Up Late*, and Abbate, *Inventing the Internet*.

21. Hafner and Lyon, *Where Wizards Stay Up Late*, 22.
22. Ibid.
23. Ibid., 35–7.
24. *Funding a Revolution: Government Support for Computing Research* (1999). Committee on Innovations in Computing and Communications: Lessons from History, Computer Science and Telecommunications Board, Commission on Physical Sciences, Mathematics, and Applications. Washington, DC: National Research Council.
25. M. M. Waldrop, *The Dream Machine: J. C. R. Licklider and the Revolution that Made Computing Personal* (New York: Penguin, 2001), 209–11.
26. *Memorandum for Members and Affiliates of the Intergalactic Computer Network*. (April 23, 1963). The memo can be accessed at: http://www. kurzweilai.net/articles/art0366.html?printable=1.
27. Ibid.
28. Waldrop, *The Dream Machine*, 207.
29. J. Markoff, "An Internet Pioneer Ponders the Next Revolution," *New York Times* (December 20, 1999). Retrieved May 28, 2008, from http://query. nytimes.com/gst/fullpage.html?res=9903E0D91539F933A15751C1A96F958 260&scp=2&sq=An + Internet + pioneer + ponders + the + next + revolution &st=nyt.
30. Ibid.
31. Hafner and Lyon, *Where Wizards Stay Up Late*, 12.
32. Ibid., 42.
33. Charles Herzfeld on ARPAnet and Computers. Retrieved July 23, 2009, from http://inventors.about.com/library/inventors/bl_Charles_Herzfeld.htm.
34. Hafner and Lyon, *Where Wizards Stay Up Late*, 10, 42.
35. From the DARPA website at http://www.darpa.mil/body/mission/.
36. NORAD was an acronym for the US Air Force's North American Air Defense command, headquartered inside a mountain near Colorado Springs, Colorado. It is now known as the US Air Force Space Command.
37. Hafner and Lyon, *Where Wizards Stay Up Late*, 45.
38. Ibid., 45–7.
39. Ibid., 32–4.
40. Abbate, *Inventing the Internet*, 78.
41. L. Kleinrock, *Communication Nets: Stochastic Message Flow and Delay* (New York: McGraw-Hill, 1964). This is Kleinrock's MIT doctoral dissertation, published later as a book.
42. Hafner and Lyon, *Where Wizards Stay Up Late*, 152–4. UCLA undergraduate Charles Kline sent the letters "LO" of the command line LOGIN to SRI in Palo Alto before the connection crashed. It points out that the network technology of the time was very fragile and buggy, but the message was sent later that day without error.
43. The "mother of all demos" was the one conducted by Douglas Engelbart in San Francisco in 1968.

44. This is a worst-case scenario for computer-based demos. Bill Gates was a participant at a Comdex demo of the plug and play capability for Microsoft Windows 98 when the system crashed. See the YouTube video: http://www. youtube.com/watch?v=RgriTO8UHvs&NR=1.

45. L. G. Roberts and R. E. Kahn, "Special Project. Participating in Demonstration of a Multi-Purpose Network Linking Dissimilar Computers and Terminals," *Proceedings of International Conference on Computer Communications* (1972), North Holland.

46. Hafner and Lyon, *Where Wizards Stay Up Late*, 178.

47. Roberts and Kahn, "Special Project."

48. There were some glitches during the ICCC demos. Graduate student Robert Metcalfe (and later inventor of Ethernet networking) was conducting a demo for ten visiting AT&T executives when the system he was demonstrating crashed. They laughed at the failure of the packet-based technology, but Metcalfe got the last laugh when telephone companies such as AT&T subsequently embraced packet switching. See Hafner and Lyon, *Where Wizards Stay Up Late*, 182.

49. E. P. Schelonka, "Resource Sharing on the Arpanet," in M. Abrams et al. (eds.), *Computer Networks* (New York: IEEE, 1976), 5–21.

50. The success of the ICCC demo had an effect on Larry Robert's career as well. He left ARPA to become president of Telenet Communications Corporation, a subsidiary created by Bolt, Berenek and Newman to commercialize packet-switching technology.

5

Internet Evolution

Part 1 – From ARPANET to Internet

Visualize an enormous, dimly lit master control room for the Internet. The scene looks like mission control at NASA, but on a much larger scale. Dozens of people monitor traffic on the global network on small personal LCD displays set into consoles and on large screens that fill one wall of the room. The largest screen displays traffic between continents and key routers in the global network. Smaller screens along the side display images of Internet traffic by continent with varying-width bands of color denoting the primary fiber backbone connections between key nodes on those networks. The image is one that J. C. R. Licklider could have visualized as a key aspect of computer-based command-and-control systems that would allow many people to see what is happening in a large network at once.[1] The problem with this vision of a master control room is that it does not exist. While there are telecommunication network control rooms operated by individual companies and governments around the world, *there is no master control room for the Internet.* How can a network as large as the Internet function without some entity managing it? The answer is at the heart of the concept of the Internet and is a key element of its phenomenal growth since 1969. Nicholas Negroponte, in his book *Being Digital*, posed an interesting analogy:[2]

Digital Universe: The Global Telecommunication Revolution, First Edition. Peter B. Seel.
© 2012 Peter B. Seel. Published 2012 by Blackwell Publishing Ltd.

Figure 5.1   A master control room for the Internet? *Photo*: NASA.

The Internet is interesting not only as a massive and pervasive global network, but also as an example of something that has evolved with no apparent designer in charge, keeping its shape very much like the formation of a flock of ducks (in flight). Nobody is the boss, and *all the pieces so far are scaling admirably. (emphasis added)*

Figure 5.2   A riddle to ponder: *Why is the Internet like migratory birds in flight? Photo*: John Benson.

Note that when Negroponte wrote this in 1995, the Internet had only 30 million users.[3] There were 2.1 *billion* users worldwide in 2011 (30 percent of the world's population).[4] Remarkably, the Internet is still "scaling admirably" with an astonishing growth rate over the past 30 years.

The Development of TCP/IP

In the 1970s, as the ARPANET evolved into what we now know as the Internet, there were many technological innovations that enhanced this growth, but few were as central as the development of Transmission Control Protocol (TCP) and Internet Protocol (IP) facilitating communication in a distributed packet-switched network. In 1970 a group of researchers in Hawaii, led by Norman Abramson, had created a unique method of packet switching using radio waves (rather than using expensive undersea telephone lines) that enabled wireless data transmission between computer facilities in the islands.[5] Using ARPA funding, this technology was developed into an inter-island radio network known as the Alohanet. The Alohanet was a practical demonstration that packet switching was feasible over networks other than those that were hard-wired.

Bob Kahn, a former MIT electrical engineering professor who had moved to Bolt, Berenek and Newman (BBN) as a researcher, assisted in developing the famed ARPANET demo at the ICCC conference in Washington in October 1972, and then moved on to ARPA later that year.[6] If this MIT–BBN–ARPA path seems familiar, it was identical to that followed a few years earlier by J. C. R. Licklider, a colleague of Kahn's at BBN. Kahn had conducted ground-breaking research in packet switching at BBN. At ARPA he expressed an interest in building on the pioneering Alohanet project by funding efforts by a professor at Stanford University named Vinton Cerf to link disparate types of digital communication networks. Cerf was a graduate of the computer science program at UCLA, where he worked on creating the first node on the ARPANET in 1969.

Kahn used ARPA funding to construct a Packet Radio (PR) network called the PRNET in the San Francisco Bay Area. It connected San Francisco, Berkeley, Palo Alto, and San Jose by using radio repeaters on peaks around the bay. It became operational in 1975 and demonstrated that packet radio could be mobile, an important application for potential military use since this technology could transmit encrypted digital messages that would be more secure than conventional radio messages.[7] During World War II, US military units in the Pacific had used Navajo "code talkers" who, by speaking in their unique language, had confounded

Japanese efforts to intercept American radio communications. Packet radio messages would be adaptable to digital scrambling such that only the receiver would know the algorithms for reassembling them.

The packet radio network in the Bay Area had been designed by Kahn and his team to be portable and rugged enough to be deployed for military use anywhere in the world. It featured omni-directional antennas that did not have to be aimed at repeater towers and a mobile van that tested reception in moving vehicles. The network was also designed to automatically keep track of all of the elements in the system and could continue to function even if elements of the network were disabled or destroyed.[8] The PRNET demonstrated that the packet radio technologies were robust, portable, and had obvious military communication applications.

ARPA was also exploring packet transmission by satellite. Voice, television images, and data had first been transmitted between the US and Europe in July 1962 by the pioneering Telstar satellite.[9] As a schoolboy in Ohio at the time, I was mesmerized by the fuzzy black and white images from Europe that we viewed live on television. It left a lifelong impression. I think that the experience was, for me, akin to the reaction that westerners had when they witnessed the first use of the telegraph at transcontinental railroad stations in Wyoming in the 1860s. The clicking key represented the instantaneous transmission of messages from New York to San Francisco. This wonder was not lost on those who saw and heard the telegraph key moving and knew that a human hand thousands of miles away was causing it. The success of satellite telecommunications meant that Americans could see live news and other television programming from around the world, a point that breathless network commentators made very clear as we viewed the live television images from Europe.[10]

Robert Kahn wanted to study whether satellite data transmission using packet technology was feasible. ARPA had an interest in transmitting data to the US from seismic monitoring stations in Scandinavia. These stations were collecting data on Soviet nuclear bomb tests, measuring their size by seismically assessing the reverberations in the ground. The stations gathered enormous amounts of data and Kahn wanted to see if packet technology could speed its transmission to the US by satellite. In 1973, the IPTO division of ARPA funded the connection of the University of Hawaii (the Alohanet creator) and University College London to the ARPANET. These first connections evolved into the SATNET project sponsored by ARPA, the British Post Office, and the Norwegian Telecommunications Authority that linked two sites in the US with one in the UK and one in Norway. The SATNET was used to test packet satellite transmission of the nuclear test seismic data gathered in Scandinavian countries.[11]

This background is needed to understand the underlying fundamental problem of connecting diverse networks to the ARPANET. The basic problem was that the PRNET, the SATNET, and the ARPANET each used different technologies, and melding them together in a common network presented a significant challenge. Kahn enlisted Vinton Cerf (the developer of the existing Network Control Protocol for the ARPANET) for the project, and they worked to solve this problem with an international group of networking experts. Kahn and Cerf have been recognized by many as "fathers" of the Internet, and credit should go not only to them, but also to the international group with whom they consulted in solving the networking problem.[12]

The open-architecture solution proposed by the team was different from the ARPANET in one significant regard: responsibility for the overall reliability of the network was assumed by the hosts rather than the network itself. This meant that if all hosts adhered to the prescribed rules of the network – the protocol – the system could scale in a way not possible if a central control center was responsible. An analogy would be an orchestra that could add an unlimited number of musicians while playing a common symphony. Each new musician would be responsible for keeping in sync with the rest of the orchestra – eliminating the need for a conductor. It was a radical idea in an era of centralized control of networks (be they telephone, television, or data), but it made possible the notion of an infinitely large network of connected networks. In May of 1974, Cerf and Kahn published a seminal paper that described how a TCP could be used to define how data would flow across the network from host to host.[13] One other key element they proposed was the development of specialized computers on the network called "gateways" that served as routers of data traffic. These crucial nodes are in fact today called "routers" and are an indispensable part of the global Internet.

Cerf, Yogen Dalal, and Carl Sunshine at Stanford published a paper in December of 1974 that included the first use of the word **Internet** derived from the term "internetting" to describe this concept of internetworking. The semi-global network of networks had a formal name.[14] Table 5.1 shows the importance of TCP and IP in defining how messages are processed and routed over the network and the key role of host systems in maintaining reliable communication. The adoption of the TCP/IP protocols was central to the growth of the Internet and its worldwide ubiquity today.

Table 5.1   Telecommunication layers

Layer 5 – **Application** (e.g., HTTP, FTP, or VoIP [Voice over IP])

Layer 4 – **Transport** (e.g., Transmission Control Protocol – TCP)

Layer 3 – **Network/Internet** (e.g., Internet Protocol – IP)

Layer 2 – **Data link** (e.g., Ethernet LAN or 802.11 wireless)

Layer 1 – **Physical** (e.g., the physical cable connecting computers in a network)

The relationship between TCP and IP is best defined with the layer model of telecommunication protocols. Internet-based applications such as Web pages addressed by Uniform Resource Locators ("URLs" defined with an HTTP prefix) are dependent on the TCP and the IP layers for the request and proper delivery of a desired website to the user's computer. TCP manages the communication in packets between the host and requesting (client) computers. IP manages the proper global routing of the stream of data packets over the Internet by many different pathways. Every computer attached to the Internet has a unique IP address. Layers 1 and 2 provide the connection to the Internet from the user's computer.

Source: P. Gralla, *How the Internet Works* (Indianapolis, IN: Que, 1999), 13.

By 1975, the ARPANET had outgrown the small research network that ARPA had funded since Licklider's first efforts to sign up participants in 1969. ARPA wanted to divest the network to focus on their primary mission of developing and funding research projects. ARPANET participants Larry Roberts and Howard Frank met with executives of AT&T to investigate if "Ma Bell" would be interested in operating the new packet-switched network.[15] This was prior to the court-ordered break up of AT&T in 1984, and at the time of the meeting with Roberts and Frank the company was one of the largest communication monopolies in the world. AT&T declined to take over the operation of the ARPANET since they were still heavily invested in the national circuit-switched telephone network and did not see a financial payoff in managing a small and still experimental system.[16]

With this lack of interest in the civilian communication sector, ARPA handed over the operation of the ARPANET to the Defense Communication Agency (DCA) in July 1975. There were some conflicts between the military managers of the DCA and ARPANET participants, especially over what the new management saw as lax controls over access to the network at member universities. The Vietnam War ended in 1975, and active hostility toward the military still existed at many US university campuses. Once DCA took over the operation of the ARPANET, there was renewed interest among the military services in using the network for command-and-control purposes.[17] One key benefit of DCA control was the ability of the Department of Defense to order all ARPANET participants to adopt the TCP/IP protocols. The system-wide adoption of the protocols accelerated the development of the network and improved overall system reliability. The Defense Communication Agency operated the network until 1983, when the MILNET was created to separate defense installations and DoD labs from the civilian net. Sixty-eight nodes formed the new civilian network named the Internet, and 45 became part of the new MILNET.[18]

The Emergence of the Personal Computer

Until 1975, the world of computing in the US, East Asia, and Europe had been dominated by large mainframe systems that were operated by teams of data-processing specialists and required special climate-controlled rooms. The concept that computers must be large and centralized changed forever in January of 1975 when the new MITS Altair 8800 personal computer appeared on the cover of *Popular Electronics* magazine (Figure 5.4). MITS was an Albuquerque, New Mexico company that made electronic kits for hobbyists. Using an early Intel 8080 processor, the Altair was a compact minicomputer that was also very affordable. It was a wildly successful product and the company sold thousands of kits at $397 in the first few months of the year to computer hobbyists.[19]

The Altair 8800 had a significant effect on the emerging computer software community. An undergraduate student at Harvard named William Gates read the *Popular Electronics* article and was motivated by the potential he envisioned in personal computing. With Seattle high school friend Paul Allen (then working as a programmer in the Boston area), Gates decided to write a version of the BASIC programming language for the Altair. They moved to Albuquerque, New Mexico, to be near MITS, the Altair's manufacturer, and started a software company they named Microsoft. Gates and Allen were early beneficiaries of the development of the personal computer.[20] At the time, no one could foresee the implications of the development of the personal computer for the development of the Internet. The ARPANET was originally designed to share resources among the users of large mainframe systems, and the network's designers could not possibly imagine that individuals would one day have fully functional computers that could sit on a desktop or laptop. The creation of personal computers had a significant effect in

Table 5.2   Evolution of the Internet from the ARPANET

Date[a]	Event	Key actors
October 29, 1969	**First connection between nodes on the ARPANET**	University of California, Los Angeles (UCLA) and Stanford Research Institute (SRI)
December 1969	**First four ARPANET nodes** are online	UCLA, SRI, University of California, Santa Barbara (UCSB), and the University of Utah
1970	First host-to-host **Network Control Protocol (NCP)** adopted. First transcontinental link between UCLA and BBN on the ARPANET	ARPANET host institutions with addition of Bolt, Berenek and Newman (BBN) in Boston. AT&T installed the link which operated at 56 Kbps
1971	The **ARPANET has 15 nodes and 23 hosts**	UCLA, SRI, UCSB, Utah, BBN, MIT, RAND, SDC, Harvard, Lincoln Lab, Stanford, Illinois, CWRU, CMU, and NASA/ Ames
1972	**ICCC's "father of all demos"** held in Washington, DC, in October. Ray Tomlinson's (BBN) **e-mail program** is adopted on ARPANET	ICCC, ARPA, ARPANET host institutions and BBN
1973	**ARPANET becomes an international network** with connections to University College London (UCL) and NORSAR	ARPANET host institutions with UCL and NORSAR, the Norwegian Seismic Array
1974	Cerf and Kahn publish details of the **Transmission Control Program (TCP)**	Vinton Cerf (Stanford University) and Robert Kahn (ARPA)
January 1975	**MITS Altair 8800** goes on sale to the general public in the US	Computer hobbyists, MITS, and Intel (maker of the 8080 CPU)

(continued)

Table 5.2   (*continued*)

Date[a]	Event	Key actors
July 1975	The **Defense Communication Agency (DCA)** assumes management of the operation of the ARPANET	ARPANET participants and DCA
1977	**Intermodal demonstration of Internet protocols** by packet radio network in San Francisco with SATNET and ARPANET	ARPA, SRI, and Atlantic SATNET
1979	PRNET demonstrates **packet data transmission via radio** using mobile vans in San Francisco Bay Area	Robert Kahn using ARPA funding with design and development by SRI
1980	**Message-based virus** crashes the ARPANET on October 27	ARPANET host institutions shared the virus
1981	**CSNET (Computer Science NETwork)** created for computer scientists not affiliated with ARPANET institutions	National Science Foundation (NSF) funded development by BBN, RAND, Purdue, and the universities of Delaware and Wisconsin
1982	DCA mandates use of **TCP/IP protocols**	DCA and ARPANET hosts
1983	All users switch from NCP and adopt TCP/IP. CSNET and ARPANET linked. **MILNET split off from the ARPANET**	ARPANET and CSNET host institutions, DCA, DoD
1984	**Domain Name System** (DNS) (e.g., edu, .com, .gov) introduced	Group of UC Berkeley students wrote UNIX implementation based on first DNS developed in 1983 by Paul Mockapetris of USC

Table 5.2   (*continued*)

Date[a]	Event	Key actors
1986	**NSF assumes management of the Internet** and funds five supercomputing centers and NSFNET	NSF with funded centers at Princeton, Pittsburgh, UC San Diego, University of Illinois at Urbana-Champaign, and Cornell
1987	**MERIT** wins bid to expand the NSFNET	NSF and MERIT (Michigan universities, state of Michigan, IBM, and MCI)
1988	**NSFNET network "backbone"speed** is upgraded to 1.544 Mbps (T1)	NSF and AT&T
1989	Number of host systems **exceeds 100,000**	NSFNET and international hosts
1990	End of the road for the ARPANET – **US network is now the NSFNET**	

[a] Dates and actors confirmed from *Hobbes' Internet Timeline*. See this useful resource at http://www.zakon.org/robert/internet/timeline/.
Sources: J. Abbate, *Inventing the Internet* (Cambridge, MA: MIT Press, 2002); M. M. Waldrop, *The Dream Machine: J. C. R. Licklider and the Revolution that Made Computing Personal* (New York: Penguin, 2001).

corporate, government, and institutional environments long before they became inexpensive enough for home use.

The first personal computer in the US was the Alto, developed at Xerox's Palo Alto Research Center (PARC) in California in 1973.[21] The Alto was a revolutionary individual workstation compared with the mainframes and minicomputers of that era. It was not a commercial product, but was widely used at Xerox PARC and a few university adopters. Its creation was influenced by Douglas Engelbart's oN-Line System (NLS) developed at SRI. The Alto featured the first commercial use of a mouse as a pointing tool, a local area network (LAN) connection for storage, and the first use of a graphical user interface (GUI) with a desktop metaphor and icons for applications that later became fundamental attributes of Apple's first Macintosh computer in 1984.

Figure 5.3   The Altair 8800 on display at the Computer History Museum in Mountain View, California. *Photo*: Michael Holley.

I vividly recall receiving my first office personal computer, an IBM 5150 PC, in 1982. The PC had been created for business and institutional use by IBM in 1981 and featured an 8-bit Intel 8088 processor that operated at the then blazing speed of 5 MHz.[22] I used the new PC for writing multimedia scripts and later used it to synchronize it with a VCR for producing and delivering video-supported computer-based-training (CBT) programs. My prior computer experience consisted of learning to write programs in BASIC in graduate school and taking stacks of research data on punch cards to the university's computer center to be processed using their DEC VAX minicomputer. I was astonished at the time that technology had advanced from expensive minicomputers such as the VAX system to desktop PCs in less than four years. This was Moore's law at work, and the Intel 8088 processor (with 29,000 transistors) used in the IBM PC is part of the linear logarithmic plot used in the calculation of the law.[23]

One phenomenon related to the rapid expansion of PCs on desktops in the 1980s was the need to connect them together in corporate/institutional networks. The design and operation of these institutional networks provided a new role for information technology departments as PCs

Figure 5.4   The Altair 8800 was featured on the January 1975 cover of *Popular Electronics*. *Photo:* Courtesy of Ziff Davis, Inc.

supplanted mainframe systems and minicomputers. Ethernet technology connected distributed PC systems into a LAN typically confined to a single institution or facility. As the ARPANET created a wide-area network (WAN) in the 1980s, thousands of LANs were being developed in companies and institutions to connect their computer resources, especially the new PCs on desktops. One often overlooked consequence of the creation of the personal computer was the need to network them together in LANs which could then be connected into ever-larger WANs.

The network of networks which became the Internet had its growth accelerated by the thousands of smaller LANs which could be interconnected at the corporate-institutional level and subsequently into regional, national, and ultimately global networks. Moore's law tracks the exponential growth of transistors on a chip which led to the creation of the personal computer and the subsequent exponential growth of networks connecting these desktop systems.

While desktop PCs typically were used in the 1980s for specific functions such as word processing and accounting (Microsoft's Office suite of applications was not introduced until 1989), their connection to larger institutional networks facilitated organizational adoption of e-mail as a communication tool. E-mail usage in companies and institutions grew rapidly as PC users discovered its utility for project updates, interoffice correspondence, and the ability to rapidly share jokes with co-workers. What was known as information technology (IT) prior to the widespread adoption of e-mail as an effective communication tool as a result evolved into information and *communication* technology (ICT) in the 1980s. This echoes Ellul's observation that all technologies have unforeseen consequences of their adoption, and the rapid adoption of e-mail makes an ideal case study of a consequence that was unforeseen by the developers of the PC and the networks that linked them together.

Internet Growth in the 1980s

Through the late 1970s and early 1980s the ARPANET added new hosts; this pattern of rapid growth continued after military users shifted to the MILNET in 1983. The newly renamed Internet needed a well-heeled patron to replace ARPA after this split. The National Science Foundation (NSF) is a US government-funded agency whose purpose is "to promote the progress of science; to advance the national health, prosperity, and welfare; to secure the national defense."[24] In the 1980s it was a major source of federal funds for computer science research. In 1981, university computer science departments in the US that were not part of ARPANET used NSF grants to create a new network called the CSNET (Computer Science NETwork) which adopted TCP/IP and thus could be linked to the Internet. [25] In 1983, a gateway was established linking CSNET universities with the ARPANET, so the formerly separate networks became one.

Mitchell Waldrop makes a key observation that one of the primary drivers for the expansion of the CSNET (and subsequently the NSFNET) were physicists who needed massive computing power to investigate the frontiers of their field in the study of astrophysics and quantum mechanics.[26] A supercomputer of that era cost millions of dollars, so physicists in the US implored the NSF to create supercomputer resources that could be shared over a network such as CSNET, much as astronomers book time for sharing access to the few large telescopes available. This plea for shared access is interesting in that it mirrored the initial rationale for constructing the ARPANET – time-shared access to expensive computer resources. It is also prescient in light of Tim Berners-Lee's creation in 1989–91 of the World Wide Web as a means for physicists to share their research.

In response, the NSF funded supercomputer centers at five universities in 1985 and a year later linked them together with a newly created network called the NSFNET. The centers were located at Cornell University, the University of Illinois at Urbana-Champaign, the University of Pittsburgh, Carnegie-Mellon University, Princeton University, and the University of California, San Diego.[27] The NSFNET was designed for academic users who needed high-speed connections (25 times that of the CSNET) and operated at the then blazing speed of 56 Kilobits per second (Kbps). The backbone speed of the NSFNET increased to 1.5 Mbps (T1 speed) in 1988 and then to 45 Mbps (T3) in 1991.[28] The additional backbone capacity was needed to handle the extraordinary growth of traffic on the network. The mix of NSFNET hosts included academic, government, and increasing numbers of commercial participants. The NSFNET benefited from the common use of TCP/IP by all host systems, and it was evolving into the network of networks envisioned by Cerf and Kahn. By 1992, over 6,000 networks were linked by the NSFNET, one-third of which were outside the United States.[29] This reflects another interesting trend – once the MILNET split off into its own network, the Internet became less US-centric and more multinational. The name Internet was intended by Cerf and his co-authors to mean an *Inter*-connected *net*work of networks, but during this period it became an Inter*national* network as well.

The burgeoning Internet was also becoming more commercial. The NSF actively sought the participation of the private sector in 1986 as part of its goal to have the NSFNET become self-supporting. It issued a request for proposals in 1987 that opened the door to commercial participation in NSF's efforts to upgrade the Internet.[30] The decision was controversial, but historians will note that this occurred during the administration of President Ronald Reagan (1981–9), who deregulated a number of US industries during his presidency. The philosophy of the Reagan administration was to reduce the role of the federal government in the regulation of businesses such as commercial aviation, railroads, trucking, and especially telecommunications. Stephen Wolff was program director for the NSFNET at that time and related:

> It had to come, because it was obvious that if it didn't come in a coordinated way, it would come in a haphazard way, and the academic community would remain aloof, on the margin. That's the wrong model – multiple networks again, rather than a single Internet. There had to be commercial activity to help support networking, to help build volume on the network. That would get the cost down for everybody, including the academic community, which is what NSF was supposed to be doing.[31]

The bid to cooperatively manage the NSFNET backbone was won in 1987 by MERIT – a consortium of the state of Michigan, several Michigan universities (led by the University of Michigan), computer manufacturer IBM, and MCI, a telecommunications company.[32] MERIT was a creation of the University of Michigan and the partners, and its staff were university employees. MCI used its expertise in telecommunications to expand capacity on the NSFNET backbone, while IBM provided the software for the network. Many academics were concerned by the participation of IBM and MCI in the public consortium and were vocal about this fundamental shift from a government-operated Internet to one that now included private, for-profit companies in central roles – and very large corporations at that.[33] In April 1995, the NSF decommissioned the backbone of the NSFNET and the Internet was no longer government-operated – the split between not-for-profit and for-profit operation of the Internet was complete.

Was the privatization of the Internet inevitable? Given the central role of the US government in creating the ARPANET and its subsequent sponsorship by the National Science Foundation, the decision to involve large corporations (e.g., IBM and MCI) in its operation was influenced by the deregulatory climate of the Reagan administration in the mid-1980s. The decision to involve MERIT and its corporate members was a contentious one and later led to a rebellion by Jon Postel and university colleagues over control of the root directory and the assignment of IP numbers on the Internet. This battle is detailed in Chapter 9, on the public and private Internet. However, to make sense of that conflict it is essential to understand the evolution from the ARPANET to the NSFNET and the eventual creation of the Internet as a global communication medium.

I would argue that the privatization of the Internet was a necessary step, in that the active involvement of global IT and telecommunication

Figure 5.5   For their roles in the development of the Internet, including the creation of TCP/IP, Vinton Cerf (left) and Robert Kahn receive the Presidential Medal of Freedom from US President George W. Bush in 2005. *Photo*: Paul Morse, White House.

companies led to a more rapid diffusion of the technology than would have been possible with only public agency support. The National Science Foundation recognized this in 1986 and pushed for the involvement of IBM and MCI as partners in expanding the backbone. This is not a black-and-white issue – the Internet has evolved today as a public–private partnership that appears to be dominated by corporate entities and Internet service providers, yet still connects thousands of public agencies and schools in countries around the globe. Recall that Facebook subscribers were originally limited to those with .edu e-mail addresses between 2004 and 2006, but the dramatic growth in their subscriber base occurred when they opened the network to all (over the age of 13) in September of 2006.

Notes

1. J. C. R. Licklider, "Man–Computer Symbiosis," *IRE Transactions on Human Factors in Electronics* (March 1960). Retrieved February 20, 2011, from http://groups.csail.mit.edu/medg/people/psz/Licklider.html.
2. N. Negroponte, *Being Digital* (New York: Alfred A. Knopf, 1995), 181.
3. Ibid.

4. Internet World Stats at http://www.internetworldstats.com/stats.htm.
5. R. E. Kahn, "The Organization of Computer Resources into a Packet Radio Network," *Proceedings of AFIPS National Computer Conference* (AFIPS Press, 1975).
6. There are two fascinating interviews with Robert Kahn in the archives of the Charles Babbage Institute in Minneapolis, MN. The first was conducted by William Aspray on March 22, 1989, and the second was conducted on April 24, 1990, by Judy O'Neill. The latter interview is available online: http://www.cbi.umn.edu/oh/pdf.phtml?id=167. Both interviews should be of interest to students of the history of the ARPANET, the Internet, and the development of TCP/IP.
7. R. E. Kahn, S. A. Gronemeyer, J. Burchfiel, and R. C. Kunzelman, "Advances in Packet Radio Technology," *Proceedings of the IEEE* 66/11 (1978), 1468–96.
8. Kahn et al., "Advances in Packet Radio Technology."
9. D. Glover, TELSTAR Fact Sheet from NASA (2008): http://roland.lerc.nasa.gov/~dglover/sat/telstar.html.
10. While Telstar communication satellites orbited the earth at relatively low altitudes (7,000 miles) which limited their utility, their development led to the later creation of geosynchronous satellites whose speed matched the rotation of the Earth by orbiting the Earth at a higher altitude of 22,000 miles. These direct broadcast satellites (DBS) made continental television transmissions possible and led to the creation of DBS services such as SkyTV, PanAmSat, Echostar, DirecTV, and STAR serving all parts of the globe.
11. I. M. Jacobs, R. Binder, and E. V. Hoversten, "General Purpose Packet Satellite Networks," *Proceedings of the IEEE* 66/11 (1978), 1448–67.
12. Within the ARPANET community, Yogan Dalal, Richard Karp, and Carl Sunshine were credited with influential roles in the creation of TCP/IP. Cerf credits the International Network Working Group (INWG) that he chaired between 1972 and 1976, and specifically cited Hubert Zimmerman and Louis Pouzin of the French Cyclades networking research group. The concept of host responsibility was first developed by the Cyclades group.
13. V. Cerf, and R. Kahn, "A Protocol for Packet Network Intercommunication," *IEEE Transactions on Communications* (May 1974). Retrieved April 22, 2009, from http://www.cs.princeton.edu/courses/archive/fall06/cos561/papers/cerf74.pdf.
14. V. Cerf, Y. Dolal, and C. Sunshine, *Specification of Internet Transmission Control Program*. International Network Working Group, RFC 675 (December 1974). Retrieved April 22, 2009, from http://www.ietf.org/rfc/rfc0675.txt.
15. L. G. Roberts, "The Evolution of Packet Switching," *Proceedings of the IEEE* 66/11(1978), 1307–13.
16. J. Abbate, *Inventing the Internet* (Cambridge, MA: MIT Press, 1999), 135.
17. Kahn, O'Neill interview (1990); see n. 6 above.

18. Abbate, *Inventing the Internet*, 143.
19. M. M. Waldrop, *The Dream Machine: J. C. R. Licklider and the Revolution that Made Computing Personal* (New York: Penguin, 2001), 431.
20. Ibid., 431.
21. Retrieved December 30, 2009, from http://www.parc.com/about/milestones.html.
22. The first IBM PC was officially named model 5150. The Intel 8088 specifications are from a datasheet retrieved January 2, 2010, from http://datasheets.chipdb.org/Intel/x86/808x/datashts/8088/231456-006.pdf.
23. See Intel pages on Moore's law at http://download.intel.com/pressroom/kits/events/moores_law_40th/MLTimeline.pdf.
24. From the National Science Foundation (NSF) website: http://www.nsf.gov.
25. NSF, *The Internet: Changing the Way We Communicate* (2009). The website provides an interesting history of NSF involvement in computer science research and the development of the Internet. Retrieved January 4, 2009, from http://www.nsf.gov/about/history/nsf0050/internet/launch.htm.
26. Waldrop, *The Dream Machine*, 459.
27. NSF, *The Internet: Changing the Way We Communicate* website.
28. Waldrop, *The Dream Machine*, 460.
29. All statistics on NSFNET growth are from NSF, *The Internet: Changing the Way We Communicate* website.
30. Waldrop, *The Dream Machine*, 463.
31. NSF, *The Internet: Changing the Way We Communicate* website.
32. Waldrop, *The Dream Machine*, 464. MERIT was renamed in 1990 as Merit Network Inc.
33. After Vinton Cerf left DARPA in 1982, he went to work as vice president of MCI Digital Information Services. There he worked on the development of MCI Mail, the first commercial e-mail service to be connected to the Internet. He later returned to work for MCI in 1994–2005 as senior vice president of technology strategy. Cerf has been vice president and chief Internet evangelist at Google Inc. since September 2005.

6

The Web

The First Web of Information

Paul Otlet, a Belgian bibliographer, peace activist, and information science pioneer, with colleague Henri La Fontaine, in 1904 created the Universal Decimal Classification (UDC) system based on the American Dewey Decimal cataloging system.[1] Otlet actively promoted the adoption of the UDC in Europe by cataloging more than bibliographic information about books and articles; he sought to expand the UDC system to include other media such as photographs, drawings, and films. It was fundamentally a paper-based system of index cards that contained information on the 14 million multimedia items classified and accessed using the UDC. This system was unique in that its cross-index was an analog precursor of the hypertext links found in websites today.[2] In 1934, he had a radical idea for improving public access to this information. He proposed building an electronic system that he called an "International Network for Universal Documentation" that would allow a user "in his armchair to be able to contemplate the whole of creation."[3] He created a system where users could telegraph or telephone a library where archivists would look up the requested information and then reply to the client electronically. Named the Mundaneum by Otlet, the library represented one of the first practical electronic client–host information accession systems, even if the information storage medium was paper index cards, the state of the art at that time.[4]

Digital Universe: The Global Telecommunication Revolution, First Edition. Peter B. Seel.
© 2012 Peter B. Seel. Published 2012 by Blackwell Publishing Ltd.

Figure 6.1   Archivists access index cards for the 14 million items catalogued in Paul Otlet's Mundaneum in Brussels. *Photo*: Courtesy of Mundaneum.

Otlet predicted the creation of massive media libraries linked to a user's television display screen by telephone and telegraph lines. He foresaw a future where all information could be cross-linked by keywords and accessible on request using electronic media. Otlet stated:

Figure 6.2   Paul Otlet was a visionary force in developing a universally accessible bibliography of all human knowledge and creative work. *Photo*: Courtesy of Mundaneum.

Phonographs, radio, television, telephone – these instruments taken as substitutes for the book will in fact become the new book, the most powerful work for the diffusion of human thoughts. This will be the *radiated library, and the televised book.*[5] (*emphasis added*)

If he were alive today, I expect that Otlet would be delighted to surf the Web on a tablet computer or hold an e-book display in his hands as the manifestation of his dreams in the 1930s. He had a vision of an information future that the radio and telephone technology of his day could not readily support, but which would come to fruition in the era of the personal computer after 1973. He was a pioneer in the use of terms to cross-link formation (later named "hypertext"), and the linking of images and films to text in what is now known as multimedia. The tragedy is that much of the Mundaneum and Otlet's life work in the Palais Mondial in Brussels was destroyed during the German occupation of Belgium during World War II. Surviving examples of his card catalog and other personal artifacts are located in Mons, Belgium, in a museum dedicated to the *Mundaneum* and Otlet's creative genius.[6]

Ted Nelson's Dream of Xanadu and Douglas Engelbart's on-Line System

Information scientist Ted Nelson started exploring computer-based methods of linking and accessing information while a first-year graduate student at Harvard University in 1960.[7] Building on Vannevar Bush's concept of developing "trails" of information relationships with the proposed Memex technology, Nelson coined the name "hypertext" in 1965 to refer to text in a document that will lead the reader to other related information.[8] Nelson's Project Xanadu was designed as a method of accessing information on a global basis using hypertext and paying a small royalty to authors as readers accessed what they had written.[9] Nelson's dream was unique in that he looked beyond hypertext to making all media linkable through what he called "hypermedia," a term that is not widely used today, but which is familiar to any Web user who clicks on embedded online links to access images, music, and video. Nelson sought to clarify this point in a 1992 publication:

> By now the word "hypertext" has become generally accepted for branching and responding text, but the corresponding word "hypermedia," meaning complexes of branching and responding graphics, movies and sound – as

well as text – is much less used. Instead they use the strange term "interactive multimedia" – four syllables longer, and not expressing the idea that it extends hypertext.[10]

While Project Xanadu evolved through a series of iterations in the 1980s and 1990s, it failed to achieve widespread adoption and was a commercial failure.[11] Hypertext is a familiar name to Internet users today, and most would certainly be familiar with the "http://www..." that begins most website addresses. The "http" is short for Hypertext Transfer Protocol, and all global website addresses are an acknowledgment to Ted Nelson and his creation of hypertext in the 1960s. The diffusion of the World Wide Web in the early 1990s finally created the hypertext-linked information universe envisioned by Paul Otlet, Vannevar Bush, and Ted Nelson.

When J. C. R. Licklider went to work for ARPA at the Pentagon in 1962, one of the first applicants for computer science funding was Douglas Engelbart at the Stanford Research Institute (SRI).[12] During service in World War II as a radar technician, Engelbart had read Vannevar Bush's "As we may think" article in the July 1945 issue of *Life Magazine*, and it

Figure 6.3   Ted Nelson speaking at Keio University in Japan in 2011. *Photo*: Daniel Gies.

Figure 6.4   Douglas Engelbart in 1984 with the prototype (in his left hand) of the computer mouse created by his Augmentation Research Center at SRI. Engelbart and the ARC were pioneers in the field of human–computer interaction. *Source*: Christina Engelbart.

had a profound influence on him.[13] As a radar technician, he worked daily with electronic graphic display systems, even if very crude ones at that early stage of their development. In 1950, while working at the Ames Research Center in Mountain View, California, he had an epiphany where he envisioned himself sitting at a CRT-type screen that could electronically display and process information.[14] He later said that the system he envisioned would replace microfilm as the medium of information storage (as designed by Vannevar Bush for his Memex) with computer-based storage and processing.[15] This would include the ability to create electronic "associative trails" (as Bush called them), to link related information together. As Engelbart later told interviewer Howard Rheingold:

> I started sketching a system in which a computer draws symbols on the screen for you and you can steer it through different domains with knobs and levers and transducers. I was designing all kinds of things you might want to

do if you had [such] a system ... how to expand it to a theater-like environment, for example, where you could sit with a colleague and exchange information. God! Think of how that would let you cut loose in solving problems.[16]

He developed this vision into a concept for a computer-based system that would combine the ability to electronically process text and images *in a way that would augment the human intellect*. Extend his concept to the present day and we see a universe of linked computers with graphical user interfaces (GUIs) doing exactly what Engelbart had envisioned in 1950. Extend it forward in time and we can visualize police detective John Anderton (played by Tom Cruise) in the film *Minority Report* using a 3-D computer interface system that appears to float in mid-air. Engelbart's problem in 1950 was that his unique vision outpaced the computing technology of that era.

Engelbart enrolled in a graduate program at UC Berkeley in electrical engineering with a focus on computers. As a new graduate in October 1957, he was hired by SRI in Palo Alto and did his initial research on magnetic logic devices. He deferred working on his HCI-augmentation concepts until 1959, as he was warned when he first arrived that they would probably not receive a warm reception at SRI.[17] With funding from the US Air Force's Office of Scientific Research and new-found support from his superiors at SRI, he created the Augmentation Research Center (with the obligatory acronym, ARC). The primary focus of ARC was Human–Computer Interaction (HCI), the interface of human senses with computers that was a central theme in Licklider's prescient "Man–Computer Symbiosis" article in 1960.[18] While early computer technology was designed for the storage and processing of data, Engelbart stressed that humans excelled at using "hunches" and "cut and try" approaches to problem solving.[19] He felt that machine intelligence could enhance the ability of humans to deal with the rising tidal wave of knowledge for the purpose of solving the problems facing humanity. These lines of thought flow directly from Paul Otlet and Vannevar Bush to both Engelbart and Licklider.

To this end, Engelbart and his staff at the ARC developed the oN-Line System (or NLS) which was designed to allow a user to draw upon the power of digital systems in document creation, storage, and revision. The contemporary use of the word "online" describes any activity accomplished when connected to a digital interactive network, typically the Internet, and the word has its roots with Engelbart and ARC.[20] The NLS advanced the concept of hypertext to new levels in very practical ways in linking keywords between documents and related databases. While much attention then (and now) focused on ARC's development of interface tools such as the digital mouse and black text on white display screens, the practical application of hypertext to augment human intelligence by Engelbart and his team at SRI is often overlooked as a significant step forward in the history of information and communication technology.

At the Fall Joint Computer Conference held at the convention center in San Francisco on December 9, 1968, Engelbart and ARC staff members (stationed in the auditorium and at SRI) staged an online demonstration of the NLS to a packed house of 1,000 attendees. Engelbart wore a headset to narrate the presentation, and the computer display was projected onto a large screen at the front of the room.[21] Although he was a bit plodding at times and had to deal with a few software problems, the demonstration was electrifying to the audience. They were witnessing the future of computing, text processing, and the innovative application of hypertext. For many in the audience it was their first exposure to the use of a mouse, graphical displays, text processing, e-mail, and teleconferencing. It has since become known as "the mother of all demos" and it made Engelbart a celebrity in the Bay Area computing community.[22]

Engelbart had demonstrated the power of the computer for information processing and display – he then sought to explore how these online systems could be networked. In April 1967, at a meeting of ARPA's principal investigators hosted by Robert Taylor in Ann Arbor, Michigan, Engelbart volunteered the ARC to host the Network Information Center (the NIC) for the ARPANET.[23] As a key ARPA research facility, SRI was one of the first sites to be connected on the new national network. He and the ARC staff played a key role in developing the NIC as an online repository for data about the network and its daily operations. While UCLA gets credit for being the first host system on the ARPANET, many overlook that the other node was located at SRI. TCP/IP creator Vinton Cerf stated that Engelbart's development of the NLS and the NIC was a central factor in the construction of the ARPANET, and that he should have received equivalent credit for his key role in the creation of the Internet.[24]

While Engelbart is best known today as the "inventor" of the mouse as a widely used HCI tool, this narrow view overlooks his contributions related to human–computer interaction, especially hypertext. In 50 years, the mouse may be seen as a quaint relic of the early days of personal computing as we communicate wirelessly with ubiquitous digital systems with lightweight headbands reading our brain waves. Future students of the history of information technology will focus less on the specific tools created by Engelbart and his team at the ARC and more on the key role they played in making the computer a much easier tool to use for solving human problems – whether that be the mundane task of paying a monthly household bill or seeking to understand changes in global climate. His ideas about augmenting human intelligence advanced the predictions of Paul Otlet, Vannevar Bush, and J. C. R. Licklider in a profound way, and helped set the stage for the development of the Internet and the World Wide Web.

The Development of the Web

In the early days of the ARPANET, physicists at the University of Illinois (an ARPANET node) were able to surreptitiously connect to the physicist community at the Centre Européenne pour la Recherche Nucléaire (CERN) research center located near Geneva, Switzerland. CERN was not part of the early ARPANET. The international community of physicists is a close one, and they collaborate on a regular basis on research projects. The connection had to be sub rosa because public telecommunication networks in Europe prohibited a direct packet-switched connection between scientists at Illinois and those at CERN.[25] Messages and files were sent from Illinois to the Rutherford lab at Cambridge University in the UK (an ARPANET node), then forwarded from Rutherford to CERN. The scientists at CERN became an unofficial extension of the ARPANET and the staff in Geneva followed developments in the US as the network expanded in the 1970s.

One of those staff members was a young scientist with a degree in physics from Oxford University and an intense interest in exploring the potential for using hypertext in networked systems. Tim Berners-Lee worked as a computer programmer in the UK after graduation in 1976, and later went to work at CERN for six months in 1980 as a contract computer scientist. He created a software system that he called EN-QUIRE after a favorite book from his childhood, *Enquire Within Upon Everything*.[26] The book was an 1890 Victorian-era guide on all forms of essential knowledge – ranging from removing stains in fabric to making financial investments. Berners-Lee liked its encyclopedic focus (if primitive at that time) and compared it to a magical "portal to a world of information."[27] The ENQUIRE system included some of the concepts that Berners-Lee later developed into the prototype Web, including the use of

Figure 6.5   Tim Berners-Lee at the TED conference in California in 2009. *Photo*: Veni Markovski.

hyperlinks to navigate within a database of information, but it was not a publicly accessible technology.

After working in the UK as a computer scientist between 1980 and 1984, he returned to work at CERN to develop the ideas that became the Web. In May 1990, with Belgian colleague Robert Cailliau, Berners-Lee submitted a revised proposal to managers at CERN for a global document-sharing system they called "Mesh."[28] It was approved in 1990 and Berners-Lee purchased a then state-of-the-art computer called the NeXT, developed by a company led by Steve Jobs (of Apple renown). Using the NeXTSTEP operating system, Berners-Lee wrote the HTML code for a browser and text editor for what he called the World Wide Web, and it went online on December 25, 1990.[29] A NeXT computer also became the first server on the new Web. The first specially created website was also developed at CERN and went online in August of 1991.

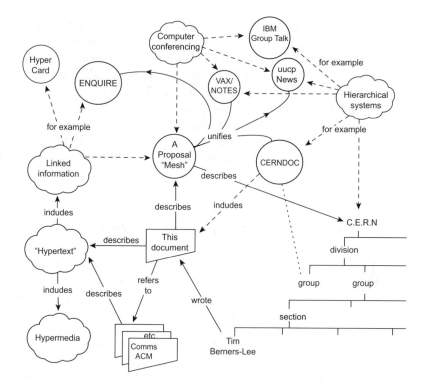

Figure 6.6   Tim Berners-Lee's schematic diagram for the "Mesh" document-sharing system at CERN that became the World Wide Web. Note the references to hypertext and hypermedia in the clouds at left. *Source:* CERN.

When Berners-Lee was asked to summarize his contributions to the development of the Web, he modestly stated:

> I just had to take the hypertext idea and connect it to the Transmission Control Protocol and domain name system ideas and – ta-da! – the World Wide Web.[30]

Inventors do stand on the shoulders of giants and the creation of the World Wide Web was based on the prior ideas and contributions of Paul Otlet, Vannevar Bush, Ted Nelson, Douglas Engelbart, Steve Jobs, and hundreds of other computer scientists, not to mention his partner and chief booster at CERN, Robert Cailliau. While postmodern scholars often debunk the "great man" historical model of invention, noting the many contributions made by an inventor's predecessors and peers, this diminishes the often dramatic effect on society of one person with the right skills having the right idea at the right time (and with the right tools to make it possible). All these elements aligned for Tim Berners-Lee at CERN, and the Web was quickly adopted as an efficient means of sharing hyperlinked documents by physicists around the world. The technology worked across diverse computer platforms and operating systems – as long as the user followed the basic protocols for creating pages with HTML code and then serving documents to users. The Web initially was a system for sharing text-based documents, but as time passed it became a multimedia platform capable of displaying photos, graphics, and motion media.

Mosaic, AOL, and the growth of the Web

Unlike the Internet (which took a decade to reach critical mass in adoption), the World Wide Web had a very rapid adoption curve.[31] Note in Table 6.1 the dramatic increase in host systems after the creation of the Web in 1990. From 1992 to 1997 there was almost a doubling of the number of host computers from year to year. The Mosaic browser was developed in 1992 by a team at the National Center for Supercomputing Applications (NCSA) at the University of Illinois at Urbana-Champaign.[32] They were led by graduate student Marc Andreessen and staff member Eric Bina. While Andreessen used newsgroups to poll Web users about what they were seeking in an improved browser, Bina wrote the code needed to make these functions work. When Mosaic was released online by NCSA in February 1993 it was an immediate success in terms of adoption. As Tim Berners-Lee noted,

> I tried it at CERN. It was easy to download and install, and required very little learning before I had point-and-click access to the Web. Because of these traits, Mosaic was picked up more rapidly than other browsers. Mosaic was much more of a product.[33]

Note the dramatic increase in the number of Internet hosts in 1993 to over one million from 727,000 in 1992. The Web was a powerful tool and the diffusion of improved browsers such as Mosaic fueled the doubling of host systems in that critical year.

Another key innovation that influenced the rapid growth of the World Wide Web in the US was the introduction in 1993 of a new dial-up Internet service called America Online (AOL).[34] It is what is known as a "walled garden" site in that it offers unique content and communication services

Table 6.1   Internet hosts

1981	213
1982	235
1983	562
1984	1,024
1985	1,961
1986	2,308
1987	5,089
1988	28,174
1989	80,000
1990	**313,000 (Tim Berners-Lee creates Mesh at CERN)**
1991	**535,000 (first World Wide Web site online at CERN)**
1992	727,000
1993	**1,313,000 (AOL 1.0 for Windows and 2.0 for Macintosh released in January and Mosaic browser introduced by NCSA in February)**
1994	2,217,000
1995	4,852,000
1996	**9,472,000 (AOL moves to $20/month flat rate fee for access)**
1997	16,146,000
1998	29,670,000
1999	43,230,000
2000	72,398,100*
2001	109,574,500*
2002	**162,128,500* (AOL reaches a peak of 27 million U.S. subscribers)**
2003	171,638,300*
2004	233,101,000*
2005	317,646,100*
2006	394,991,600*

(continued)

Table 6.1   (*continued*)

2007	433,193,200*
2008	541,677,400*
2009	625,226,500*
2010	732,740,400*
2011	818,374,269

*rounded to nearest hundred.
Source: Internet host data from Internet Systems Consortium Inc. Used with permission.
Points added in bold are the author's.

(e.g., unique chat rooms) to its paying clients. For first-time Internet users in the 1990s, AOL was akin to a set of training wheels providing one-click access to a wide variety of online information services. It facilitated access to chat rooms and bulletin board sites that had become popular in the late 1980s. It featured an easy-to-use graphical user interface that was a key feature in mass adoption by clients in that era. As a result of being one of the first companies to mass-market Internet access (along with CompuServe and a few others), AOL experienced rapid growth after 1996, when the company moved to a flat-rate fee of $20 per month for online access. One major drawback to AOL was that, as a walled-garden site, it emphasized its proprietary services and inhibited access to the rest of the Internet. The number of subscribers peaked at 27 million in 2002 and steadily declined to 4.1 million by 2011.[35] The Web and its thousands of online services had become so easy to access that walled-garden services such as AOL had become an anachronism by the beginning of the 21st century.

Web 2.0 and the Architecture of Participation

If companies such as AOL represented the world of Web 1.0, a plethora of innovative services are helping define the evolving nature of the Web in the new century.

Web 2.0 is term that describes the evolution of the Web from a static one-to-many environment to an interactive many-to-many collaborative online universe.[36] Tim O'Reilly expanded this concept in a 2004 article, "The Architecture of Participation," in which he states that the relative simplicity of HTML coding made the Web an inherently open-source community where anyone familiar with HTML could add content.[37] We have now progressed to the point where this is no longer required as templates, fill-in-the-box forms, and click-here-to-upload buttons are now commonplace tools for online contributors. The code is still there a click away on a browser window, but users do not need to know HTML or XHTML coding to create websites or add online content.

Where Web 1.0 was characterized by users pulling content from the Internet, the Web 2.0 universe is inherently more interactive. Not only are users routinely going to the Web to look up movie times and read e-mail, they are uploading photos and posting comments on social networking sites. Posting content online used to require building a specialized website and then writing the code needed to add new content. Posting new content is now as easy as picking the files to be uploaded and perhaps writing some comments about them. The democratization of the Internet has been enhanced by the one-click upload and the technology that makes this possible.

The Web 2.0 service YouTube has transformed the display of video content online. Once the sole purview of film studios and television distribution networks, YouTube has democratized the delivery of motion media to mass audiences. Anyone with a camcorder can now be a broadcaster on the Web. An observer who has spent more than a few minutes looking at videos on YouTube knows that the sublime and the ridiculous are no more than a click apart. This is part of the success of the site – anyone can post almost anything as long as the content is not indecent, obscene, or copyrighted. YouTube is also a remarkable repository for formerly perishable mass media content such as television commercials and music videos. The impermanence of electronic media, decried by Harold Innis, takes a new twist as online sites such as YouTube have become massive archives of "perishable" pop culture content. As someone with a lifelong interest in music, especially classic rock and roll, I found nirvana in the treasure trove of music videos on YouTube. While the image resolution is low-definition and the audio quality is often poor, these videos were typically inaccessible to mass audiences before the creation of YouTube. It is a shrewd strategic move by record labels to make these videos available online, as I expect they will kindle interest in many "ancient" genres of popular music in new generations of viewers and listeners.

Central to the evolution from 1.0 to 2.0 (and on to 3.0) is the use of the Web as a communication medium. One high-growth area is the use of the Web for social networking. The phenomenal growth rates of sites such as Facebook (see below) and LinkedIn since 2005 illustrate the compelling attraction of these venues as a forum for sharing information, personal interests, photos, and videos. The vision of Ted Nelson of the Internet as a forum for hypermedia has been realized not only in e-commerce and mass media, but now in the form of shared personal media. It's a rare person under 30 in wired nations who does not have a social networking site filled with photos, text, and video.

Facebook as a Case Study

Facebook makes an interesting case study when analyzing the phenomenal adoption rate of social networking sites. It was started in 2004 by then Harvard sophomore Mark Zuckerberg and two roommates, Chris Hughes, and Dustin Moskovitz.[38] It was intended to be an online version of a publication that Zuckerberg had seen at his preparatory school that featured the names and photographs of all students.[39] At Harvard in November 2003, Zuckerberg hacked into a university database of photos of students living in on-campus housing and posted pairs of the images on a website he created named "Facemash."[40] His idea was that students would vote on which of the pair was more attractive. He sent the site's URL to a few friends and then posted it on several university list-serves. In a single day the site was visited by 450 students who voted 22,000 times on the photos.[41] While the site was popular with these students (and outraged many others), Harvard administrators were upset about Zuckerberg's unauthorized access to their photo database. The site was ordered offline and Zuckerberg was called before Harvard's Administrative Board for disciplinary action.

He was allowed to return to Harvard for the spring term in 2004 and, along with Hughes and Moskovitz, decided to expand the Facemash concept into a social networking site. The revised site debuted on February 4, 2004 as "Thefacebook" and included a (non-hacked) color photo provided by each student subscriber with information about their major, relationship status, interests, and contact information.[42] As the film *The Social Network* made clear, one key factor driving users to the site was seeing the relationship status of a person of interest. The basic format remains unchanged today, but it has been tweaked to include Twitter-like "what's on your mind" boxes for posting information about current activities or thoughts.

The site was an immediate success at Harvard and soon expanded to other colleges and universities – a ".edu" university e-mail address was required for registration. In 2006 the site opened membership to anyone over 13 with an e-mail address, a move which was opposed by some members who wished to keep it a site exclusively for college students. However, this was a key strategic move as it greatly expanded the subscriber base.

Facebook is one of the fastest-growing sites (of any kind) on the Web, with over 800 million subscribers worldwide, an increase of 700 million since 2008.[43] These users are no longer predominantly from the US – 70 percent reside elsewhere, a statistic that has been influenced by the creation of Facebook access in multiple languages.[44] Facebook access in North Africa has been credited as a primary medium for mobilizing popular protest in the overthrow of repressive governments in Tunisia and Egypt in January 2011.[45] While the 18–25 age group represents the greatest number of US Facebook users, the fastest-growing segment is users over the age of 25.[46] Aunt Marge and Uncle George are signing up for Facebook, as are Grandma and Grandpa. Not only are the demographics of site users skewing toward them being older and more diverse, but users are spending more time on the site. The average Facebook user spends 4.5 hours a month online at the site, compared with 3 hours on Yahoo, 2.75 hours on AOL, and 2.5 hours on Google.[47]

You may know someone who spends 4.5 hours *a day* on Facebook or a similar site. What is the appeal of social networking sites in general, and Facebook in particular? It is no mystery that human beings enjoy communicating with each other. We like connecting with our friends and family with our cell phones, via e-mail, and now with social networking sites. They allow us to share photos, see what our friends are doing each day, make amusing comments about them, and renew connections with old friends and classmates. Facebook's goal is to encourage users to make site visits a daily habit and to promote linkages with other frequently visited websites. The rapid growth in the number of Facebook's subscribers, combined with the "stickiness" of the site (the time spent on the site), has generated increasing revenues for the parent company. The privately held company does not release profit and loss statistics, but analysts estimate that it had revenues in 2010 of over $2 billion.[48] The site will become even more profitable in the future as the cross-linking alliances yield new advertising revenue. Selling access to 800 million global subscribers for advertising and marketing purposes has tremendous revenue potential, but at the risk of alienating these members, as Facebook's *Beacon* project did in 2007. These and other privacy concerns with social networking sites will be analyzed in detail in Chapter 11.

The interval from Paul Otlet's dream of a global electronic information accession system in 1934 to its realization in the World Wide Web in the

1990s spanned less than a generation – 60 years. In those six decades enormous leaps were made in information and communication technology. Electronic computers had to be created that could process large amounts of data quickly and efficiently. Electronic technology had to evolve from vacuum tubes in the 1950s, to transistors as individual components, then to millions of transistors embedded in chips. The doubling of chip capacity driven by Moore's law not only reduced the size of digital systems, it halved their prices every two years. While devices were doubling in speed and capacity, networks had to be constructed to connect them. The Cold War may have been part of the impetus for their construction in the US, but ultimately it was a desire to share information and computing resources that led to the rapid growth of the Internet and then the Web. The addition of *communication* to information technology, first in the form of e-mail and now in the form of hypermedia and all-purpose mobile phones, has led to the explosion in social media that will continue to expand in this century. The irony is that this wireless digital universe is dependent on a network of cables that spans the globe – the wiring of the planet is the theme of Chapter 7.

Notes

1. P. Otlet, *International Organisation and Dissemination of Knowledge: Selected Essays of Paul Otlet*, ed. W. B. Rayward (London: Elsevier, 1990). Otlet's colleague Henri La Fontaine was a key partner in organizing the Mundaneum.
2. A. Wright, "The Web Time Forgot," *New York Times* (June 17, 2008). Retrieved September 3, 2009, from http://www.nytimes.com/2008/06/17/science/17mund.html?_r=2.
3. Ibid.
4. The name *Mundaneum* is derived from root word *mondial* for world. Otlet's original vision called for it to be part of a "world city" dedicated to global peace. The predecessor to the Mundaneum was the Palais Mondial in Brussels, Belgium.
5. Otlet, *International Organisation and Dissemination of Knowledge.*
6. The museum is about one hour by train from Brussels. See Wright, "The Web Time Forgot."
7. G. Wolf, "The Curse of Xanadu," *Wired* (June 1995). Retrieved September 3, 2009, from http://www.wired.com/wired/archive/3.06/xanadu.html.
8. Ibid.
9. Ibid.
10. T. H. Nelson, *Literary Machines: The Report On, and Of, Project Xanadu Concerning Word Processing, Electronic Publishing, Hypertext, Thinkertoys,*

Tomorrow's Intellectual Revolution, and Certain Other Topics Including Knowledge, Education and Freedom (Sausalito, CA: Mindful Press, 1981).

11. Wolf, "The Curse of Xanadu."

12. M. M. Waldrop, *The Dream Machine: J. C. R. Licklider and the Revolution That Made Computing Personal* (New York: Viking Penguin, 2001), 210–11. Engelbart had previously applied for National Institute of Mental Health funding in 1961, but they rejected the proposal saying that "since your Palo Alto area is so far from the centers of computer expertise, we don't think that you could staff your project adequately" (ibid., 216). This comment is amusing today, as SRI is located on the northern end of Silicon Valley, but in 1961 it was far from the established computer science centers in the eastern US.

13. Ibid., 215.

14. D. Engelbart, "The Augmented Knowledge Workshop," in A. Goldberg (ed.), *A History of Personal Workstations* (New York: ACM Press, 1988), 189.

15. Ibid., 215.

16. H. Rheingold, *Tools for Thought* (New York: Simon & Schuster, 1985), ch. 9. Retrieved August 6, 2009, from http://www.rheingold.com/texts/tft/9.html.

17. M. M. Waldrop, *The Dream Machine: J. C. R. Licklider and the Revolution that Made Computing Personal* (New York: Penguin, 2001), 212.

18. The widely used acronym HCI can mean either Human–Computer Interaction or Human–Computer Interface. The latter term is more narrowly defined as the tools that allow humans to input and receive analog information from a digital computer – e.g., a display screen, speakers, keyboard, and a mouse.

19. D. Engelbart, *Augmenting Human Intellect: A Conceptual Framework*, Report to the Director of Information Sciences, Air Force Office of Scientific Research (Menlo Park, CA: Stanford Research Institute, 1962). Available online: http://dougengelbart.org. See section III, where Engelbart analyzes Vannevar Bush's *As We May Think* ideas in detail.

20. The term *online* is defined in Federal Standard 1037C, *Glossary of Telecommunication Terms* (http://www.its.bldrdoc.gov/fs-1037/fs-1037c.htm): 1. In computer technology, the state or condition of a device or equipment that is under the direct control of another device. 2. In computer technology, the status of a device that is functional and ready for service.

21. A grainy, low-resolution film of the "mother of all demos" is accessible online at YouTube: http://www.youtube.com/watch?v=JfIgzSoTMOs. Recall that this presentation was made in 1968, in the early days of computing history.

22. The term "mother of all demos" is from S. Levy, *Insanely Great: The Life and Times of Macintosh, the Computer that Changed Everything* (Harmondsworth: Penguin, 1994), 42.

23. K. Hafner and M. Lyon, *Where Wizards Stay Up Late: The Origins of the Internet* (New York: Touchstone, 1996), 78.

24. V. Cerf, "Rants & Raves," letter published in *Wired* 9/3 (September 1995). The letter is accessible online at http://www.wired.com/wired/archive/3.09/rants.html.

25. J. Abbate, *Inventing the Internet* (Cambridge, MA: MIT Press, 1999), 94.

26. T. Berners-Lee, *Weaving the Web* (New York: HarperCollins, 1999), 1. *Enquire Within Upon Everything* (1890) has been reprinted and is available online: http://www.amazon.com/Enquire-Within-upon-Everything-1890/dp/187359030X/ref=sr_1_1?ie=UTF8&s=books&qid=1215026795&sr=8-1.

27. Berners-Lee, *Weaving the Web*, 1.

28. Ibid., 26. See also *A Little History of the World Wide Web* page at the W3C site: http://www.w3.org/History.html.

29. Berners-Lee, *Weaving the Web*, 30.

30. See the *Answers for Young People* site at W3C: http://www.w3.org/People/Berners-Lee/Kids.

31. It is also important to not confuse the Web with the Internet. The Web is an application that is a *subset* of the Internet, and subsumes many prior functions that had to be accomplished by writing instructions in Unix code. As new and easy-to-use GUI browsers were developed such as Mosaic in 1993 and Netscape Navigator in 1994, the Web became accessible to millions of computer users.

32. Berners-Lee, *Weaving the Web*, 68.

33. Ibid., 69.

34. The company is officially known as AOL LLC, a company formerly operated by Time Warner. Dial-up meant that subscribers had to connect via a special phone line at what is today a very slow access speed – 56 kbps.

35. S. Yin, "75% of AOL Subscribers Don't Need to Pay, Says Report," *PC Magazine* (January 24, 2011). Retrieved January 30, 2011, from http://www.pcmag.com/article2/0,2817,2376167,00.asp#.

36. D. DiNucci, "Fragmented Future," *Print* 53/4 (1999), 32. While Darcy DiNucci is cited as the source for the term Web 2.0, many others have contributed to its elaboration since 1999.

37. T. O'Reilly, "The Architecture of Participation" (June 2004). O'Reilly Media Inc. website. Retrieved July 10, 2009, from http://www.oreillynet.com/pub/a/oreilly/tim/articles/architecture_of_participation.html.

38. C. Hoffman, "The Battle for Facebook," *Rolling Stone* (June 26, 2008). Retrieved July 30, 2009, from http://www.rollingstone.com/news/story/21129674/the_battle_for_facebook/. This article includes claims from three other Harvard students who contributed to the Facebook concept, but were shut out of the company.

39. Zuckerberg attended Phillips Exeter Academy in New Hampshire, which published a generically named "facebook" with each student's name and photograph.

40. K. A. Kaplan, "Facemash Creator Survives Ad Board," *The Harvard Crimson* (November 19, 2003). Retrieved July 30, 2009, from http://www.thecrimson.com/printerfriendly.aspx?ref=350143.

41. Ibid.

42. Hoffman, "The Battle for Facebook."

43. Facebook statistics. Retrieved September 4, 2011, from http://www.facebook.com/press/info.php?statistics.

44. B. Stone, "Is Facebook Growing Up Too Fast?", *New York Times* (March 29, 2009). Retrieved August 3, 2009, from http://www.nytimes.com/2009/03/29/technology/internet/29face.html.

45. A. Shah, "Egypt's New Hero: Can Geek-Activist Wael Ghonim Overthrow Mubarak?", *Time* (February 8, 2011). Retrieved February 14, 2011, from http://www.time.com/time/world/article/0,8599,2047006,00.html.

46. J. Smith, "Number of U.S. Facebook Users Over 35 Nearly Doubles in Last 30 Days," *Inside Facebook* (March 25, 2009). Retrieved July 30, 2009, from http://www.insidefacebook.com/2009/03/25/number-of-us-facebook-users-over-35-nearly-doubles-in-last-60-days/.

47. M. Megna, "Facebook Rules in Time Spent Online," *Internetnews.com* (July 14, 2009). Retrieved July 22, 2009, from http://www.internetnews.com/webcontent/article.php/3829801/Facebook + Rules + in + Time + Spent + Online.htm.

48. J. O'Dell, "Facebook On Track for $2B in Revenue in 2010," *Mashable* (December 16, 2010). Retrieved January 16, 2011, from http://mashable.com/2010/12/16/facebook-2-billion-revenue/.

Part III

Telecommunication and Media Convergence

7

Telecommunication and the "Flat" World

"What hath God wrought"

The dramatic message from the Bible was transmitted 34 miles from the Supreme Court building in Washington to a railroad station in Baltimore, Maryland on May 24, 1844. It was part of a demonstration for members of the US Congress of telegraphy, then a new communication technology.[1] Note that the message is a statement and not a question. It does not question the divine linkage to this new technology, it celebrates it. The message reflected the perspective in that era that this new technology was divinely inspired as a powerful tool to assist human communication. This viewpoint may seem atypical today in a world suffused with secular communication technologies, but at the time the hand of God was seen as the motive force behind the mysterious powers that made telegraphy, and later telephony, possible. Subsequent advances in science explained the electromagnetic forces at work in electrical communication and progressively demystified them. In the 19th century, however, it enhanced the public acceptance of these technologies to invoke their supposedly divine origins.

Digital Universe: The Global Telecommunication Revolution, First Edition. Peter B. Seel.
© 2012 Peter B. Seel. Published 2012 by Blackwell Publishing Ltd.

Figure 7.1   Samuel F. B. Morse, photographed circa 1866 by Mathew Brady. The date of the photo is uncertain. Photographic historians place it as being taken in Brady's Washington studio after 1865 and before Morse's death in 1872. A distinguished painter, Morse was also a pioneer in photography, studying under Daguerre in Paris and then undertaking portrait photography in the United States on his return. *Source*: US Library of Congress.

Samuel F. B. Morse and his partner Alfred Vail had developed a unique system of batteries to periodically amplify the telegraph signal, and used Vail's system of dot-dash code (named for Morse) to demonstrate to a Congressional audience that telegraphy could be an effective means of instantaneous communication. The key term is *instantaneous* – observers of the demonstration in Baltimore's Mount Clare railway depot were awed by the fact that the clicking key was being moved by Morse's hand on the sending key in Washington at that same instant. Centuries-long

Figure 7.2 The actual telegraph key used in Morse's 1844 demonstration in the Supreme Court building in Washington, DC. The key is on display in the Smithsonian's National Museum of American History, located one mile west of the site of the 1844 demonstration in the US Supreme Court building. *Source*: Smithsonian Institution, National Museum of American History.

barriers to human communication posed by distance were smashed by the creation of telegraphy, a coined word from the Greek *tele-* (far) and *graphein* (to write) – far-writing. As telegraph wires were deployed around the world in the 1800s with the construction of new railroad lines, citizens ventured down to local railway stations to hear and see the telegraph key click. It is a common sight in movies about that era today, but at the time the telegraph was viewed as a magical instrument activated by unseen hands hundreds or thousands of miles away. For perspective, it is helpful to recall Arthur C. Clarke's classic observation that "any sufficiently advanced technology is indistinguishable from magic," to imagine how observers of that era reacted to the new medium of telegraphy.[2]

Visitors to the National Museum of American History in Washington can see Morse's telegraph key used in the 1844 demonstration. It is important to remember that Morse did not "invent" the telegraph – he is credited with improving on designs created earlier by others. While optical telegraphs using semaphore signals spanned many parts of Europe in the 1700s, the first electrically powered telegraphs were developed in Europe by Gauss and Weber in Germany in 1833 and by Cooke and Wheatstone in Great Britain in 1837. The English system was designed to improve intelligence about trains operating along the Great

Western Railway's single-track line from London's Paddington Station to West Drayton in the borough of Hillingdon.[3] An instantaneous communication system was required to shift trains onto sidings to prevent head-on collisions. It was a command-and-control system designed to operate in real time over long distances (13 miles in this case). Morse made the telegraph commercially successful in the US and Europe and introduced his improved electromagnetic version at a time when a need emerged for the widespread diffusion of the invention.

Communication historian Brian Winston has expanded upon French historian Fernand Braudel's concept of braking and accelerating factors in the history of technology to create a useful model (Figure 7.3) that analyzes why some inventions succeed and others fail to diffuse in society.[4] One key principle for Winston is that human technologies, including those for communication, are fundamentally embedded in what he terms the "social sphere." Winston situates the creation of new inventions along an axis in the social sphere between science (representing competence) and technology (performance) and defining a lateral axis as "past" and "future." In this model, ideas for inventions evolve from science into a prototype stage, where they are tested and then modified by their creators. Winston describes a key stage between prototyping and invention as requiring a *supervening social necessity*.[5] Borrowing from the cliché that "necessity is the mother of invention," Winston elaborates on this theme with a number of technological histories as examples. The "supervening social necessity" for telegraphy to move to the invention

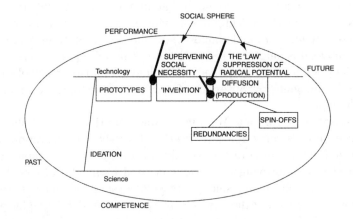

Figure 7.3   Winston's telecommunication diffusion model. *Source*: B. Winston, *Media Technology and Society* (1998).

stage in Winston's analysis was initially railway safety, but this was soon superseded by business and journalistic applications (telegraphed stock quotations and news bulletins sent by telegram). Media historian and critic Harold Innis also noted the key role played by the telegraph in news dissemination after 1850 that led to the formation of newspaper cooperatives to share the latest news and commodity information.[6]

Winston defines four distinct areas that influence the diffusion of a new communication technology,[7] and brakes and/or accelerators can be found in each area:

1. **Needs of companies**. In the case of telegraphy, railway companies seized upon the new technology as a method of keeping track of train locations for safety and management purposes. These were accelerating factors in the diffusion of the technology. There were few braking or inhibiting factors as this was the first widespread adoption of an electrical communication technology.

2. **Requirements of other technologies**. The success of Morse's telegraphy system was dependent on a superior coding system (Morse code) which could be transmitted as short or long bursts of current (dots and dashes). Morse and Vail also had the perceptive insight to visit a printer's shop to investigate the optimal coding scheme based on the frequency of letters used in publications.[8] Thus, the familiar S-O-S distress call is rendered in International Morse Code as dot-dot-dot (S); dash-dash-dash (O); dot-dot-dot (S), as this message could be quickly transmitted in an emergency with three sets of three common key impressions in succession.[9]

3. **Regulatory and legal actions**. The US government supported the development of telegraphy by funding the short line from Washington to Baltimore in 1844. As noted above, Morse's public demonstration of his system was for members of the US Congress, and it was adopted by the US Postal Service the following year.[10] Diffusion in Great Britain was more complicated. Early attempts to develop an electric telegraph were rejected by the British Admiralty in 1814 (developed by Wedgwood) and 1816 (by Ronalds).[11] Ships at sea used flags and semaphore to signal each other, and the Admiralty saw no need for this impractical *wired* technology. The reception in other countries was even more hostile. Diplomat Pavel Schilling developed a working prototype system in 1832 in St. Petersburg, but Emperor Nicholas I viewed it as an instrument of subversion (one obviously without divine origins) and forbade its diffusion in Russia.[12]

4. **General social forces**. As the industrial revolution exploded in the second half of the 19th century, thousands of miles of railroad track were laid to connect cities throughout the world. Telegraph poles followed the rails as a command-and-control system, but other uses for instantaneous communication soon usurped railroad applications by transmitting stock quotes and news bulletins. Telegraphy could be used to link nations – and ultimately continents – for business, military, and mass media purposes.

The Atlantic Cable

'Tis done! The angry sea consents,
The nations stand no more apart,
With claspèd hands the continents
Feel throbbings of each other's hearts
Speed, speed the cable; let it run
A loving girdle round the earth
Till all the nations 'neath the sun
Shall be as brothers of one hearth.
(Anonymous poem composed in 1858 on the
completion of the Atlantic Cable)[13]

In 1843 (a year before his successful Washington demonstration), Samuel Morse had expressed his opinion that a trans-Atlantic cable was feasible.[14] A group of American entrepreneurs led by New York merchant Cyrus W. Field created a company in 1856 that proposed to link the United States and Canada with southern Ireland, which was then part of Great Britain.[15] It was a wildly ambitious idea since the distance to be spanned was almost 2,000 miles across the often stormy North Atlantic. Manufacturing a cable of that length that could withstand the extreme pressures two miles below the surface and the corrosive effects of salt water seemed to be a technical impossibility given the state of metallurgy and wire insulation of that era just before the US Civil War. While undersea cables had been laid under other bodies of water at this time (including the English Channel between Britain and France in 1851), these distances were relatively short (25 nautical miles under the Channel) and the depths were shallow compared with that of the Atlantic.

By the mid-1850s, telegraph lines extended east in North America to the far islands of eastern Canada and west from London under the Irish Sea and on to the west coast of Ireland. Cyrus Field and fellow investors created the New York, Newfoundland, and London Telegraph Company to purchase the 2,000 miles of cable and lay it under the North Atlantic.[16] Field was the motive force behind this undertaking and successfully enlisted the support of the governments of the United States and Great Britain.[17] Given the technical challenges it was a very risky undertaking. Skeptics considered the proposed cable a technical impossibility, and many thought it was a shady scheme to fleece unwary investors.

The technical challenges were imposing. Manufacturing 2,000 miles of cable that could withstand the intense pressure under 14,000 feet of sea water was daunting enough. Making a flexible cable with a copper inner core (to conduct the telegraphic signal) and a protective iron outer covering that would not corrode in sea water was another challenge. Other undersea cables of that era utilized a newly found material, gutta-percha, to insulate the inner core and protect it from sea water that might

Figure 7.4   A poster celebrates the successful completion of the Atlantic Cable in 1866 with the British lion at left, Neptune in the center, and the American eagle at right. The new telegraphic connection between North America and Europe was touted here as the Eighth Wonder of the World. *Source:* US Library of Congress.

cause it to short-circuit. Gutta-percha is the white latex sap from the tree of the same name found on the Malay peninsula of Southeast Asia. At the time, it was considered a miraculous substance that, while brittle in the open air, could be softened and molded when immersed in hot water. In the cold depths of the North Atlantic it would solidify into an ideal insulator for the cable. Gutta-percha was shipped in vast quantities from Malaya (now Malaysia) to factories in England to be coated over the inner copper core of the cable. This was then wrapped in an outer sheath of spiraled iron wires to strengthen the cable and protect it from being damaged by ship's anchors in shallow waters at the ends of the cable.

The *USS Niagara*, an American warship converted to cable-laying duties for the project, set off from Valentia Island off Ireland in August 1857, with 1,800 miles of cable aboard. Moving slowly at four knots to avoid stress to the cable reeling off its stern, it had been at sea barely three days when the cable separated and 335 miles of it were lost to the depths. This was just the beginning of a nine-year struggle to lay the Atlantic Cable that would severely test the engineers, scientists, and investors involved.

The company stored the remaining cable in Britain over the winter of 1857 and started again with a fleet of cable-laying vessels in June of 1858. This time they began in the middle of the Atlantic by splicing together two halves of the cable, and then one group sailed west toward Newfoundland and the other east toward Ireland. They progressed slowly to avoid breaking the cable, but after the *HMS Agamemnon* had laid 255 miles to the east, the line failed again. The fleet sailed to Ireland to resupply, and then started again at mid-ocean. Proceeding with great care to smoothly pay out the cable, the *USS Niagara* reached Trinity Bay in Newfoundland on August 5, and the *Agamemnon* set anchor off Valentia Island on the same day. The ends of the Atlantic Cable were ferried ashore and connected to the North American and European telegraph networks. Company engineers sent a message down the 1,950 miles of wire under the North Atlantic and it was successfully received in Ireland. The first non-test message sent was "Glory to God in the highest; on earth, peace and good will toward men." Confounding all the skeptics, the Atlantic Cable worked.[18]

Contemporary reaction to the news of the successful completion of the Atlantic Cable on August 5, 1858 was dramatic. The public response was comparable to the outpouring of international good will that accompanied the landing of human beings on the moon 111 years later in July of 1969. When news of the cable connection arrived in New York, a spontaneous celebration erupted in the streets. In Boston, 100 guns were fired on the Common and church bells rang for one hour. Queen Victoria sent a congratulatory telegraphic message over the cable to President James Buchanan.[19] Hundreds of messages flowed back and forth between the Old and New Worlds over the completed cable link.

The city of New York held an official civic celebration on September 1, 1858 to honor Cyrus Field, Atlantic Cable investors, the captains of the cable-laying ships, and the scientific and engineering staff who worked on the project. A massive procession marched from the Battery north to what is now midtown Manhattan. The day concluded with a torchlight parade conducted by the city's firemen. Ironically and sadly, the celebrated Atlantic Cable stopped functioning that same day – corrosive salt water somewhere along the 2,000 miles of wire had intruded past the gutta-percha insulation under enormous pressure and shorted out the conductor.

The cable had worked for one day short of four weeks, and its failure caused much gloom on both sides of the Atlantic. However, it was a successful (albeit brief) proof of concept that emboldened efforts to replace it. Cyrus Field immediately planned to lay a new, more durable cable, but the outbreak of the Civil War in the US was to delay its completion for almost seven years. The new cable was designed to address the design and construction flaws with the first conduit. It was better insulated with gutta-percha and had a stronger steel wire casing.

In July of 1865 the *Great Eastern*, the world's largest ship at that time, sailed west from Ireland paying out 2,000 miles of cable stowed in her hold. Only a ship as large as the *Great Eastern* could carry the improved cable, which weighed thousands of tons (3,500 pounds per mile). On August 2, after 1,216 miles of cable had been laid, the line separated and, despite immediate efforts to capture the end of the cable, it sank to the bottom of the sea two miles below. At this point one would expect those with less motivation to simply give up and walk away from the enterprise. Cyrus Field was not a person to be easily discouraged. Later that year, new cable was manufactured in a British factory to replace what had been lost, and the *Great Eastern* sailed again in the summer of 1866 from Ireland. New machinery had been created to smoothly pay out the cable (Figure 7.5), and the new cable had greater buoyancy to facilitate its gradual descent to the bottom of the Atlantic. After 20 days at sea, on July 28, 1866 the *Great Eastern* set anchor off the small village of Heart's Content in Newfoundland and the end of the cable was carried ashore to the telegraph station there.[20] This cable worked flawlessly for years and was the forerunner of many other trans-oceanic telegraph cables.

Figure 7.5   Cable-laying machinery aboard the HMS *Great Eastern* in 1866. The improved feed mechanism reduced stress on the cable as it was paid out into the depths of the Atlantic. *Source*: US Library of Congress.

By the turn of the century in 1900, undersea cables spanned the globe from North and South America to Europe, through the Mediterranean Sea to the Middle East, Africa, and on to India, Indonesia, China, and Australia.[21] The technical struggles involved in creating and laying the Atlantic Cable made possible the global linkages between all of the planet's temperate continents. It is instructive to apply Winston's model to the Atlantic Cable as the first of its kind. The supervening social necessity was the need to link the economic capitals of two of the world's great powers, New York and London. Remnants of the animosity from the war of 1812 had been supplanted by active trade between the two nations. This trade was dependent on the need to share intelligence on commodity prices and related investment information. A telegraphic connection would allow real-time communication between the continents at a time when it took almost two weeks for mail to cross the Atlantic by ship. In April 1865, it took 12 days for news of Abraham Lincoln's assassination on the 14th to reach London by ship.[22] The relative advantage (to borrow from Rogers) of telegraphic cable over mail sent by sea was dramatic and part of the cause for the short-lived celebration on both continents in 1858. Winston's diffusion model can be applied to the Atlantic Cable:

1. **Needs of companies.** The Atlantic Cable was the *raison d'être* of Field's New York, Newfoundland, and London Telegraph Company. The company's success was directly dependent on laying a durable cable that would provide the message transmission capacity or bandwidth needed to make the service economically sound. There was no alternative to telegraphy for instantaneous trans-oceanic communication at the time (communication satellites were not an option until 1962). Mail was a very small portion of trans-Atlantic trade, so shipping companies were not opposed to the laying of the cable.

2. **Requirements of other technologies.** The success of the Atlantic Cable was dependent on technical advances in three distinct areas: oceanography, materials science (with gutta-percha and metallurgy), and cable-laying technology. Multiple surveys of the Atlantic Ocean floor in the 1850s along the planned cable route were made by both the US and British navies. Pioneer oceanographer Lt. Matthew Maury identified an undersea "telegraphic plateau" as the ideal route for the Atlantic Cable.[23] The use of gutta-percha as a rubber-like insulating material was a key element in protecting the successful deep-water cable. Methods had to be developed for processing the tree sap and molding it around the inner copper wire that carried the signals. The development of machinery that could spin a protective layer of steel wire around the cable was also important in "armoring" the conduit. Lastly, the art of cable placement in deep water had to be perfected so that it could be fed smoothly from a ship without the unwanted stresses that snapped early versions.

3. **Regulatory and legal actions.** As noted above, both the US and British governments actively supported the risky endeavor. Government support reduced the risks involved by making direct subsidies and grants to the Atlantic Telegraph Company. The government of Great Britain pledged the use of Royal Navy ships for surveys of the planned route and for laying the telegraph cable. In addition, the British government pledged to pay the company £14,000 per year until its net profit exceeded 6 percent, at which point the subsidy would drop to £10,000 for the subsequent 25 years.[24] In 1857, the US Congress approved a similar subsidy with an equivalent $70,000 per year at first and then $50,000 a year after the 6 percent threshold was reached.[25] The US Navy also supplied two ships for cable laying in 1857, the new *USS Niagara* and the *USS Susquehanna*. It was a unique partnership for two nations that had been at each other's throats in 1812.

4. **General social forces.** There was intense public interest in the Atlantic Cable, which was made manifest during the premature celebrations in 1858 in both Great Britain and the US. Citizens in both nations had observed the implications of instantaneous communication provided by the telegraph as the technology diffused along the rail lines that spread like spider's webs in the 1850 and 1860s. Intercontinental electronic communication has become such a commonplace today that it is difficult to imagine a world without it. The world before the Atlantic Cable must have seemed much larger to the average citizen compared with their perceptions of global distances after it was successfully completed in 1866. The public sense of the "death of distance" exemplified by trans-oceanic telegraph lines was later amplified by the international development of telephone lines across continents and under the seas.[26]

Communication, Empire, and Harold Innis

Harold Innis (1894–1952) was an influential Canadian communication scholar who studied the linkages between communication, transportation, and the rise and fall of empires.[27] His doctoral dissertation in economics was on the history of the Canadian Pacific Railroad and how its construction in the 1880s profoundly affected Canadian life, especially in the west.[28] Railroads in North America were a figurative communication medium in the 19th century, spreading western culture along their roadbeds, and, as we have seen, they were also a literal communication conduit as the telegraph followed the line of the rails. Innis became well known, first in Canada and then internationally, for his economic studies of the role played in Canadian national development by natural goods such as fish, fur, and wood products.[29] Later in his career he studied the history of the evolution of speech and writing in ancient empires. His interest in communication led him to define media as either time-binding or space-binding – terms he defined as a differentiating a "bias" in communication.[30] Durable messages such as inscriptions chiseled into stone columns in Egyptian or Greek monuments were "time-bound," according to Innis. They had a permanence that endured for centuries.[31] More modern media such as newspapers, radio, and television were defined by Innis as "space-binding" and were inherently less durable and more ephemeral.

"Space-bound" electronic media sounds like a contradiction in terminology since one theme of this chapter is that modern media "flatten" the earth by shrinking both space and time in a process that Frances

Cairncross refers to as the "death of distance."[32] Innis criticized "mechanized" contemporary post-war media such as newspapers, radio, and television for their impermanence compared with "time-bound" media such as books. Space-bound media served an advertising and consumerist agenda that he despised. He also felt that impermanent space-bound media contributed to the diminishment of the oral tradition in all cultures, especially in Canada.[33] He felt that the imbalance between space-bound and time-bound media needed to be addressed in the education of young people, especially at the university level.

If Innis thought that radio and television were adversely affecting the cultural education of young people in the early 1950s, he would be apoplectic observing the use of space-bound media by students of all ages at present. Not only are young people communicating using mobile phones during most of their waking hours, they are sending electronic messages that are completely transitory. It is a rare e-mail that is printed as hard copy, and very few text messages are ever saved. Websites on the Internet are notoriously transitory in design and location, so much so that archives have been created to preserve the appearance of sites that have since been redesigned many times.[34]

One irony, noted elsewhere in this text, is that the Internet and the World Wide Web have actually made radio, television, and newspaper content *more* accessible than in Innis' lifetime. These space-bound media are now actually *less* transitory in terms of access to their content through online search engines and digital archives. Internet users can access radio and television stations around the world as they listen and watch live streamed broadcasts – and most media companies archive prior broadcasts for playback at will. Accessing newspaper archives once meant either a visit to the publisher or spending hours loading and viewing microfilm reels of newspaper archives in a library. Today most large newspapers and magazines have online digital archives extending back decades, and access is much faster and simpler.

Innis would also be astonished at the use of multimedia by faculty and students in the modern university classroom. I have gone to great lengths to add projected images, video segments, and live Web links to my classroom lectures and online modules. The Web has made this content accessible and its addition has provided a richness and depth to these "lectures" that was not possible even a decade ago. Students are asked to participate in online dialogs about course content in classroom discussion websites, as I have found that many students who are reluctant to talk in a large lecture hall are much more expressive in these online fora. Some faculty are experimenting with blended classrooms where some students are present in the room while the rest participate at a distance.

Some students prefer being physically present in the room, while others prefer to take the class at home or work due to family or job demands. A few faculty have extended this concept to internationally blended classes, where some students are in one location and others are taking the course from other continents. The concept that makes this possible is the notion of the "flat world."

Evolution of the Flat World

As we have seen, the wiring of the world through undersea cables is not a recent phenomenon. The successful operation of the English Channel telegraph cable in 1851 and the final success of the Atlantic Cable in 1866 led to many public–private partnerships to extend cable lines across continents and under the world's oceans. By 1891 a cable could be sent between all six temperate continents and most of the major cities of the world were linked together by telegraph wires (see Figure 7.6). These

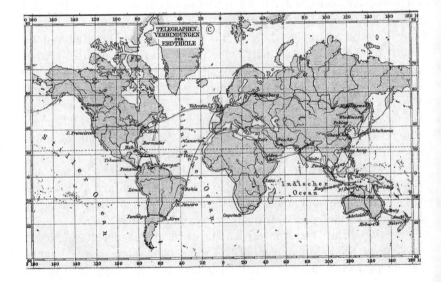

Figure 7.6   Transcontinental telegraph lines crossed North and South America as well as linking Europe with Asia. Undersea cables connected the western hemisphere with Europe, looped around Africa, extended through the Mediterranean Sea to the Indian Ocean, and continued on to Southeast Asia, Australia, and New Zealand. The world was electrically connected by the beginning of the 20th century. *Source:* Telegraph Connections (Telegraphen Verbindungen), *Stielers Hand-Atlas* (1891), plate 5, Weltkarte in Mercator projection. Creative Commons.

routes were later expanded to include undersea *telephone* cables that also linked the world's continents.

The importance of these connections for the command and control of overseas colonial assets by the world's dominant powers should not be understated. Undersea cable and telephone connections enhanced Great Britain's control of colonial governments in Canada, India, East Africa, Australia, and New Zealand. Other European powers depended on these telecommunication linkages for the same purpose in Africa, the Americas, and Asia. No longer would under-secretaries of state, national finance ministers, and business executives have to wait for trade reports to arrive by ship many weeks after they were sent. Daily reports arrived by telegram (and subsequently by telephone) from their counterparts in colonial nations. This real-time intelligence enhanced the development of global empires in the 19th century and helped sustain their operation into the 20th.

The construction of undersea cables consisted of copper wire cores until the 1970s, when the development of glass fiber-optic conduits began to supplant heavy and expensive copper cables. Fiber-optic cables are much lighter and have a carrying capacity many times that of copper. In 1967, the first Telstar communication satellite was successfully launched by AT&T and a consortium of European telecommunication providers.[35] Satellites offered a global telecommunication alternative to undersea cables, but they are very expensive to construct, launch, and operate. They are also risky to operate due to threats posed by cosmic radiation, micrometeorites, and the increasing risk of being hit by human-made debris in space.[36] Undersea cables are typically protected in the deep oceans by thousands of feet of water – the primary threats to their operation come from ship's anchors, fishing nets, and the occasional undersea earthquake.

The carrying capacity of fiber-optic cables has increased dramatically since 1990, especially using light multiplexed in multiple colors. The cables work by converting electrical signals from devices such as computers and telephones into pulses of light that flick on and off millions of times each second. These pulses of light can vary by color so that each hue acts as its own independent channel inside a fiber-optic cable. At the other end of the cable, a receiving device decodes the stream of multicolor light bursts and converts it back into electrical pulses that a computer or phone can decode. The website from a server in Hong Kong that is viewed on a mobile phone in Paris is transmitted over undersea cables as millions of pulses of light.

Thomas Friedman, in his 2005 book The *World Is Flat*, notes that the passage of the Telecommunications Act of 1996 in the United States led to the installation of thousands of miles of new fiber-optic cable around the world.[37] By deregulating large telecommunication companies in the US, the Act led to intense competition between these companies (and their overseas partners) to install extensive new fiber networks. The companies expected the rapid growth they experienced during the go-go 1990s to continue indefinitely. When the dot-com market crashed in the spring of 2000, many over-extended telecommunication firms folded, and the survivors purchased their fiber infrastructure for pennies on the dollar.[38] The forces of excessive supply and lower demand in telecommunication led to lower rates for long-distance transmissions. As Friedman notes, long-distance telephone charges went from $2 a minute to 10 cents, and data transmission costs fell almost to zero.[39] Ironically, the dot-com crash, while it led to a shake-out of many early Internet services, had a significant silver lining in the form of "dark fiber" that was installed, but unused at the time. Since the year 2000 much of that installed fiber-optic cable has been reconnected, and this expanded carrying capacity around the world has contributed to the dramatic growth of new services on the Internet, such as YouTube and Facebook, that have benefited from the expansion in bandwidth.

In *The World Is Flat*, Friedman explores the implications for global trade and how international relations are affected by a world linked by telecommunication systems that operate at the speed of fiber-optic light.[40] Friedman's thesis is that these linkages, especially the Internet, have transformed how and where information is processed around the world. He describes ten primary "flattening" factors:[41]

1. **November 9, 1989** is the date that the Berlin Wall came down – with the earth-shaking geopolitical transformations that followed. For Friedman, the collapse of the USSR and its proxies in eastern Europe was a triumph for capitalist societies and the free flow of information and trade between nations.
2. **August 9, 1995** is the date that the Netscape Corporation went public. The (short-lived) success of their browser, for Friedman, was symbolic of the rise of the Internet in the 1990s as a widely adopted communication and information transmission medium.
3. The development of **work-flow software** facilitated the digitization of information so that it could be processed or analyzed anywhere in the world. He used the example of animated films being developed in California, with cell animation accomplished in India, voice recording near each actor's home, and final editing in California.

4. **Open-sourcing** is the creation of computer code and Internet content by "self-organizing collaborative communities." Examples profiled include open-source Apache software for Web servers and Wikipedia as an open-source global encyclopedia with thousands of contributors in multiple languages.

5. **Outsourcing** is the delegation of tasks outside a company or organization. Friedman cites outsourcing the task of correcting computer code to avoid system failures at the start of the year 2000. Software companies in India solved the "Y2K" problem for their clients by rewriting the defective code, and proved that they could successfully take on similar outsourced programming tasks.

6. **Offshoring** is the shift of production to the lowest-cost global manufacturer or service provider. Friedman profiles the rise of China as a competitive producer of manufactured goods and the establishment of the "China price" as a benchmark for competitors to match.

7. **Supply-chaining** is the design of an end-to-end system for the purchase and delivery of goods and services from a supplier to a customer. Friedman analyzes Wal-Mart's computerized supply chain that immediately re-orders products from suppliers as they are purchased in their stores.

8. **In-sourcing** is a process whereby a company invites a vendor to provide key services within an organization. United Parcel Service (UPS) is profiled for its range of logistical services for clients that have expanded beyond package delivery.

9. **In-forming** is Friedman's description for search engines and their providers. He profiles Google's rise to prominence in this field and examines the implications for society of making all the world's information accessible to all.

10. **"The steroids"** are four factors that enhance the trends outlined above: **digital, mobile, personal,** and **virtual.** Analog media and information are being converted to digital formats that can be quickly accessed and transmitted. Mobile phones and other wireless devices are making content accessible to all without the need to be connected by wires. Newly developed applications allow media and similar digital content to be personalized for each user, e.g. in a Facebook account. The advent of cloud computing means that users won't need to carry their digital files when traveling. Users will access virtual files stored on remote servers and use shareware software to process and distribute information.

Friedman then linked these flattening factors to what he calls the "Triple Convergence:"

> The net result of this [triple] convergence was the creation of a global, Web-enabled playing field that allows for multiple forms of collaboration – the sharing of knowledge and work – in real time, without regard to geography, distance, or, in the near future, even language. No, not everyone has access yet to this platform, this playing field, but it is open today to more people in more places on more days in more ways than anything like it ever before in the history of the world. This is what I mean when I say that the world has been flattened. It is the complementary convergence of the ten flatteners creating this new global playing field for multiple forms of collaboration.[42]

Of the ten flattening factors that Friedman describes, several are directly dependent upon telecommunication technology, especially on the cables that span the world and enable the global Internet. These fiber-optic linkages – for better or for worse – make possible open-sourcing, outsourcing, offshoring, insourcing, in-forming, and each of his steroid factors. Even mobility is dependent on the connection of mobile devices to the global wired network. For Friedman, the primary benefit of the flattened world is personal empowerment as these technologies allow anyone with connections to the network to gather information and develop new services that enable humans to collaborate and communicate more effectively.[43]

These technologies also allow governments, corporations, and non-profit organizations to create global teams for problem solving (e.g., collaboration on climate change issues), product development and marketing, and for command-and-control purposes. All large companies are now competing using the global Internet. The same technologies that facilitate global competition can also be used to export employment to the lowest-cost labor markets in the world. Those who have lost their positions in higher-wage nations to an offshore information worker can purchase a T-shirt with a photo of Thomas Friedman that says, "I lost my job to India and *The New York Times* foreign-affairs columnist couldn't care less."

From an Ellulian perspective, the flattening of the world facilitated by the Internet makes an ideal case study. As Ellul stated in 1962, the favorable effects of technology are inseparable from the negative ones and these "contradictory elements" are "indissolubly connected."[44] To Ellul this did not mean that technology should be seen as a neutral force in society. Our perception of information and communication technology will be colored by whether one sees it as a life-affirming force or as something that has degraded the individual's quality of life. These perspectives are also situational – one might resent having Internet access surveilled by management at work, yet enjoy uploading personal or family photos to a social networking site accessed by a large circle of friends.

Information and communication technology provides the means for digital work to be accomplished in any nation with a highly educated workforce. Global teams are assembled by companies and organizations that draw upon group member expertise with regional markets and unique cultural needs. Utilizing continental time differences, information processing is accomplished quickly and efficiently around the clock. Radiologists in India analyze digital X-rays of American patients overnight and the results are transmitted to the US by the next morning.[45]

Since 2000, significant numbers of information workers in more developed countries have lost their jobs to workers in lower-wage nations. I recently talked with a colleague at a high-technology company in Colorado who was actually asked to train the overseas worker taking his position. He did it to retain his severance benefits. This process is known in business terminology as "rationalization," or a reduction in workforce in higher-wage countries countered by an expansion of similar positions in less wealthy countries. Some might argue that this is also a rationale for the more equal distribution of wealth around the globe, but those who have lost their jobs and careers to this trend may fail to see the logic, as expressed in the T-shirt slogan criticizing Thomas Friedman. The exportation of jobs in information processing and provision (call centers and help lines) has enhanced the economies of developing nations able to provide the required training. It has also led to reconsideration of careers in fields such as computer programming by young people in more developed nations. They are understandably reluctant to invest in an occupation where jobs may migrate overseas during their working lifetime. Friedman notes that creative positions in engineering, science, and the arts are less likely to be exported due to the highly specialized knowledge or skill required. However, with improved technical education around the globe, workers in every information-oriented occupation will be collaborating – and competing – with their peers in other developed nations. As the creators of the telegraph and the Atlantic Cable noted, the blessing is that the barriers of distance that inhibited global communication are gone, but we now live in a world where one's job can suddenly disappear overseas in the interest of "rationalization."

notes

1. C. Mabee, *The American Leonardo: A Life of Samuel F. B. Morse* (New York: Knopf, 1943). This book won the Pulitzer Prize for biography in 1944. The telegraph message is an exclamation from the Bible (Numbers 23:23) and was selected by Annie Ellsworth, the daughter of US Commissioner of Patents Henry L. Ellsworth, a college classmate of Morse at Yale University.

2. A. C. Clarke, "Clarke's Third Law," *Profiles of the Future* (London: Phoenix, 1961).

3. B. Winston, *Media Technology and Society* (London: Routledge, 1998).

4. Ibid. F. Braudel, *Civilization and Capitalism: 15th to 18th Century* (New York: Harper & Row, 1981), 430.

5. See also B. Winston, "How Are Media Born and Developed?", in J. Downing, A. Mohammadi, and A. Sreberny-Mohammadi (eds.), *Questioning the Media: A Critical Introduction* (Thousand Oaks, CA: Sage Publications, 1995), 54–74.

6. H. A. Innis, *The Bias of Communication* (Toronto: University of Toronto Press, 1951), 167–8.

7. Winston, *Media Technology and Society*.

8. Ibid., 26.

9. The SOS code in International Morse Code used by ships at sea differs from that in American Morse Code, which would be converted as three dots, a dot-pause-dot for "O," then three dots.

10. Winston notes that government support was an accelerating factor in the adoption of telegraphy in the US. In fact, the $30,000 appropriation from Congress for the 1844 Washington–Baltimore demonstration line was made through the US Postal Service. However, Winston notes that the Postal Service lost money operating the first US commercial telegraphy lines. It was then privatized in what became known as the Western Union Company. This set a precedent for the operation of telecommunication services in the US as private enterprises. In Europe they were folded into government-operated communication entities later known as the PTTs – Postal Telegraph and Telephone services. Note that they are listed in the order created.

11. Winston, *Media Technology and Society*.

12. R. L. Thompson, *Wiring a Continent* (Princeton, NJ: Princeton University Press, 1947), 317.

13. Cited in B. Dibner, *The Atlantic Cable* (New York: Blaisdell, 1964). An online version (1959) of this classic history is available from the Smithsonian Institution: http://www.sil.si.edu/digitalcollections/hst/atlantic-cable/. It includes a number of excellent illustrations of the ships involved and the cable-laying technology used. It would be of interest to all students of telecommunication history.

14. Morse wrote this in a letter circa 1843 (Dibner, *The Atlantic Cable*, 7). What is remarkable is that this letter was written barely 30 years after the British had burned the White House to the ground in 1814 during the war of 1812.

Apparently commercial ties between the United States and Great Britain overwhelmed any lingering hostility between the two nations.

15. Dibner. *The Atlantic Cable*, pp. 10–11.

16. The first institution that Field created was the New York, Newfoundland, and London Telegraph Company. In 1856 the cable-laying organization was renamed the Atlantic Cable Company.

17. The governmental support of the US and Britain was financial and in-kind, enlisting the assistance of the navies of each nation. The US Congress supported the Atlantic Cable effort in 1857 with a bill that passed by just one vote. Secretary of State William Seward stated at the bill's passage, "My own hope is, that after the telegraphic wire is once laid, there will be no more war between the United States and Great Britain." (Cited in Dibner, *The Atlantic Cable*, 27.)

18. Dibner, *The Atlantic Cable*, 28–73.

19. Ibid.

20. Ibid., 77.

21. The laying of a cable that spanned the vast Pacific Ocean did not occur until 1902.

22. IET.org. *The Transatlantic Telegraph Cables 1865–1866*. Retrieved August 11, 2009, from http://www.theiet.org/about/libarc/archives/featured/trans-cable1865.cfm.

23. C. G. Hearn, *Circuits in the Sea* (Westport, CT: Praeger, 2004), 37–41.

24. Ibid., 48. An additional agenda for the British government was to establish telegraphic communication with its rapidly growing dominion in Canada. After the loss of the American colonies in the 18th century, Great Britain sought to strengthen its connections with Canada, and the undersea cable from Ireland to Nova Scotia enhanced this.

25. Ibid., 54.

26. F. Cairncross, *The Death of Distance* (London: Orion, 1997).

27. H. A. Innis, *Empire and Communications* (Oxford: Clarendon Press, 1950); Innis, *The Bias of Communication*.

28. H. A. Innis, *A History of the Canadian Pacific Railway* (Toronto: University of Toronto Press, 1971).

29. P. Heyer, *Harold Innis* (Lanham, MD: Rowman & Littlefield, 2003).

30. Innis, *The Bias of Communication*.

31. The 1799 discovery of the Rosetta Stone, an ancient Egyptian artifact, was a key find in decoding text that was inscrutable to modern eyes. Its inclusion of identical text in Greek and two Egyptian languages (one hieroglyphic) meant that the latter two could finally be decoded. It is on display in the British Museum in London.

32. See Cairncross's book, *The Death of Distance*.

33. Innis, *The Bias of Communication*.

34. One of the largest and most comprehensive sites is the Internet Archive at http://www.archive.org/index.php. Their *Way Back Machine* has archived

over 150 billion Web pages since its inception. See early site designs for Yahoo.com and Google.com (and note how little the latter home page has changed since November 1998).

35. H. Gavaghan, *Something New Under the Sun: Satellites and the Beginning of the Space Age* (New York: Copernicus, 1998).

36. The threat of a cascading series of collisions with debris in space is known as the Kessler Syndrome, named for NASA scientist Donald Kessler, who first described the potential catastrophic threat to all spacecraft in Earth orbit. Such an exponentially expanding series of collisions could destroy essential satellites that nations are dependent upon for telecommunication, navigation, and defense. See D. J. Kessler and B. G. Cour-Palais, "Collision Frequency of Artificial Satellites: The Creation of a Debris Belt," *Journal of Geophysical Research* 83 (1978), A6. See also J. Schefter, "The Growing Peril of Space Debris," *Popular Science* (July 1982), 48–51.

37. T. Friedman, *The World Is Flat: A Brief History of the 21st Century* (New York: Farrar, Straus & Giroux, 2005).

38. Most were victims of poor business plans, but one telecommunications company, Worldcom, was charged with accounting fraud to the tune of $11 billion, and its CEO and founder Bernie Ebbers was sentenced in 2005 to 25 years in a US prison.

39. Friedman, *The World Is Flat*, 68.

40. Ibid.

41. Ibid., 48–172.

42. Ibid., 176–7.

43. Friedman has been criticized for a somewhat Pollyanna-ish worldview that nations that collaborate together (via trade and other partnerships) are unlikely to go to war with each other, but his observations concerning the role of telecommunication in the creation of networks that bind the citizens of the world together are perceptive.

44. J. Ellul, "The Technological Order," *Technology and Culture* 3/4 (Fall 1962), 412.

45. A. Pollack, "Who's Reading Your X-ray?", *New York Times* (November 16, 2003). Retrieved March 23, 2009, from http://www.nytimes.com/2003/11/16/business/yourmoney/16hosp.html?pagewanted=1.

8

Digital Media Convergence

Convergence

Pavlik and McIntosh define convergence as "the coming together of computing, telecommunications, and media in a digital environment." They state that convergence has effects in four key areas:[1]

- The content of communication
- The relationships between media organizations and their publics
- The structure of communication organizations
- How communication professionals do their work

Several of these points are illustrated in Figure 8.1. It is a rare journalist today who carries only a notepad on an assignment. The photo of CNN journalist Phillip Littleton shows him editing a video segment in a hotel room on location in 2007 with Anderson Cooper's *AC360* program in Brazil. Field video is downloaded from the camera to a laptop computer, where each shot is trimmed and then organized in a linear timeline with a soundtrack. Once the story is edited, it is either sent electronically to CNN or inserted into a live shot of Anderson Cooper from a satellite

Digital Universe: The Global Telecommunication Revolution, First Edition. Peter B. Seel.
© 2012 Peter B. Seel. Published 2012 by Blackwell Publishing Ltd.

Figure 8.1   Reporter Phillip Littleton uses digital news gathering (DNG) tools to electronically write and edit a segment for CNN's *AC360* program on location in Brazil. *Photo:* Jeff Hutchens / Reportage by Getty Images for CNN.

truck. The journalist or a producer would then rewrite the story for posting on CNN's website. Before bedtime the journalist might be expected to post a daily entry as a blog on a site dedicated to a newscast or cable news program. To perform this multimedia hat trick,[2] a journalist must be a reporter, a videographer to shoot the needed footage, a video editor to cut the footage into a 90-second story, a writer for online news, and last, but certainly not least, a skilled blogger. To say the least, this requires e-journalists to become a jill or jack of all trades.

The content being communicated is influenced by the ability of a multimedia journalist to "go light" (compared with a three- or four-person television news crew prior to 2000). There are obvious pros and cons to the "one-person band" model of convergent news-gathering at many local television stations in the US. What is gained in capturing spontaneous content may be lost in marginal video or audio, acquired by a reporter who is now a producer, videographer, and sound person. Convergence is affecting how media organizations relate to their publics as these companies strive to provide global coverage of news events with fewer reporters. It is not enough in this competitive environment to feature an edited video package on the 6 p.m. newscast – there needs to be a reporter introducing the story live on location. If the story features breaking news, it might be posted on the channel's website before it is aired, lest the competition post it on their site first.

The emphasis on speed is paramount, and digital technology makes it routine to telecast news as it occurs. Millions of television viewers worldwide watched the terrorist attacks on the World Trade Center in New York (and the Pentagon in Washington) as they occurred on September 11, 2001. Much of the viewer's horror and anguish was induced by the knowledge that people were dying as they watched the towers collapsing and the Pentagon burning. The attack on Pearl Harbor by Japanese carrier pilots on December 7, 1941 galvanized the US into mobilization for World War II, but most Americans heard about this event hours later on the radio. Film footage of the attacks did not appear in newsreels in movie theaters until several weeks had elapsed. Media organizations now routinely air newsworthy events as they occur, and there is an expectation that they will continue to do so. In Thomas Friedman's "flat" world outlined in Chapter 7, news travels globally at the speed of light, and there is concern that terrorist groups count on this factor to maximize the global horror caused by their attacks.

Convergence is not only affecting how media professionals do their jobs, but it is also changing the structure of their companies. Many US television stations are phasing out specialized professions such as videographers and tape editors in favor of convergent "all-platform" journalists who can report, shoot, and edit their stories, often on the road. Newspapers worldwide have been adversely affected by the double whammy of declining readership and falling ad revenue as readers and advertisers migrate to the Internet. They have responded by reducing staff, cutting pages, and closing foreign bureaus. The negative aspects of convergence are exemplified by its effect on traditional news sources. It is a wonderful thing to read news for free on websites, but not if there are fewer sources of news and fewer trained journalists to report the news. In the near future, online readers may have to accept poor-quality content with factual errors written by amateur reporters or pay for a subscription to access higher-quality content created by professional journalists.

Convergence is placing new demands not only on journalists, but on everyone who communicates information as part of their profession. It is a rare organizational presentation that is not accompanied with a projected talk that includes not only text, but also images, sound effects, and video. PowerPoint® and similar presentation technologies make it possible to enthrall an audience with multimedia content – or torture them with an endless stream of slides filled edge to edge with poorly edited text, irrelevant images, and nonsensical animation.[3] I would argue only half-facetiously that a government agency (the Bureau of Digital Presentations?) should require a license for those who plan to give digital presentations. Before they can speak to any group larger than three people, PowerPoint® users would need to take a class on the principles of good design and effective communication – and then prove to a tough examiner that they can use the technology effectively. Imagine how this might transform education and business communication on a global basis.

Analog to Digital

Humans are analog creatures. We cannot see or hear digital media unless we convert them to an analog form that we can process through our senses. Our vision depends on waves and particles to convey light and its color frequencies to the retina in the eye. Our eardrums and the tiny bones in the auditory channel vibrate in direct relation to sounds generated in our sensory environment. Human senses have evolved over thousands of years, and it is much easier to adapt communication technologies to human sight, hearing, and touch than to re-engineer our bodies.

First and foremost, we are fundamentally visual creatures so visual displays are the most common interface between humans and digital devices. Speakers are attached to most electronic displays to provide the auditory link to digital content. Some type of tracking device, such as a mouse or virtual buttons, allows users to point and click on desired content on screen. We often take this ability for granted, but as Lewis Mumford noted, any widely adopted technology becomes "invisible" to casual observation. We walk up to a digital display and immediately look for the mouse or some means to interact with the images on screen. In the future this process will increasingly be voice- (and, eventually, thought-) activated. Digital technologies designed for hands-free mobile phone and music access in cars are examples of this type of interface.

Smell is one human sense that technology rarely attempts to reach. Peripheral devices for personal computers were created in the late 1990s that were designed to create smells that could be triggered by a website link. For example, when one visited an online provider of floral arrangements, the user could actually smell flowers as they surfed the site. When visitors went to a site for a company that delivered pizza to the home the device would create similar smells. However, because the human sense of smell is so subjective, a digitally created replica of pizza scent that smelled delicious to one user might smell like a wet dog to another. Interface devices that provide a sense of smell still need more refinement before they are widely adopted. However, there is great inventive potential here since our sense of smell powerfully affects our sense of taste and even our response to other people. The multibillion-dollar fragrance industry attests to the appeal of attractive scents.

Figure 8.2   The Alto workstation developed by Robert Taylor's team at Xerox PARC. Note the vertical screen for editing documents. It was one of the first personal computers and featured a number of advanced technologies for its era. *Photo*: Creative Commons.

Figure 8.3 The Macintosh computer developed by Steve Jobs, Steve Wozniak, and their team at Apple. The icons on the screen "desktop" allowed users to point and click to access applications instead of writing lines of code. *Source*: Creative Commons.

Xerox's PARC

As analog creatures, we need interface devices between our senses and our digital tools. Significant research in computer science has been devoted to this since the 1950s and 1960s. J. C. R. Licklider devoted much of his classic "Man–Computer Symbiosis" article[4] in 1960 to appeals for the creation of new human–computer interface (HCI) technologies. In the article, Licklider called for the development of digital speech recognition systems, interactive graphic tablets, large-screen digital projection systems, and mass storage technologies – all were subsequently developed by computer scientists inspired by Licklider's vision of a digital multimedia future. They recognized that the use of computers by laypersons was dependent on the creation of less complex human interfaces that did not require the typing of lines of code or the interpretation of raw data.

Douglas Engelbart and his team in the Augmentation Research Center (ARC) at the Stanford Research Institute (SRI) in Palo Alto, California, performed significant pioneering work on HCI (outlined in Chapter 6). After Department of Defense funding for ARC declined in the late 1960s, several key staff members went to work for the Xerox Corporation at their nearby Palo Alto Research Center. Commonly known by its acronym PARC, the now legendary lab was founded in 1970 by chief scientist Jack Goldman and physicist George Pake.[5] Xerox was flush with cash as businesses throughout the world bought thousands of photocopying machines to help create what would later be described by Xerox, without obvious irony, as the "paperless office." To create the office of the future, the company sought to expand beyond copiers into computer-based information systems, and charged Goldman and Pake with creating an ICT-oriented version of Bell Labs in Palo Alto. The site in Stanford University's nearby industrial park was selected for proximity to their advanced computer science and engineering programs.[6] Stanford's research spinoffs included Fairchild Semiconductor and its own spinoff, Intel, co-founded by Gordon Moore, of Moore's law renown. Silicon Valley was still to be named in the future, but by 1970 there was already a critical mass of new electronics companies in the areas west and south of San Francisco Bay.

In the fall of 1970, Goldman and Pake went on a headhunting search to recruit the best minds in US computer science to Xerox PARC. Scientists and engineers from SRI, UC Berkeley, Utah, Carnegie Mellon, MIT, and Xerox's own Rochester, New York lab were hired or transferred to research positions at PARC. To manage the Computer Systems Division at PARC, Pake and Goldman hired Robert Taylor from the University of Utah. As readers will recall from Chapter 4, Taylor had been instrumental in the late 1960s in creating the early ARPANET as the director of the Advanced Research Projects Agency.[7] He was actively recruited because of his extensive ARPA contacts in the computer science community, especially with researchers building computer networks. Taylor was co-author with J. C. R. Licklider of an influential article in 1968 titled "The Computer as a Communication Device," in which they predicted that communication would become a primary function of computers.[8] Recall that this article appeared more than two decades before e-mail was widely adopted in organizations and when large mainframe computers were still the dominant technology. Visionaries such as Taylor and Licklider could foresee a future with personal computers on every office desktop, linked in networks to other computers in a company, nation, and across the globe. Led by Goldman, Pake, and Taylor, scientists at PARC set out to create this technology.

In retrospect, the research group they assembled was the information and communication science version of a 1970s "dream team." From the University of Utah came Alan Kay, a recent Ph.D. with an interest in personal computers as a teaching and learning tool. From UC Berkeley came Chuck Thacker, Butler Lampson, and a team that developed the BCC 500 computer that could process data for 500 users simultaneously.[9] The key team members were not all external hires. Gary Starkweather worked at Xerox's existing research center in Rochester, New York, and he sought a transfer to the new PARC facility. His background in physics and optics led to insights about using the tightly focused beam of light from the newly invented laser to print documents. Two years of work at PARC led to the creation of the first practical laser printer. From Doug Engelbart's Augmentation Research Center at SRI, the PARC team recruited chief engineer Bill English and other key ARC staff. Their background included the development of innovative HCI devices such as the computer mouse and screens that display black text on a white or gray background. At that time most digital screens could only display white or green letters against a black background. Innovations were also made in software – the research group led by Alan Kay and Adele Goldman created an interface called Smalltalk that featured overlapping windows for accessing multiple applications at once, a mouse-driven cursor, and on-screen icons. Chuck Thacker's team developed a program that allowed users to link graphic elements for architectural and engineering design which later led to computer-assisted design (CAD) programs. A team led by Butler Lampson and Charles Simonyi created Bravo, a WYSIWYG[10] text editor that displayed fonts the way they would look in print and allowed easy cut-and-paste editing. Simonyi later left Xerox and moved to Microsoft, where he converted this word-processing technology into a very successful product called Microsoft Word.[11]

The descendants of what they created at PARC are sitting on every desktop and reside in every laptop and mobile phone. Computer scientists and communication researchers at PARC created graphical user interfaces (GUIs) for computers so users would not need to type lines of code to access and use applications. The touchscreen "keys" on 4G mobile phones are a direct descendant of this now-essential human–computer interface. PARC researchers advanced the science of client–server computing that laid the foundations for both the Internet and the Web. Their research on local and wide-area networks (LANs and WANs) led to the creation of Ethernet by Robert Metcalf. In short, the networked world we use every day to access news, messages, and entertainment owes much to the research teams at Xerox's PARC.[12]

Despite the creativity shown by the staff at PARC, poor decision-making by Xerox's senior management in that era has become a cautionary business school case study. For more than a decade they fumbled multiple efforts to move innovative products from the lab to the marketplace. Xerox was led in the mid-1970s by a group of bottom-line finance experts concerned with protecting their dominance in copiers and who could not understand the potential of networked computers and their peripherals.[13] Innovations such as the Alto computer, the Smalltalk GUI interface, and the Bravo text editor are cited as examples of technologies that were years ahead of their competition that Xerox failed to capitalize on. However, Waldrop makes the salient point that Xerox more than recouped their investment in the PARC lab with their perfection of laser printing as an essential computer output device.[14] The patents on this single invention made millions for Xerox as these printers siphoned away future income from the market for photocopiers. The larger legacy of PARC was its influence on a new generation of computer engineers and entrepreneurs. In December 1979, Steve Jobs and a team from Apple Computer visited PARC and received two demonstrations of the innovations developed at the PARC. While Apple had already incorporated on-screen windows and other GUI technologies in their new Lisa computer, what Jobs and team witnessed in the demonstrations at PARC was the future of personal computing.[15]

Much of the success of Apple's Macintosh personal computer (see Figure 8.3) was due to its adoption of a GUI that replicated a scene familiar to users – a desk top. In fact, it was probably exactly what most users saw in front of them, a computer sitting on a desk top. Apple succeeded in incorporating this then-unique interface into computers that were affordable by the masses. I recall seeing my first Macintosh and marveling at the icons on the screen – it was a wonderful concept, compared with writing lines of code, which you had to do with other computers of that time. Virtual folders could be created to store files and they could be dragged to the trash can icon and dropped there to dispose of them. Apple engineers had harnessed the power of computer technology to create a virtual world on a graphic desktop that modeled what users were familiar with in the real world. The trend continues, as creative engineers are presently leveraging dramatic increases in computing power in all devices (Moore's law again), from mobile phones to 3-D digital displays to provide human–computer interfaces that are more intuitive and realistic to users.

The creation of digital content in an analog world is an encoding process that requires decoding on the receiving end. Binary code is expressed in bits (short for *B*inary dig*IT*) of either 1 (*on* in a circuit) or 0 (*off*). The digital universe is constructed in this dyad of off and on, black and white, low and high voltage, and the miracle is that technology has converted a stark binary world into one that is filled with beautiful music and remarkable digital images. Moore's law and the expansion of media-processing and storage capabilities have given us a digital palette of millions of colors in 3-D images (e.g., in the film *Avatar*) combined with rich sounds delivered to our ears through headphones or through multi-speaker surround-sound systems. The key to this process is sampling, which enables any analog wave to be converted to numbers and then bits. The process is illustrated in Figure 8.4.

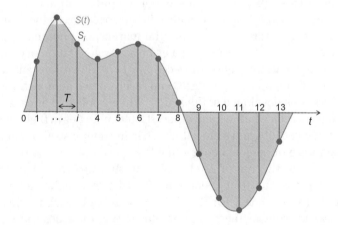

Figure 8.4   Sampling: A sound or light wave is sampled at periodic time intervals and a numerical value is determined for that interval. The value is then encoded as binary digits and saved as part of a digital file. The larger the number of samples in a given time period, the better the fidelity to the original content. When played back in a digital device, the media is decoded and converted back into an analog format audible or visible to humans. *Source*: Creative Commons.

Atoms and Bits – Benefits to Digitization

Nicholas Negroponte makes a key point about the benefits of digitizing media content. Once analog content has been converted to a digital format, it is far less costly to distribute. Bits can be transmitted electronically for a fraction of the cost of shipping data or text in hard-copy form (or as "atoms").[16] Once the content has been created, the incremental costs of online distribution are minimal (especially if the user is paying for the online access). If the content is user-generated as with a wiki (e.g., via Wikipedia), access to it is usually free. As a child, I recall a salesman imploring my parents to purchase a new edition of the *Encyclopaedia Britannica* as an essential home education aid, but it cost more than $1,000. He implied that unless they made this purchase the education of my brother, sister, and I would be severely shortchanged. Somehow we became educated adults by using an outdated 20-year-old version that we inherited. We did acquire a sense of the perishability of information related to science, technology, and geography in the older encyclopedia and learned to identify when we needed to find a more up-to-date source. This proved to be a very useful skill and one that users of online sources may not acquire, especially if sources or revision dates are not identified.

The content of the printed encyclopedia was usually quickly outdated since major revisions were made only every 10–15 years. In the 20th century the *Encyclopaedia Britannica* was written to be *the* authoritative source on human knowledge in the arts and sciences, but it has struggled to stay in business with the advent of online communication. The company offers online access to their encyclopedia content via subscription at $70 per year, while the hard-copy edition costs $1,395.[17] This illustrates the cost differential between the "atomic" hard-copy version of the encyclopedia and the online "bit" version, but what is not apparent is the struggle the company has endured to stay in business since 2000 with greatly reduced hard-copy sales. It does market a version of the *Encyclopaedia Britannica* on CD/DVD for $50 while their nearest digital competitor is Microsoft's Encarta with a retail price of $45. The key point is that the online and digital versions can be produced, updated, and distributed at a much lower cost than the multi-volume hard-copy editions.

A recent innovation has been the creation of the e-book reader, best known by the first-to-market Kindle sold by online retailer Amazon Inc. E-book displays are designed to look like the pages of a text – the virtual book. The text appears in black on white or gray pages and its virtual "pages" are turned using buttons along the side. Much like electronic encyclopedias, novels and other printed publications can be distributed much less expensively in electronic form. Readers such as the Kindle can receive new texts wirelessly in Internet hot spots or by mobile phone transmission. Amazon Inc. sold 500,000 Kindles in 2009, and during the 2009 holiday season it sold more electronic versions of books (from 390,000 available e-titles) than it did hard-copy editions.[18] E-books will revolutionize the K-12 and university textbook markets, with school districts and college students leasing new editions rather than paying high prices for soon-to-be-obsolete hard copies. From a logistical and environmental viewpoint, e-books are a significant improvement over hard copies in that millions of tons of paper and the forests from which they are processed can be saved by book distribution as bits instead of atoms. E-texts can include live links to the Internet (and these have been integrated into citations for the electronic edition of this book). From Harold Innis' 20th-century point of view, the e-book is a travesty. Books, to Innis, were "time-bound," with a permanence that "space-bound" media such as radio and televisions did not have. The e-book with its text in bit form makes books more ephemeral and more like electronic mass media. Hard-copy texts will not disappear anytime soon, but readers will have to pay more if they desire to hold an actual book in their hands.

Five Digital Attributes

It is helpful for those living and working in the digital universe to understand five key attributes that affect the production, storage, and transmission of digital media:

1. **Scalability** is a wonderful digital attribute that allows users of digital media to make tradeoffs in sound or image quality in order to create smaller file sizes. Readers who exchange digital images have likely received a photo from a friend or relative that has not been resized. When the photo is opened it is so large that the viewer can see only an eye or an ear of the subject – the results can be startling to the receiver. It is a simple matter with image editing software such as Photoshop® or GIMP to resize a horizontal image from 2,500 pixels in width to any smaller size desired. The file size shrinks accordingly and the photo can be sent easily to a friend or family member without overwhelming their e-mail in-box. All types of digital media – music, photos, or video – can be scaled in quality to make them easier to store, email, or save. This is a key attribute for posting media on websites so that pages will load quickly. Long-time users of the Web

will remember the days before broadband connections when images would load from top to bottom or load out of focus and add interlaced detail as the viewer watched. Scalability provides the media creator with an infinite ability to scale digital media to the level desired, based on network bandwidth and storage capability.

Digital compression is the technology that makes scalability possible. It involves the use of complex algorithms to shrink file sizes in ways that should not be noticeable to the human eye or ear. It is a form of technical voodoo that is best known to digital citizens who download music to mobile phones or portable players. The MP3 file compression format discards up to 90 percent of the data from music files found on CDs.[19] An experienced audiophile can easily hear the difference in music quality between the uncompressed and compressed versions, but most users are happier to have more songs available on their player than complain about sonic quality issues. Compression is used with all types of digital media to make files more compact and thus make more data fit in a given storage medium.

2. **Extensibility** refers to the ability of software producers to create new and improved versions of software without making earlier versions obsolete. Users of the older versions can continue to use them without the need to upgrade with every new iteration. This is a very smart move by software creators to maintain their customer base over many years and through multiple software upgrades. It does complicate the lives of software developers in maintaining backward compatibility as they add new features, but consumers appreciate not having to purchase completely new versions every year or two. A major problem arises when a company such as Microsoft introduces a new operating system such as Vista which makes older software obsolete. Many consumers stayed with the XP operating system due to perceived flaws with Vista prior to upgrading to Windows version 7.

3. **Replicability** is the ability to make unlimited exact copies of a digital file. The 1,000th copy should have the same bits of information as the original file. One of the problems in making copies of *analog* media is that the copies quickly degrade with each generation created. Anyone who copied an analog VHS videotape could see a visible quality loss in the dubbed version – the image softened and the colors smeared. Digital video files can be copied repeatedly without any loss of quality if the files are not compressed. Replicability is one of the most useful of all digital attributes. A digital photo can be copied and the copy creatively

altered using image-manipulation software – the original digital file is saved unaltered as a source for future altered versions. Exact copies can be made from the original or the copies can be altered as the user sees fit. The trick is to preserve all the data in the original file unaltered and intact.

Thus, one of the most important commands for anyone working in the Digital Universe is *duplicate* (or *copy* with its CTRL + C shortcut). The ability to make unlimited copies is a powerful tool for anyone working with digital documents, media files, or data sets. It also allows anyone to make a perfect digital copy of a copyrighted song, photo, or movie. This has led to an explosion in the digital piracy of copyrighted media, an unintended consequence of digitization. This unintended consequence of the conversion of analog media to digital formats again highlights Ellul's critique that the positive effects of technology adoption are inseparable from the negative ones. This topic will be addressed in the next chapter, on the public and private Internet.

4. **Interoperability** does just what it says. Ideally, it makes digital hardware and software function together in a smooth and seamless manner – and usually it does. Some manufacturers and software developers are better at this than others. Apple has an excellent reputation for the interoperability of their operating systems, computer hardware, and application software. Much of the success of the iMac, iPod, iPad, and iPhone is based on Apple's skill at making the interface between hardware, software, and end user as seamless as possible.

ICT users are more likely to notice interoperability when it is missing. In the rush to get a product to market, hardware manufacturers and software developers will fail to fully test it with potential users. Consumers then become unwitting and typically unwilling beta testers in debugging the product or service, and become angry and frustrated when they are not able to use it as advertised. Some of this trend is related to "complexification" as a phenomenon outlined in Chapter 2. As devices add more features, it becomes progressively more difficult to fully test them all in the product itself or in their interaction with other services. So users become the beta testers in uncovering defects with device hardware or software; problems which manufacturers then provide a patch for or fix in subsequent versions. This problem will keep recurring as long as the providers of ICT goods and services sell them to customers without fully testing them first.

5. **Metadata** is another key attribute of digital media and literally means data about data. This may seem like an abstract concept, but will be familiar to anyone who accesses digital music or photos. When a user listens to a song on satellite radio or on any digital player, they can see the name of artist, the name of the song, the source album, and typically an image of the album. This, to me, is one of the most wonderful attributes of digital media. Back in the analog dark ages, we had to hope that a radio DJ would identify the song they had just played. It was maddening to hear a song that one liked, only to have the DJ segue to a commercial and never identify it. For digital photographers, every image file contains basic data about the date and time it was taken, along with metadata about the camera used and basic exposure settings. RAW files created by high-end digital cameras contain even more image data and allow for subsequent manipulation of photo contrast, color, and brightness. Each RAW image file includes the data that makes infinite alterations possible in the "digital darkroom."

These five attributes have transformed the acquisition, processing, and distribution of digital media. They facilitate media convergence and are key factors in creating a media-saturated world where virtually any connected person can produce and share digital content. By making digital text, photos, video, and sounds more usable, digitization has encouraged the use of devices to access them, often to the point that we may feel disoriented without them. These devices and their digital content have become extensions of our senses and their use will increase as the applications become more powerful. The digital–analog (human) symbiosis envisioned by J.C.R. Licklider more than half a century ago is now commonplace in technologically advanced societies and will become even more pervasive on a global scale in the future as convergence becomes a universal digital attribute.

notes

1. J. Pavlik and S. McIntosh, "Convergence and its Consequences," in E. P. Bucy (ed.), *Living in the Information Age: A New Media Reader* (Belmont, CA: Wadsworth, 2005), 68.
2. In ice hockey a "hat trick" is three goals scored by a player in a single game, but the term is used in other sports as well.
3. D. McMillian, *Life after Death by PowerPoint* (2007). Retrieved January 11, 2010, from http://www.youtube.com/watch?v=ORxFwBR4smE.

4. J. C. R. Licklider, "Man–Computer Symbiosis," *IRE Transactions on Human Factors in Electronics* (March 1960), 4–11. Retrieved February 20, 2011, from http://groups.csail.mit.edu/medg/people/psz/Licklider.html.

5. M. Waldrop, *The Dream Machine: J. C. R. Licklider and the Revolution that Made Computing Personal* (New York: Penguin, 2001), 333–410.

6. Ibid., 338.

7. J. Abbate, *Inventing the Internet* (Cambridge, MA: MIT Press, 1999), 43–55.

8. J. C. R. Licklider and R. W. Taylor, "The Computer as a Communication Device," *Science and Technology* (April 1968). Retrieved January 7, 2010, from http://gatekeeper.dec.com/pub/DEC/SRC/publications/taylor/licklider-taylor.pdf.

9. Waldrop, *The Dream Machine*, 346.

10. WYSIWYG is an acronym for *What You See Is What You Get* in text-editing and graphic design software, and was a revolutionary concept at its inception.

11. Waldrop, *The Dream Machine*, 383–6.

12. Ibid., 380–2.

13. D. K. Smith and R. C. Alexander, *Fumbling the Future: How Xerox Invented, then Ignored, the First Personal Computer* (New York: William Morrow, 1988).

14. Waldrop, *The Dream Machine*, 387–410.

15. M. Hiltzik, *Dealers of Lightning: Xerox PARC and the Dawn of the Computer Age* (New York: HarperBusiness, 1999). Xerox invested $1 million in Apple in April of 1979, and this relationship (though soon severed) is what allowed Jobs and his design team to demand that they be shown PARC's proprietary technology. The Apple group was especially interested in the demonstration of Smalltalk, and after seeing it Jobs exclaimed: "Why hasn't this company brought this to market? What's going on here? I don't get it!" Apple's engineers later replicated the Smalltalk features they had seen in the PARC demonstration and included them in the Lisa and Macintosh computers in 1983 and 1984.

16. N. Negroponte, *Being Digital* (New York: Alfred A. Knopf, 1995), 11–20.

17. Price data for the online and hard copy editions is from the *Encyclopaedia Britannica* website: https://safe.britannica.com/registration/freeTrial.do?partnerCode=EBO_DWHEADER.

18. K. Allen, "Amazon E-Book Sales Overtake Print for First Time," *Guardian* (December 28, 2009). Retrieved January 15, 2010, from http://www.guardian.co.uk/business/2009/dec/28/amazon-ebook-kindle-sales-surge.

19. MP3 represents the MPEG-1 Audio Layer 3 compression scheme for music file size reduction. Compression algorithms can be either "lossless" or "lossy." The former preserves most of the data in the original file and the latter discards more of the data and typically results in a much smaller file. High-quality TIFF files for images are typically lossless and JPG files of the same image are lossy, and are typically smaller than their TIFF versions.

Part IV

Internet Control, Cyberculture, and Dystopian Views

9

The Public and Private Internet

"Information wants to be free. Information also wants to be expensive ... that tension will not go away."
(Philosopher, writer, and editor Stewart Brand, 1987)[1]

The first sentence of Brand's quote is widely cited as the part of the essential mantra of the Internet. The second part of the quote is rarely addressed, but serious attention should be paid to it. Information that has strategic and economic value to corporations, organizations, and nations can be very expensive to acquire and often provides a competitive advantage to the holder. A classic case would be the information required to build the first atomic bomb, coupled with the great lengths to which the US government went to keep that information secret, and the subsequent initiatives by the USSR to steal the weapon's construction details. In a more recent example, I gather data annually on digital television (DTV) set sales in the US and other nations as part of my research concerning the global diffusion of DTV. Key US data in this area is collected by the Consumer Electronics Association (CEA), and the sale of its annual reports on consumer adoption represents a significant source of income for the organization. While some generic electronics sales figures are

Digital Universe: The Global Telecommunication Revolution, First Edition. Peter B. Seel.
© 2012 Peter B. Seel. Published 2012 by Blackwell Publishing Ltd.

issued in press releases, the complete data set is available to non-members of the association for $2,000.[2] Most marketing data of this type is proprietary and its sale generates millions of dollars, euros, and yen for the organizations that collect, analyze, and market it. Some information wants to be expensive, as Brand noted.

In an interesting variation on this theme, a key tenet of cyberpunk philosophy states that information *should* be free, but media titan Rupert Murdoch's News Corporation has a different perspective. For years prior to its acquisition by News Corporation in 2007, the *Wall Street Journal* required payment for online access by non-subscribers to its hard-copy editions (subscribers had free access to the online edition). Murdoch is expanding a similar "paywall" around other News Corporation media properties that will require payment for access to information. Their competitors are following suit. The *New York Times* moved to a fee-for-access model in 2011 that allows up to 20 free downloads each month, then require a $15 per month subscription for articles accessed beyond that point.[3] Formerly free online media will now charge a fee for access. This should not be a surprise to users as media organizations struggle to cover their costs for reporters, editors, and overhead expenses in an era where their online editions have been typically accessible for free.

A key term for understanding the economics of Internet media is "monetization." Three basic models are dominant for *monetizing* online content:

1. **Free ad-supported sites** that direct their users' attention to advertisers seeking to market products to this audience (this is also the traditional economic model for radio and television broadcasting).
2. **A premium membership model** where users pay a monthly or yearly fee to access "free" sites with the ads deleted.
3. **A pay-per-view model** in which users pay only for what they access.

Unique online information of value to the reader will increasingly require payment in the future. Beyond the basic topic of paying for media content online, another significant issue concerns *who* controls access to the Internet as all media forms migrate to it. Information may want to be free, but nations and media corporations have diverse interests in limiting access based on national political agendas and the pursuit of corporate profits.

Internet Management and Governance

One of the Internet's most contentious issues over the past three decades concerns control. That is, who makes decisions about fundamental issues such as the assignment of domain names and control of the *root* – the 13 top-level root servers that govern traffic on the Net? What should be the role of governments in deciding which Internet content their citizens can access? Should nations restrict access to sites posted by hate groups, terrorist organizations, or religious groups such as the Falun Gong in China? What role should telecommunication companies have as gatekeepers for Internet access by their customers? International battles over control continue to this day with conflict between the US government (which still oversees the root) and increasing demands from governments, agencies, and individuals outside the United States for greater international control. Within the US, a debate is under way in Congress over the ability of telecommunication corporations to act as gatekeepers to broadband access by their customers; this is the *net neutrality* controversy. As control of the Internet passed from the US Department of Defense to the National Science Foundation and then on to the US Commerce Department (where ultimate control of the root resides today), there was increasing pressure both to privatize its operations and internationalize its governance. The US government supported the former trend, but not the latter. This chapter examines this evolution and the related governance conflicts that continue to the present.

Regulation of industry at the federal level in the US tends to swing like a pendulum between less regulation and more regulation, depending on which political party is in power. When conservative Republicans were in power during the administration of President Ronald Reagan between 1981 and 1989, there was a significant emphasis on deregulation. During his administration (and afterward under his successor George H. W. Bush from 1989 to 1993), federal government regulation was reduced for major industry segments such as transportation, finance, and telecommunications. The gradual shift in management of the burgeoning Internet from the federal government to private industry between 1987 and 1995 must be seen within this political context under two conservative Republican presidents.

In 1984, the National Science Foundation (NSF) initiated a new Office of Advanced Scientific Computing that funded the creation of supercomputer research centers in San Diego, Urbana-Champaign in Illinois, Pittsburgh, and Princeton, New Jersey.[4] To link these new centers with existing regional computer facilities, the NSF proposed creating a new national digital backbone, the NSFNET. The creation of this new high-speed national network made the 15-year-old ARPANET look slow and antiquated. One of the regional networks to be linked to the high-speed backbone was the Michigan Educational Research Information Triad (MERIT). The consortium was selected in 1987 in a competitive bidding process by NSF and awarded a five-year contract to upgrade and operate the rapidly growing NSFNET.[5] While MERIT was a not-for-profit consortium of Michigan state universities, its corporate partners also included computer maker IBM, and MCI, a telecommunications company.[6]

One significant problem for NSF managers was the agency's Acceptable Use Policy, which prohibited commercial use of the NSFNET – the backbone was reserved for "open research and education."[7] NSF managers (with the blessing of a deregulatory Reagan administration) sought privatization of the network as a way around their own Acceptable Use Policy. The privatization of the NSFNET was inevitable as increasing numbers of commercial interests sought to provide services on the new higher-speed network. These companies included MERIT partners IBM and MCI, as well as regional service providers such as PSINet in northern Virginia.

The ARPANET had been very successful in nurturing the expansion of the nascent Internet, but it was formally decommissioned on February 28, 1990. Janet Abbate notes that this was more than a literal "passing of the baton" within the federal government from ARPA to the NSF; the transition represented the end of US military *control* of the global network.[8] The irony in this transition is that two decades later the US Department of Defense spent $100 million in 2009 as part of the creation of a new Cyber Command (Cybercom). The purpose of the new command is to enhance offensive cyberwar capabilities against other nations while simultaneously building defensive firewalls to prevent these same powers from attacking American institutions and digital networks.[9] We'll return to the theme of global cyberwar in Chapter 14, on the future of the Internet.

Privatization of the US Internet in the 1990s

One of the key tasks in the operation of the Internet is the assignment of Internet Protocol (IP) addresses to new users as they join the global network of networks. An IP number represents a distinct address for the routing of data to and from that system.[10] What users see as their personal site name (e.g., as "mysite.net") is actually a 128-bit string of numbers that is the searchable IP address. Until 1990 the right to assign IP addresses was provided by the Internet Assigned Numbers Authority (IANA), and this was controlled by Dr. Jon Postel at the Information Sciences Institute (ISI) at the University of Southern California (USC). He volunteered to take on this thankless task in 1988, but it ultimately turned out to be a powerful role as Internet usage increased dramatically in the late 1980s.

Postel had helped create the Domain Name System (DNS – the .com, .edu, .gov, and all national country codes outside the US) familiar to every user of the Internet. The "root" was the top-level domain, and control of the DNS root was maintained by IANA. In the privatization process, ultimate control of the DNS root was up for grabs to the highest bidder.[11] Privatization of the Internet picked up steam in 1990 when a non-governmental entity, Network Solutions Inc. (NSI), won the right in May to assign Internet names and IP numbers as a subcontractor to Government Systems Inc. (GSI), which had won a federal bid to operate the NSFNET. In their privatization efforts, officials at the National Science Foundation sought to involve non-governmental firms in the management and operation of the national network, a development that was not universally applauded in all quarters. In retrospect, it was a development that had to occur if the Internet was ever going to become more than a network of university computer systems and government agencies. In the summer of 1991, the Commercial Internet Exchange (CIX) was created by PSINet, CERFNet, and Alternet to facilitate use of the burgeoning Internet by commercial interests.

The early 1990s were characterized by the discovery of the Internet as a communication and information exchange network by thousands of new users who were not affiliated with universities or government agencies. This period saw the rise of new Internet services called Bulletin Board Systems (BBSs) that featured dial-up access for their paying subscribers. BBS users could log in from a home or office personal computer and exchange messages with other subscribers as e-mail or in chat rooms and share news and software. One of the first of these systems was the WELL (for Whole Earth 'Lectronic Link), founded in 1985 in the San Francisco Bay Area by Stewart Brand (the source of the opening quote to this chapter) and Larry Brilliant.[12] It began as a dial-up BBS, morphed into a dial-up ISP, then shifted shape again into an online forum for subscribers operated by Salon.com. The BBSs were linked by a global meta-network known as Fidonet that mirrored the larger construction of the Internet as a network of networks.[13]

By the mid-1990s a "parallel universe" (to government users) of commercial Internet Service Providers (ISPs) had emerged. This was a useful development as the rise of commercial ISPs enabled the network of networks in the US to grow much more rapidly than if the federal government (by either the Department of Defense or the National Science Foundation) had retained strict control. The problem was that the success of the rapidly expanding network was causing growing pains, some of them related to the monetization of Internet services. In 1995, NSI was given the right to charge for Internet domain names, a change in policy that caused anger among users concerned about the effects of privatization and the perception by some that NSI was gouging users. NSI began charging $100 to register a domain name for two years, then charged $50 each year after that.[14] While this was a modest sum for commercial sites, some personal users felt that the fees were excessive. This was at a time when an online gold rush began as entrepreneurs "staked out" and laid claim to valuable generic domain names such as "toys.com," "business.com," and "flowers.com." The explosion in the registration of domain names led to rapidly growing income for NSI, and the company collected more than $200 million in registration fees in 1999 alone. Network Solutions was viewed by many of the more altruistic founders of the Internet as a greedy organization that cared more about maximizing the remarkable profits gleaned from domain registrations than about expanding services.[15]

As non-governmental use of the Internet expanded in the 1990s, it became a lively forum for the free exchange of ideas, opinions, media, and also adult content. A number of adult-themed bulletin board sites were created as purveyors of pornography realized that online sites could generate significant revenue at relatively low cost. Pornographers and their customers have consistently been "early adopters" of new media technologies, from the VCR to CDs and DVDs, and now online high-definition video content. They will undoubtedly lead the way in developing and adopting new 3-D, 4-D, and holographic technologies in the near future.[16] While it is one thing for adults to freely access this content (and zealous local prosecutors gave up pursuing them as pornography moved online in the 1990s), most global societies seek to prevent children from viewing pornography – and there is near-universal criminalization of pornography involving children. In this context, US lawmakers sought to block children from viewing adult content on the Internet as pornographic websites began proliferating in the 1990s.

On February 8, 1996, the Telecommunications Act of 1996 was signed into law in the Library of Congress by President Bill Clinton.[17] The legislation was designed to promote competition between US telecommunication companies by removing regulations that inhibited the provision of new services that used similar transmission systems (e.g., broadband services by cable and telephone companies). By deregulating these companies, the intent of Congress was that increased competition would lead to enhanced telecommunication services and, ideally, lower rates for customers. While the primary focus of the law was telecommunication deregulation, the most contentious part of the Act involved new anti-pornography regulation in the form of Title V, the Communications Decency Act (CDA). This provision made it a criminal act to provide online materials that were judged to be "obscene or indecent" to anyone under the age of 18 in the US.[18]

In reaction to the passage of the Telecommunications Act of 1996 (and especially the inclusion of the CDA), essayist John Perry Barlow published online a *Declaration of the Independence of Cyberspace* the following day, February 9.[19] Barlow had been one of the co-founders of the Electronic Frontier Foundation (EFF) in 1990 with Mitch Kapor (CEO of Lotus software) and John Gilmore (employee number five at Sun Microsystems and one of the creators of Cygnus Solutions).[20] In the declaration, Barlow stated:

> Governments of the Industrial World, you weary giants of flesh and steel, I come from Cyberspace, the new home of Mind. On behalf of the future, I ask you of the past to leave us alone. You are not welcome among us. You have no sovereignty where we gather … Cyberspace consists of transactions, relationships, and thought itself, arrayed like a standing wave in the web of our communications. Ours is a world that is both everywhere and nowhere, but it is not where bodies live. We are creating a world that all may enter without privilege or prejudice accorded by race, economic power, military force, or station of birth. We are creating a world where anyone, anywhere may express his or her beliefs, no matter how singular, without fear of being coerced into silence or conformity. Your legal concepts of property, expression, identity, movement, and context do not apply to us. They are all based on matter, and there is no matter here.[21]

It was a utopian vision of the Internet as an unbounded new frontier that is a uniquely American perspective, and is unsurprising coming from a man raised on a cattle ranch in northwest Wyoming. The spirit of the pioneers who settled the west lives on in Barlow and others such as Stewart Brand and John Gilmore who envisioned the Internet in similar terms as an easily accessed forum where free speech would prevail and where huge investments were not required to be a publisher or broadcaster. As Barlow stated in a 1991 journal article:

> Imagine discovering a continent so vast that it may have no end to its dimensions. Imagine a new world with more resources than all our future

Figure 9.1   John Perry Barlow. *Photo*: Joichi Ito.

greed might exhaust, more opportunities than there will ever be entrepreneurs enough to exploit, and a peculiar kind of real estate that expands with development. Imagine a place where trespassers leave no footprints, where goods can be stolen an infinite number of times and yet remain in the possession of their original owners, where business you never heard of can own the history of your personal affairs.[22]

This vision of cyberspace as an unbounded forum for the free expression of ideas was colliding head-on with those who sought to impose censorship on its content (in the name of protecting America's children). The flaw in the legislation was that it was so strictly written that some online literary works, works of art, health information, and medical diagrams might be construed in more conservative areas of the United States as being "obscene or indecent." The American Civil Liberties Union (ACLU) filed suit against the US Department of Justice and Attorney General Janet Reno and argued that the CDA was unconstitutional. To the credit of the American legal system, two lower courts agreed with the ACLU's position and their decisions were appealed by the federal government to the US Supreme Court.[23]

In one of the most significant US legal decisions concerning telecommunication in modern times, the Supreme Court ruled 7–2 on June 26, 1997 in *Reno v. ACLU* that the Communications Decency Act was unconstitutional. The majority found that the term "patently offensive" as applied in the law was overly vague and that the law infringed the First Amendment rights of parents in establishing what their children should be able to access online. The decision supported the First Amendment rights of adults in the US as a higher priority for society than censoring the Internet. The decision had far-reaching repercussions extending beyond attempts by Congress to censor content on the Internet. In his brief as part of the majority opinion, Justice John Paul Stevens noted that the Internet was a "unique medium – known to its users as cyberspace – located in no particular geographical location but available to anyone, anywhere in the world."[24] He further stated that, *"no single organization controls any membership in the Web, nor is there any centralized point from which individual Websites or services can be blocked from the Web"* (emphasis added).[25] While Justice Stevens was technically correct on this first point, we'll see that the US government is still first among equals in terms of control of the root-level structure of the Internet. In regard to his second point, we'll examine several specific cases where nations systematically block access to websites they consider subversive or illegal.

The International Struggle Over Internet Governance

In 1997, several groups sought to create a new international governance structure for the Internet as an alternative to control of the Domain Name System by Network Solutions. Internet pioneer Vinton Cerf, co-author of TCP/IP, had been instrumental in creating the Internet Society (ISOC) in 1992.[26] As the US government was taking steps in 1991–2 to privatize the Internet, Cerf and the newly formed ISOC were seeking an alternate international privatization system to "provide a governing structure, institutional home, and source of funding independent from the US Defense Department and, more generally, the US government," as Goldsmith and Wu note.[27] Many of the founders of the Internet, including Cerf, were involved in the creation of ISOC, and clearly preferred the idea of an international organization governing the privatized Internet instead of a for-profit US corporation such as NSI.

To this end, in 1998 ISOC created a "blue-ribbon" International Ad Hoc Committee (IAHC) comprised of powerful organizations with diverse interests in Internet policy and governance. It was chaired by Don Heath, ISOC chief executive, and included two representatives from the Internet Engineering Task Force appointed by Jon Postel of IANA. There were also representatives of the World Intellectual Property Association (WIPO) and the International Trademark Association, both organizations with interests in maintaining control of copyrights and trademarks online. Of the eleven members of the IAHC, the only representative of the US government was George Strawn of the National Science Foundation, the administrator of US control of the root at the time.[28]

The IAHC drafted a key document outlining significant changes in Internet governance, titled the "Generic Top-Level Domain Memorandum of Understanding" – with the convoluted acronym gTLD-MoU.[29] The unwieldy acronym was to be a prescient symbol for the rocky reception it received from organizations and corporations opposed to the transfer of governance to an international body. The gTLD-MoU proposed to place significant control over Internet governance in the hands of a Swiss non-governmental organization, CORE (formally known as the International Council of Registrars) – and the Internet Society. In doing so, it would take away domain registration from Network Solutions and control of the root from the US government. The MoU also proposed adding seven new generic top-level domains such as .web and .shop. Another key supporter of the gTLD-MoU was the International Telecommunications Union (ITU) based in Geneva, Switzerland. The ITU regulates supranational communication, including the international assignment of radio frequencies and telecommunication satellite orbits.[30]

When asked by a reporter if the Internet Society would need the approval of the US to implement its proposal, CEO Don Heath stated that the federal government, "has no choice."[31] This confidence that the US government would willingly submit to a transfer of power to an international body was seriously mistaken. The day after 57 organizations signed the gTLD-MoU in Geneva on May 1, 1997, a US government official (most likely White House Internet policy expert Ira Magaziner) stated to CNet News:

> We are explicitly saying that we are not supporting the ad hoc committee's plan in its current form. It's not entirely clear what the role of [UN] organizations like the ITU and WIPO is going to be, but we are concerned about the possibility that those organizations will have too great a role in the process and we won't have a private sector-driven process. There are also some concerns about addressing an Internet-related issue in a forum that has traditionally done telecommunications regulation, like the ITU.[32]

While the official did not state that the US government was opposed to the potential loss of its control over the root, this was one of the most significant reasons for its opposition. The conversion to control by the Internet Society-led international consortium was due to take place on January 1, 1998 – it did not. In a Green Paper released on January 28 as a formal Notice of Proposed Rulemaking requesting comments from interested parties, the National Telecommunications and Information Administration (NTIA) objected to this potential loss of control of the root and suggested that management of Internet assigned numbers be transferred to private organization. It was a direct rejection of the gTLD-MoU and the proposed transfer of power to the Internet Society and CORE. Their supporters in the United States, especially one of the key architects, Jon Postel, were demoralized by this rejection of their efforts to internationalize Internet governance.

Table 9.1 Key events in 20th-century Internet governance, 1984–1999

Date	Event	Primary actors
1984	Top-level Domain Name System (DNS) (.edu, .com, .gov) introduced.	Jon Postel, USC, ARPANET, MILNET, CSNET, Paul Mockapetris, and USENET hosts and users.
1985	Information Sciences Institute (ISI) at the University of Southern California (USC) assigned responsibility by DCA for Domain Name System root management. Dr. Jon Postel is manager.	ISI, Defense Communication Agency (DCA), USC, Jon Postel.
1986	Internet Engineering Task Force (IETF) formed. The group is influential in shaping Internet policy and technology by consensus and collaboration.	Created by Internet Activities Board, itself a creation of the Internet Configuration Control Board (ICCB).
1987	Michigan Educational Research Information Triad (MERIT) wins contract to co-manage the NSFNET.	National Science Foundation and the MERIT consortium.
December 1988	Internet Assigned Numbers Authority (IANA) established at USC. Jon Postel is named as its director.	Information Sciences Institute at USC and SRI.

(*continued*)

Table 9.1 (*continued*)

Date	Event	Primary actors
1989	Reseaux IP Européennes (RIPE) formed by European ISPs to coordinate their IP network.	Reseaux IP Européennes.
May 1990	Network Solutions Inc. (NSI) wins right to assign Internet names and IP numbers as subcontractor to winning bidder Government Systems Inc.	NSI, Government Systems Inc., and the National Science Foundation.
July 1990	Electronic Frontier Foundation (EFF) formed.	John Perry Barlow, John Gilmore, and Mitch Kapor.
July 1991	Commercial Internet Exchange (CIX) created to provide Internet access for commercial users.	PSINet, CERFNet, and Alternet.
April 30, 1995	Merit Networks terminates the NSFNET backbone, effectively "ending U.S. government ownership of the Internet's infrastructure."[a]	Merit Networks and the National Science Foundation.
September 14, 1995	$50 annual fee implemented for registering formerly free domain names. NSI wins contract to register names	NSI.
February 8, 1996	Telecommunications Act of 1996 signed into law, including Title V – Communications Decency Act.	President William J. Clinton and the US Congress.
February 9, 1996	*A Declaration of the Independence of Cyberspace* is published online.	John Perry Barlow and the Electronic Frontier Foundation.
May 1, 1997	The Generic Top-Level Domain Memorandum of Understanding (gTLD-MoU) is signed in Geneva, Switzerland, proposing an international governance scheme for management of the Internet.	International Ad Hoc Committee, the Internet Society, and the International Telecommunication Union (ITU).
May 2, 1997	Officials of the US government state that they will not support the gTLD-MoU.	Ira Magaziner and the federal Interagency Task Force.

Table 9.1   (*continued*)

Date	Event	Primary actors
June 26, 1997	US Supreme Court rules 7:2 in *Reno v. ACLU* that the Communications Decency Act is unconstitutional.	US Supreme Court, Department of Justice, American Civil Liberties Union (ACLU), EFF.
January 1, 1998	Planned date of transfer of control of the Internet to the Internet Society and CORE in Geneva. The US government objects to this transfer and it does not take place.	Internet Society, International Council of Registrars (CORE), US government, and the ITU.
January 28, 1998	Jon Postel redirects segments of the root zone file from NSI to IANA at USC.	Jon Postel and the root administrators for eight areas in the US.
January 30, 1998	NTIA issues Green Paper Notice of Proposed Rulemaking asserting continued US control of the root.	US Department of Commerce's National Telecommunications and Information Agency (NTIA).
February 4, 1998	Postel returns root directory control to NSI after showdown with Ira Magaziner and USC officials.	Jon Postel, Ira Magaziner, USC administration, and NSI.
July 1998	White Paper conference proposes international Internet governance through creation of an "Internet Corporation for Assigned Names and Numbers" (ICANN).	The Internet Society, IANA, US government, CIX, Educause, IBM, MCI, and Cisco.
September 19, 1998	ICANN created under contract to US Commerce Department.	ICANN, US Department of Commerce.
January 1, 1999	IANA's role as gTLD manager is transferred to ICANN.	ICANN, IANA, ISI, and USC.

Sources: J. Abbate, *Inventing the Internet* (Cambridge: MIT Press, 1999); J. Goldsmith and T. Wu, *Who Controls the Internet? Illusions of a Borderless World* (Oxford: Oxford University Press, 2006); K. Hafner, and M. Lyon, *Where Wizards Stay Up Late: The Origins of the Internet* (New York: Touchstone, 1996); *Hobbes Internet Time Line* (2010); M. L. Mueller, *Ruling the Root* (Cambridge, MA: MIT Press, 2002).
a Abbate, *Inventing the Internet*, 199.

The Day that Jon Postel Seized Control
of the Top-Level Domains

Jonathan Postel (1943–98) was an Internet pioneer, first working with fellow graduate student Vinton Cerf and Professor Leonard Kleinrock on the first ARPANET node at UCLA (see Chapter 4), and subsequently working at the Information Sciences Institute at the University of Southern California in Los Angeles.[33] Under a contract from SRI he was the editor at USC of the *Request for Comments* (*RFC*) series that documented the technical operations of the Internet. *RFC*s govern the day-to-day functioning of the massive international network, and Postel played a central role in these operations prior to his death. There is no master control for the Internet, but if it existed prior to 1998 the chief technical officer would have been Jon Postel. In an era when many computer scientists were often iconoclasts, Postel was a kindred spirit with long hair and a beard who wore jeans and sandals to work. He was a kind and gentle person who could be remarkably stubborn about issues in which he was a stakeholder.[34] This background knowledge is important when analyzing why Postel seized partial control of the Internet on January 28, 1998.

As director of the Internet Assigned Numbers Authority based at USC, Postel had great power in making decisions about the domain name system and how unique IP addresses were assigned to computers connected to the Internet.[35] Any university, company, ISP, or agency in the world who wished to connect with the Internet had to work with the IANA to define which root server they would use, and this would in turn determine which unique IP addresses would be assigned to computers in their networks. As the global address designation authority, IANA not only had governance over the top-level domain structure (.edu, .com, .gov), it also had naming control over the assignment of a unique IP address for every computer connected to the Internet.

After National Science Foundation management of the NSFNET ended in 1987 with the selection of MERIT as the vendor, control of the root and IP address assignments still rested with IANA. However, when Government Systems won the management contract in 1990, they sub-contracted domain name rights to Network Solutions Inc. Postel chaffed at what he perceived to be their arrogant attitude as a government-sanctioned monopoly. The fact that they were earning millions of dollars in domain registrations each year as a monopoly surely rankled him as a champion of shared governance. As IANA director, he managed the

Figure 9.2   Dr. Jon Postel of USC's Information Sciences Institute managed IP address assignment policies for the Internet from 1969 until his death in 1998. *Photo:* Irene Fertik, USC News Service. Copyright 1994, USC.

transparent process by which IP addresses were assigned, but all registration revenue accrued to NSI. Postel become one of chief supporters (with his high-school and college friend Vinton Cerf) of the Internet Society and its participation in the creation of the gTLD-MoU in 1997 with 57 international agencies and companies.

Given his sources in both government and industry, Postel must have had some inkling of the positions NTIA planned to take with its forthcoming Green Paper. The NTIA's Notice of Proposed Rulemaking, issued on January 30, 1998, explicitly stated US government opposition to a transfer of network governance to the Internet Society, effectively killing the gTLD-MoU, in which hundreds of individuals in the consortium had invested thousands of hours. At 5 p.m. on the afternoon of January 28, he sent e-mails from IANA in Los Angeles to eight individuals who controlled the secondary Internet root servers in their areas. In a remarkable act of chutzpah, he instructed them to redirect their servers from the A root at NSI to a computer he controlled at IANA. Four US government root

Figure 9.3   Ira Magaziner, Clinton White House telecommunication and health policy expert, makes a speech in 2007. *Photo:* Joichi Ito.

servers at NASA, NSF, and two military networks were not redirected.[36] As a measure of their trust and faith in Postel, all eight operators did as instructed, although server K manager Paul Vixie told his family that he might be going to jail for his actions.[37] Even though Postel did not control all 12 secondary root servers, if he wished he could have arbitrarily added the seven new domain names sought in the gTLD-MoU.[38] Internet scholar Milton Mueller notes that "there can be little doubt that the redirection was a direct challenge to the US government."[39] In an interview Mueller conducted in 2000 with Paul Vixie about Postel's motives, he said, "He [Postel] was firing a shot across the bow, saying [to NSI] you may have COM, but I've got the dot."[40]

Most users of the Internet at that time did not notice any change in the operation of the network, but national security officials in the US government did. Clinton administration Internet policy expert Ira Magaziner was attending the World Economic Forum in Davos, Switzerland when he was informed of the redirection. Magaziner was acquainted with Postel as he had consulted with him concerning US opposition to the gTLD-MoU. He immediately called Postel (and his ISI supervisor) at USC to inquire what he was doing. Postel claimed it was only a test, and when his supervisor expressed consternation at this statement, Postel promised to redirect the eight secondary servers back to NSI.[41] When the Green Paper appeared two days later, wording had been added that any unauthorized alteration of the root structure would henceforth be a federal crime in the US.

The legendary Postel "rebellion" demonstrates that, when push comes to shove, the federal government can shove very hard when officials perceive that national security and economic issues are at stake. While NSI had been actively lobbying members of Congress and the administration to protect their monopoly control of domain name registration, others in the US government were more concerned about cybersecurity as the Internet was becoming a powerful global communications medium. There is an old legal cliché that states that "possession is nine-tenths of the law." Ira Magaziner put it succinctly when he stated in an interview that "The United States paid for the Internet, the Net was created under its auspices, and most importantly everything that Jon [Postel] and Network Solutions did was pursuant to government contracts."[42]

ICANN as the Middle Path

After the abortive attempt to seize control of the secondary Internet root servers in early 1998 by Postel and partners, the Clinton Administration (led by telecommunications policy maven Ira Magaziner) proposed that an international organization be created to manage the awarding of domain names. This concept was introduced at a White Paper conference held in the Washington suburb of Reston, Virginia in July of 1998. While the administration suggested the creation of an "Internet Corporation for Assigned Names and Numbers" (ICANN), with an internationally constituted board of directors, the US did not wish to cede control of the root authority to ICANN.

In September of 1998 ICANN was formally founded, with headquarters located in Marina del Rey, California and regional offices in Palo Alto, California, Washington, DC, Brussels, in Belgium, and Sydney, Australia.[43] The original charter for ICANN was for five years, and it was extended in 2006 for another five-year period. However, in July 2008 the US Department of Commerce (via the NTIA) sent a letter to ICANN stating that the government had "no plans to transition management of the authoritative root zone file to ICANN."[44] It is clear that the US government has no immediate (or long-term) interest in ceding ultimate control over the root to ICANN or to any other non-governmental body.

The Internet as a Medium of Democratic Communication

Just after midnight Cairo time, in the early hours of Friday, January 27, 2011, the government of Egypt shut down national access to the Internet. Almost instantly, Internet traffic to and from a nation of 80 million people plummeted 90 percent.[45] Originally led by regional Google executive Wael Ghonim, anti-government protesters had used Facebook and Twitter over the prior week to organize rallies in several Egyptian cities, including Cairo. Ghonim had created a Facebook site in memory of Khaled Said, a young Alexandrian businessman murdered by local police. The site was labeled "We Are All Khaled Said" and featured horrific photos of the injuries suffered by Said. The site quickly became a focal point for the citizen rebellion against long-time dictator Hosni Mubarak, so much so that creator Ghonim was arrested by the Egyptian secret police and held incommunicado for 18 days. By then, the site had attracted 350,000 Facebook users, who mobilized street protests that continued after Ghonim's arrest.[46] Mubarak resigned the presidency of Egypt on February 11, the second dictator of a North African nation toppled by citizens mobilized by Facebook and Twitter.

Internet-based communication technologies had proved very useful in bypassing government efforts to censor the mass media after the fall of the Tunisian dictator Ali Ben Ali, which had also been orchestrated by Internet-mobilized protests. Apparently, the Egyptian government had the ability to shut off national Internet access as if switching off a light (and most Vodaphone mobile phone service as well).[47] The protests in Egypt and the government's reaction to them demonstrated that dictators such as President Mubarak understand the power of new communication technologies to foment rebellion against autocratic rule and will take steps to block public access to them. Information wants to be free, and repressive governments will go to great lengths to prevent the free flow of ideas.

In their perceptive text *Who Controls the Internet?* (2006), Jack Goldsmith and Tim Wu explore the relationship between geography and the Internet, which they state is splitting apart and becoming "a bordered network."[48] This theme contradicts Thomas Friedman's concept of a "flat world" where Internet connections universally transcend national boundaries. Wu and Goldsmith make a convincing case that the public image of the Internet as an unfettered, unordered network that leaps national boundaries is an illusion. They state that the "bordered Internet accommodates real and important differences among peoples in different places, and makes the Internet a more effective and useful communication tool as a result."[49] The popular uprisings in North Africa and the Middle East confirm the power of the Internet as a tool to promote democratic communication, and illustrate why repressive governments seek to control access to free-speech applications such as Facebook and Twitter. Who would have thought that 140-character messages could have the power to topple governments? However, recent events in Egypt and Tunisia have demonstrated the power of the Internet as a medium of protest.

The Egyptian shutdown of the Internet raised the question in many US-based blogs – "Does the United States government have access to a kill switch?" They were assured by experts that the Internet in the US is too diverse to be easily shut down by a dictator or repressive regime. There is no central chokepoint for information flowing into or out of the US, as it moves through hundreds of undersea cables. However, as Jon Postel demonstrated on January 28, 1998, the agency that controls the root of the Internet has the power to allow or deny access to it. This may be why the United States government is reluctant to surrender control of the root and ICANN.

The Social Embeddedness of the Internet

The Internet is defined by some as a largely invisible global network of fiber-optic lines, digital routers, and millions of connected computers. While this viewpoint is factually correct, it is an obvious oversimplification to see it in such literal terms. As this chapter makes clear, the Internet has become a battleground over who controls its structure, operation, and governance. The US government has asserted that, since it funded the creation and early development of the Net, it should be first among equals in making basic decisions concerning its governance. The battles over governance highlight the social embeddedness of the Internet as a universal global communication network that transcends national boundaries and cultures. It also illustrates related efforts by some governments to impose national boundaries on the free flow of information. Information wants to be free, and this philosophy is of great concern to some dictatorial regimes.

It is clear that the US government sees significant national security rationales in maintaining control of root-level servers for the Internet. These interests extend beyond global e-commerce trade by US companies, as these governance policies have to do with fundamental control issues. It should not come as a surprise that Rod Beckstrom, ICANN's president and CEO, was formerly director of the National Cybersecurity Center, part of the US Department of Homeland Security.[50] Governments worldwide have watched the Internet-fueled protests in Tunisia and Egypt with great interest. Repressive regimes such as those in Iran and China see free access to the Internet as a threat to their legitimacy, while nations which allow free Net access are not breathing easy. A populist uprising could occur in any nation where large groups of citizens feel disenfranchised and have access to a medium of communication that governments cannot control. Communication scholar Ithiel de Sola Pool wrote in 1983 of the use of new communication media, such as the Internet, as "technologies of freedom" – he would have been very pleased to see the populist use of the Internet in Egypt and Tunisia.[51]

Notes

1. S. Brand, *The Media Lab: Inventing the Future at MIT* (New York: Viking Penguin, 1987), 202. Stewart Brand's initial comment on this issue was at the first Hackers Conference in 1984 and was printed in *The Whole Earth Review* (May 1985, p. 49) as "On the one hand information wants to be expensive, because it's so valuable. The right information in the right place just changes your life. On the other hand, information wants to be free, because the cost of getting it out is getting lower and lower all the time. So you have these two fighting against each other."

2. Consumer Electronics Association, *U.S. Consumer Electronics Sales and Forecasts* (2010). Cost retrieved January 30, 2010, from http://mycea.ce.org/Default.aspx?tabid=129.

3. A. O. Sulzberger, "A Letter to Our Readers about Digital Subscriptions," *New York Times* (March 17, 2011). Retrieved March 18, 2011, from http://www.ny times.com/2011/03/18/opinion/l18times.html?_r=1&scp=1&sq=A%20letter %20to%20our%20readers%20about%20digital%20subscriptions&st=cse.

4. J. Abbate, *Inventing the Internet* (Cambridge, MA: MIT Press, 1999), 191–3.

5. Ibid., 193.

6. The government partners included Michigan State University, the University of Michigan, and Wayne State University. The operations center for the network is based at the University of Michigan.

7. E. Krol, *The Whole Internet User's Guide & Catalog* (Sebastopol, CA: O'Reilly & Associates, 1992), 353–4. http://www.archive.org/details/whole internet00krolmiss.

8. Abbate, *Inventing the Internet*, 195.

9. CBS News, "Pentagon Bill to Fix Cyber Attacks: $100M" (2009).

10. Until 1995, IP addresses developed under Internet Protocol Version 4 (IPv4) were written as a 32-bit code typically expressed as a string of 11 numbers (e.g., 205.78.526.815). Due to the rapid growth of the Internet since 1995, IP addresses will be expressed as a 128-bit code under Internet Protocol Version 6 (IPv6).

11. A complete database of all generic (gTLD) and country code (ccTLD) Top Level Domains can be viewed online at the IANA website: http://www.iana. org/domains/root/.

12. K. Haftner, *The WELL: A Story of Love-Death and Real Life in the Seminal Online Community* (New York: Carroll & Graf, 2001).

13. Fidonet now links 10,000 smaller networks. See the global Fidonet website at http://www.fidonet.org.

14. J. Goldsmith and T. Wu, *Who Controls the Internet? Illusions of a Borderless World* (Oxford: Oxford University Press, 2006), 35.

15. Ibid., 36.

16. 4-D content involves the transmission of sensory information to the viewer that goes beyond 3-D sight and surround-sound. Holographic imagery would allow the viewer to move around a filmed object and see all sides if it.

17. Public Law No: 104-104: Telecommunications Act of 1996. http://frwebgate. access.gpo.gov/cgi-bin/getdoc.cgi?dbname=104_cong_public_laws&docid =f:publ104.104.

18. Ibid. While Title V of the Act primarily banned the carriage of obscene content on cable television, Section 507 made it a criminal offense to transmit indecent or obscene content by anyone who "(A) Uses an inter-active computer service to send to a specific person or persons under 18 years of age, or (B) Uses any interactive computer service to display in a manner available to a person under 18 years of age, any comment, request, suggestion, proposal, image, or other communication that, in context, depicts or describes, in terms patently offensive as measured by contem-porary community standards, sexual or excretory activities or organs."

19. J. P. Barlow, *Declaration of the Independence of Cyberspace* (1996). Retrieved November 20, 2010, from the EFF site at https://projects.eff. org/~barlow/Declaration-Final.html. As a writer for *Wired* magazine in the 1990s and as a co-founder of the EFF, John Perry Barlow played a key role in promoting a "hands-off" philosophy toward Internet control by governments and corporations. He was born in Sublette County in northwest Wyoming near the town of Pinedale, and maintained a ranch there for many years. As a teenager he met future Grateful Dead member Bob Weir while attending a private boarding school in Colorado, and this later led to a productive

collaboration writing songs for the band. He joined the WELL online community in 1986 and later worked with John Gilmore and Mitch Kapor to create the EFF in 1990.

20. The Electronic Frontier Foundation has taken a lead role in defending and litigating key issues related to free speech and privacy, among others, related to regulation of the Internet and new media. The EFF website (http://www.eff.org/) contains interesting information about their history and current projects.

21. Barlow, *Declaration of the Independence of Cyberspace.*

22. J. P. Barlow, "Electronic Frontier: Coming into the Country," *Communications of the ACM* 34/3 (March 1991).

23. Federal district courts in Philadelphia and New York ruled, respectively, that the CDA as drafted would unfairly restrict the First Amendment free speech rights of adults, and in New York stated that aspects of the Act intended to protect children from "obscene or indecent" content were too broadly drawn.

24. *ACLU v. Reno* (1997). 521 US 844, 851.

25. Ibid., 853.

26. ISOC has 28,000 members, who participate in 90 chapters around the world, with offices in Reston, Virginia (Washington, DC area) and Geneva, Switzerland. See the ISOC website: http://www.isoc.org/.

27. Goldsmith and Wu, *Who Controls the Internet?*, 37.

28. M. L. Mueller, *Ruling the Root* (Cambridge, MA: MIT Press, 2002), 143.

29. The term "Generic Top-Level Domain" referred to the most commonly used domain names such as .com and .org. The term "Memorandum of Understanding," or MoU, describes an agreement less formal than a contract between organizations indicating a mutually agreed course of action. The promoters of the transfer of power were known colloquially as "the MoUvement."

30. The ITU is an agency of the United Nations, with 191 nations as members. It also develops international communications standards and assists less developed nations with telecommunication infrastructure development. It has four primary divisions: the General Secretariat, Radiocommunication (ITU-R), Standardization (ITU-T), and Development (ITU-D). See the ITU website: http://www.itu.int/en/pages/default.aspx.

31. "U.S. Rejects Net Name Plan," *CNet News* (May 2, 1997). http://news.cnet.com/U.S.-rejects-Net-name-plan/2100-1023_3-279468.html.

32. Ibid.

33. M. Waldrop, *The Dream Machine: J. C. R. Licklider and the Revolution That Made Computing Personal* (New York: Penguin, 2001), 301.

34. The background information about Jon Postel comes from Vinton Cerf's eulogy "I REMEMBER IANA" that was published as RFC 2468: http://tools.ietf.org/html/rfc2468. Postel would have appreciated that this moving

eulogy was distributed as an RFC to users of the Internet who knew and worked with him. Postel died after heart surgery on October 16, 1998.

35. In fact, in 1983 Postel requested that Paul Mockapetris create the domain name system the Internet uses today.
36. Mueller, *Ruling the Root*, 161.
37. Ibid., 162.
38. Goldsmith and Wu, *Who Controls the Internet?*, 45.
39. Mueller, *Ruling the Root*, 162.
40. Ibid.
41. Goldsmith and Wu, *Who Controls the Internet?*, 46.
42. Ibid., 41.
43. Note that the headquarters of ICANN is located in the same Marina Del Rey building as USC's Information Sciences Institute, where Jon Pastel managed IANA in the years prior to ICANN's creation.
44. M. A. Baker, "Letter from Meredith A. Baker, Acting Assistant Secretary for Communication and Information, National Telecommunications and Information Administration, to Peter Dengate-Thrush, Chairman of the Board of Directors, ICANN" (2008). Retrieved December 3, 2010, from http://www.ntia.doc.gov/comments/2008/ICANN_080730.html#.
45. M. Richel, "Egypt Cuts Off Most Internet and Cellphone Service," *New York Times* (January 28, 2011). Retrieved January 30, 2011, from http://www.nytimes.com/2011/01/29/technology/internet/29cutoff.html?scp=1&sq=egypt%20and%20internet&st=cse#.
46. M. Giglio, "The Facebook Freedom Fighter," *Newsweek* (February 13, 2011). Retrieved February 19, 2011, from: http://magazine-directory.com/Newsweek.htm. Ghonim had given the username and password to the Facebook site to confederates prior to his arrest. Khaled Said had been murdered by police in Alexandria because he had posted online a video of local police helping themselves to drugs from a local bust.
47. Egyptians with satellite-provided Internet access did not have it curtailed.
48. Goldsmith and Wu, *Who Controls the Internet?*, pp. x–xi.
49. Ibid., p. xii.
50. It should be noted that Beckstrom is also a successful software entrepreneur, helped found an international peace-seeking organization, and is a director of the Environmental Defense Fund. See his biography at the ICANN website: http://www.icann.org/en/biog/beckstrom.htm.
51. I. De Sola Pool, *Technologies of Freedom* (Cambridge, MA: Belknap Press, 1983).

10

Censorship and Global Cyberculture

"The Net interprets censorship as damage and routes around it."
(John Gilmore, co-founder of the Electronic
Frontier Foundation, 1993)[1]

For many netizens there is an illusory image of the Internet as an unfettered, unbounded global network; Gilmore's well-known statement reinforces that image. The Internet is seen as a global web of connections that allows information to flow along multiple pathways around any barriers erected by police-state nations, anti-pornography censors, and companies seeking to limit social network access by their employees. As with much Net folklore, the reality is not quite so reductionist.

As cited in Chapter 9, Internet scholars Jack Goldsmith and Tim Wu described numerous examples of successful censorship of Internet content by politically repressive nations (e.g., China) and even democracies such as France.[2] They also note that on many websites the first thing a new user is asked to do is indicate their national origin by clicking on a menu of countries (or within a country by postal code). Once this is accomplished, the site then presents information that is tailored to the user's nationality, language, or community. Goldsmith and Wu note that this often makes the

Digital Universe: The Global Telecommunication Revolution, First Edition. Peter B. Seel.
© 2012 Peter B. Seel. Published 2012 by Blackwell Publishing Ltd.

information more useful by limiting it to the user's immediate needs. Local weather information is typically more useful than national data, especially in larger countries. Thus, the first step in analyzing universal access to the Internet is to differentiate between online censorship – restricting what you can see – from the filtration of content, the self-directed process of narrowing search parameters to acquire only the information sought. The rationales for Internet censorship (the intentional restriction of a citizen's or an employee's free access to information) are diverse and vary depending on the scale and scope of restriction (see Table 10.1).

Table 10.1   A Hierarchy of Internet Censorship

Scale	Scope	Example
International	Content access is *almost* universally blocked and/or prosecuted.	Pornography involving children – government condemnation is universal.
National	Some content is blocked based on national political and/or moral standards.	French prosecution of Yahoo over Nazi memorabilia sites. Egypt shuts down most national Internet access in 2011 in reaction to citizen protests.
State or province	Content is blocked based on regional standards.	Cities and regions in Russia block sites such as YouTube and the Internet Archive.
Company or local level	Access to defined content (e.g., social networks, gambling, or pornography sites) is blocked based on company or organization standards.	Use of technologies such as keyword blockers to monitor and/or inhibit employee Internet access on an employer's computers.
Personal	Censorship applied by parents at home for their children. Self-censorship based on social, organizational, or religious norms.	Installation of password-protected blocking software on home computers. Avoidance of gambling or pornographic sites in places of employment.

Censoring the Internet

Pornography featuring images of children is condemned worldwide. Children are abused and exploited to create these images, which provides a rationale for the prosecution of those who create this type of pornography and, in many legal jurisdictions, for the possession of such content. While legal standards for the creation and adult use of pornography vary dramatically from nation to nation (the Netherlands compared with Saudi Arabia, for example), creating or accessing child pornography elicits universal condemnation. The problem with attempting to block the distribution of child pornography is that the same Internet attribute of promoting the creation of global affinity groups unbounded by geography also enables networks of pedophiles to share this morally offensive content. Recall Jacques Ellul's *La Technique* (see Chapter 3), where the good and bad effects of the diffusion of technology take place simultaneously and are inseparable. The same technology that enables groups to mobilize to protest government abuses of power (e.g., in Egypt), also enables pedophiles to share child pornography, or hate groups to incite violence.

In April of 2000, a French court charged the Silicon Valley-based Internet search company Yahoo with a violation of the law banning the sale of Nazi memorabilia to French citizens. One of the plaintiffs, the Ligue Contre le Racisme et l'Antisémitisme (The Anti-Racism and Anti-Semitism League, LICRA for short), discovered that the memorabilia sold on the site hosted by Yahoo included concentration camp photos, Nazi flags, and replicas of the Zyklon B gas canisters used to execute prisoners in death camp gas chambers. LICRA filed suit against Yahoo in a French court to have it removed.[3] The 90,000 French Jews killed in Nazi concentration camps during World War II are memorialized in Paris and other French cities – the Holocaust is not an abstract issue in France.[4]

Yahoo's defense was based on three fundamental concepts: (1) that French courts did not have jurisdiction over Internet content based on servers in the US; (2) that the First Amendment rights of Americans would be abridged by requiring content to meet the internal legal standards of other nations; and, most critically, (3) that it would be technically impossible to filter Internet content so that it could not be viewed by French citizens.[5] During the trial of the lawsuit in Paris, Judge Jean-Jacques Gomez discovered that technology *was* available to filter Web content based on the user's IP address and their Internet Service Provider (ISP). It was also discovered that Yahoo's servers were actually physically based in Stockholm, Sweden, and the California site simply mirrored this. The judge appointed a panel of three technical experts (which included Internet pioneer Vinton Cerf) to investigate the claim that it was impossible for Yahoo to filter content based on the nationality of the user. In fact, the experts found the opposite.

Yahoo could block up to 90 percent of French users from seeing proscribed Internet content. The court ruled, on November 20, 2000, that Yahoo had to make a reasonable "best effort" to block the Nazi sites from its French users.[6] After making part of its key defense in the French court the "impossibility" of blocking Net users based on geography, Yahoo revealed that it could do this "for ad targeting purposes."[7] Years of appeals in US courts followed, but Yahoo ultimately surrendered on this issue and blocked the Nazi memorabilia sites in France. The key lesson here is that the 1990s vision of a global Internet unfettered by national boundaries, laws, and regional customs is a simplistic viewpoint that ignores efforts by nations since 2000 to restrict access to online content that their courts see as illegal, obscene, or seditious.

Internet Censorship in Iran

After the disputed national elections in Iran in June of 2009, the theocratic government attempted to shut down Internet access to the rest of the world to prevent images of street protests from being published or broadcast. As protests mounted the day after the results were announced (which were considered rigged by neutral observers), Internet access to and from Iran was shut down for 30 minutes.[8] As the government struggled to control information flowing out of the country by monitoring Internet traffic, activists turned to alternative means of communicating about the protests to the outside world. They shifted from the traditional communication modes of landline telephones, television, and e-mail (which were being blocked or censored) to the use of mobile phones and Twitter posts, which were not.

Neda Agha-Soltan was driving with three friends in central Teheran on June 20, 2009 to participate in anti-government protests, and had just parked her car. The 27-year-old music student was accompanied by her singing teacher that afternoon. Shortly after stepping out of her car, she was shot in the chest by a sniper positioned on a nearby rooftop. She collapsed to the ground as several nearby observers recorded three videos of the horrifying scene.[9] The most widely distributed video shows her prostrate on the ground as her eyes scan those around her in shock. Blood then pours from her mouth and nose, covering her face and pooling

Figure 10.1   Neda Agha-Soltan, a 27-year-old Iranian vocalist and music student killed in Teheran while participating in street protests against 2009 election results that kept president Mahmoud Amedinejad in power.

on the ground around her head as bystanders scream and call for help. Minutes later a Basij militiaman emerged from an adjacent home and was seized by protesters in the crowd who photographed him after he admitted that he had shot Agha-Soltan. He was released by the crowd and fled the scene, but was later identified by his identity card seized by the crowd. Thanks to the digital firewall erected around Iran by government censors, citizens outside the country probably never would have heard about this tragedy, and her death would have been mourned only by her family and friends.

Despite efforts by the government to censor all media coverage of the protesters, the video taken with a mobile phone soon made its way onto the Internet and ultimately onto YouTube. Twitter posts (with a #neda hash mark), both from within Iran and from outside the country, called

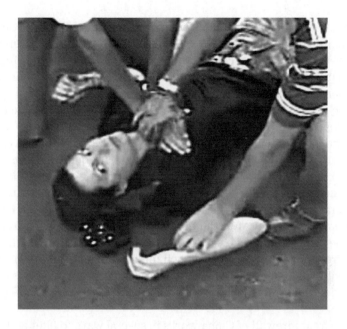

Figure 10.2   Neda Agha-Soltan was shot in the chest by a Basij militia sniper who attacked the protestors. Video images of her death were captured on a bystander's mobile phone and later uploaded to the Internet.

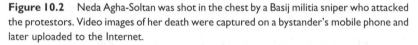

attention to the story and pointed to online sites where the videos were posted. Within a day the video was seen by millions of online viewers worldwide as the death of Ms. Agha-Soltan became a symbol for pro-democracy forces protesting the re-election of president Mahmoud Ahmedinejad. The posting of the video online demonstrated that, despite the best efforts of the Iranian government to block access to the Internet during the protest, other means of telecommunication (via mobile phones) were used to bypass these censorship barriers. While nations such as Iran and China have developed the means to control and regulate Internet access, other modes of communication can and will be used to bypass these barriers.

The Great Firewall of China

China's censorship firewall was created in 1998 in response to the rapid growth of Internet access in that country and efforts by Chinese citizens to use the Net as a forum for open political discussion and criticism of the government. Blocked online material includes politically sensitive content dealing with the banned Falun Gong religious group, the Chinese nationalist government on Taiwan, material that the Chinese government considers pornographic, content about the Dalai Lama and his efforts to have Tibet reinstated as an independent nation, and any mention of the massacre at Tiananmen Square. Sites blocked periodically in the past include CNN (after Tiananmen), BBC News, and Wikipedia. The online encyclopedia was completely blocked at the Great Firewall in October 2005 and then unblocked in October 2006 – except for the Chinese version and articles about the Falun Gong and Tiananmen Square protests.[10] It is another example of Chinese censorship of online content they find problematic, especially details about the deaths of 400–800 young pro-democracy protestors in 1989 at the hand of the Chinese army in Beijing's Tiananmen Square.[11] After the offensive content was deleted from the site, the Chinese-language version was reinstated in 2007. Ca Mingzhao, vice director of China's State Council Information Office (SCIO), met in 2008 with Wikipedia founder Jimmy Wales to discuss Wikipedia's efforts to provide uncensored content on the site, now translated in 279 language editions.[12]

The Great Firewall of China works in several ways to filter and block online content at its borders and internally. This may seem problematic in a nation that has one of the fastest-growing Internet-accessible populations in the world. As of September 2011, 485 million citizens of the People's Republic of China (PRC) are online – 36 percent of its population of 1.33 billion. What is more remarkable is the growth rate in the past decade – the number of PRC citizens who use the Internet has increased by 462 million since 2000.[13]

The Chinese government uses computer technology that involves URL and keyword filtering, along with IP address blocking – and it was created in the United States. Not only was the technology built using American expertise, its effectiveness is assisted by the willingness of US-based search firms and content providers to block forbidden content for Chinese citizens (much like the selective blocking for French citizens). The filtering and blocking technology was created in the 1990s in the US to allow corporations to monitor what their workers were seeing online and typing into their e-mails. Software would be installed on the corporate intranet to search for keywords such as blackjack, hot babes, and eBay (to block online shopping during work hours). E-mails might be scanned for similar terms, but the key aspect was the ability to search for the names of secret projects that were not to be revealed to anyone outside the company. Violations of corporate Internet access policies might lead to a counseling session in a manager's office or even termination of employment if the violation was egregious enough. The creation of the Great Firewall was facilitated by the limited number of access points to China's internal telecommunication networks. The government installed Cisco routers with blocking technology at key companies such as China Telecom. The firewall does more than just block – the technology is also a surveillance tool to catch and then prosecute those who post content the Chinese government considers seditious.

Bypassing the Great Firewall

A similar tragic story highlights efforts by the Chinese government to suppress media accounts that are unflattering or that provide evidence that high-ranking officials and members of their families are above the law. On the night of October 16, 2010, two female Hebei University students were inline skating near the campus grocery store in the city

Figure 10.3   Chen Xiaofeng, the Hebei University student who was struck and killed by drunken driver Li Qiming.

Figure 10.4   Baoding police chief Li Gang (left) making a tearful public apology on CCTV, China Television, and his son Li Qiming (right) doing the same after he was charged for causing the death of Chen Xiaofeng.

of Baoding when they were struck by a speeding car.[14] The 22-year-old driver, Li Qiming, was intoxicated and when eventually stopped by campus police he shouted at them, "Sue me if you dare. My father is Li Gang."[15] One of the students survived with a broken leg, but the other, Chen Xiaofeng, age 20, died the next day of her injuries in a local hospital. In modern China, a negative news story relating to charges of corruption or an abuse of power by party officials is often censored by the state-controlled media. A Hebei University student told *New York Times* reporter Michael Wines,

> There was a little on the school news channel at first, but then it went completely quiet. We're really disappointed in the press for stopping coverage of this major news.[16]

In this case, the facts were so egregious and the arrogance of the perpetrator in claiming that his birthright entitled him to a free pass from vehicular homicide charges was so shocking that the story quickly went viral, despite efforts by government officials to hush it up. Mainline media such as the official government news service, Xinhua, ignored the story until a blog appeared online where contributors could claim mock-violations of the law, followed by the exculpatory phrase, "My father is Li Gang." The phrase quickly became a national sardonic excuse for any minor social transgression. In the face of public outrage over this attempted abuse of power, Xinhuanet.com finally carried the story ten days later on October 27. The story stated that the children of high-ranking officials were "deviating from the basic tenet of following the Party's mass line, which is serving the people heart and soul."

Beyond the tragic death of Ms. Chen and the injuries to her friend, and the contrite apologies of son Li Qiming and father Li Gang for the son's attempted abuse of power, this story says a great deal about the desire of the Chinese people to end government censorship of unflattering stories in the state-controlled media. The use of a Chinese blog, sarcastically titled the "Ministry of Truth," enabled the story to spread virally throughout the nation, exploiting pent-up citizen anger over similar abuses of power. Ideally the role of the free press in democracies serves an equivalent function as the "Ministry of Truth" in China, but people who "live in glass houses" should not be quick to throw critical stones at China (given the distressed financial state of most US newspapers and subsequent reductions in investigative reporting budgets). Does this story indicate that critical blogs and similar online sites are systematically bypassing censorship in China? At present, probably not. As noted above, China has built a very effective digital firewall around the nation. However, the firewall did not seem to work as well in suppressing an internal story that quickly spread through a country where individuals are rapidly acquiring the advanced digital communication tools commonly found in highly developed nations.

The US Government and WikiLeaks

As outlined in Chapter 9, efforts by the US Congress to censor the Internet have been rejected by the courts as violations of the free speech protected by the First Amendment of the Constitution. In 1997 the US Supreme Court rejected the Communications Decency Act (CDA), Title V of the Telecommunications Act of 1996, as an infringement of the information accession rights of adults.[17] Members of Congress tried again to protect US children from viewing pornography on the Internet with passage of the Children's Online Protection Act (COPA) in 1998. This bill was also opposed by the American Civil Liberties Union, again as an infringement of the free-speech rights of adults. This bill was also rejected after almost ten years of lower court litigation and two US Supreme Court decisions, first enjoining its enforcement in 2004 and finally rejecting the law in 2009.[18]

Despite the good intentions of members of Congress to protect children from pornographic content on the Internet, the US judicial branch has consistently ruled against any restriction of the rights of adults to freely access information. Efforts by legislators to require the installation of website blocking software in public libraries and to require the posting of credit card information to see adult content online were rejected. One major loophole in this type of legislation is that COPA would only have applied to commercial providers of adult content based in the United States. Pornography produced by companies outside the US would not have been affected by the law. Efforts by nations to censor Internet content typically collide with the reality that the Internet is an international construct and that one nation's prohibited content may be legal in another.

The release of 251,000 secret US documents by the online WikiLeaks organization makes a relevant case study. The posting by news organizations of these secret military and foreign relations documents were a source of great concern to the US government (and with significant embarrassment at candid State Department assessments of some foreign leaders).[19] The documents were given to WikiLeaks by a US Army private with a top-secret clearance who had earlier provided them with secret footage of an army helicopter attack on a Reuters news team in Baghdad in 2007.[20] In the secret documents case, the WikiLeaks organization appeared unconcerned that revealing the unredacted names of individual US supporters in Iraq and Afghanistan might lead to their assassination. In other cases, the documents revealed that some foreign leaders had publicly rejected US policies while privately supporting them. The US government reacted to the massive disclosure of the documents by attempting to shut down the WikiLeaks websites, by successfully enjoining credit card companies from processing contributions to the organization, and by supporting Sweden's effort to extradite WikiLeaks founder Julian Assange from the UK on sex crimes charges. Despite the efforts made by the US and allied governments to shut down WikiLeaks, the organization was able to distribute many of the pilfered documents to newspapers in the US and the UK, which then printed them. The stated goal of WikiLeaks and its founders is to pull back the curtain of secrecy over what it considers "unethical behavior" by governments and institutions and provide an online transparency to issues that affect the public.[21] The Internet facilitates this process, as the combined powers of the US government and its allies have been unable to shut down WikiLeaks' mirror sites. Their next disclosures will involve secret Swiss bank accounts, which probably has made many kleptocratic dictators and global tax dodgers very nervous.[22]

Global Information and Communication Technology Use

While scholars focus on examining the roles of multinational corporations in controlling access to technology and media content, it is enlightening to visit developing nations and personally observe ICT use in urban areas and small villages. We did so aboard the ship *MV Explorer* as it voyaged around the world as part of the Semester at Sea program in the spring of 2006. I asked the 35 students in my "Communication Technology and the Wired World" course to observe ICT usage in the nine ports the ship visited. At each port students and faculty divided into small groups as we ventured into sprawling cities and small rural villages in Puerto Rico, Brazil, South Africa, Mauritius, India, Myanmar, Vietnam, China, and Japan. Students in the course were asked to create a personal journal documenting the telecommunication use they observed in each port visit and to take digital photos of what they saw. When the class resumed as the ship sailed to the next port, the students and I debriefed about we had observed. The shore visits and the students' first-person observations brought the course content to life in a way that is difficult to achieve in a classroom with four walls.

What we observed individually and as a group was enlightening. One small group voyaging up the Amazon River in Brazil outside the city of Manaus were surprised to hear the sound of a generator outside a small wooden house perched on poles next to the river. It was getting dark and as the boat went past the open-air cabin the students could see a group of children watching cartoons on a small television set that cast a blue glow on the walls of the home. It was unclear whether the program source was a videotape, DVD, or over-the-air broadcast, but the children were clearly delighted by what they were watching. Television is a ubiquitous technology in even the most remote parts of the world.

Another ubiquitous icon in the photos students took was the satellite television dish. They were found in every nation and they came in all sizes and shapes ranging from large, older, open-mesh C-band antennas to small, pizza-platter-sized dishes accessing powerful direct-broadcast television satellites. Satellite dishes were observed in every conceivable location – attached to the balconies of favelas in Rio de Janeiro, bolted to the rooftops of shanties in the vast townships of South Africa, attached to poles outside thatch-roofed huts in India, and secured to the sides of new high-rise apartments in Hong Kong. Satellite technology provides television programs to all global citizens with access to electrical power, rich and poor, urban and rural, around the world.

Mobile phones were another ubiquitous technology we observed. As with television, we observed their use by all socioeconomic classes in

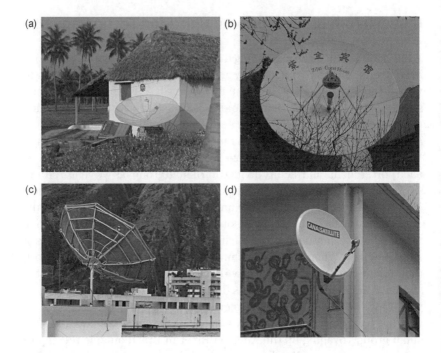

Figure 10.5   Satellite television dishes around the world: (a) India; (b) China; (c) Brazil; and (d) Mauritius. *Photos*: India: Paul Lankford; China, Mauritius, and Brazil: author.

both developed and developing nations. The primary difference compared with satellite television is that mobile phones require a network of towers to operate and thus were observed primarily in urban areas. As in parts of the United States, remote and rural areas lack mobile phone service. One interesting exception was South Africa. In driving across the vast inland desert known as the Karoo we expected not to have mobile phone service. We were surprised to see solar-powered towers spaced every 10 miles along the highway in that expansive area with working mobile phone service the entire distance. On the remote island nation of Mauritius in the southern Indian Ocean there were conventional-looking cell towers spaced at regular intervals to ensure seamless service. One tower that caught our attention was located in an upscale resort area and was disguised as an unnaturally straight palm tree (Figure 10.6). People talking on mobile phones seemed to appear everywhere we went – even in some remote locations. One student photographed her tour guide talking on a mobile phone on a boat tour of the Mekong Delta in southern Vietnam. In Japan we were surprised to see hundreds of local people photographing

Figure 10.6   A mobile phone tower disguised as a palm tree on the island nation of Mauritius in the southern Indian Ocean. As these towers become more ubiquitous there is increasing social pressure to conceal them. *Photo:* Author.

the remarkable spectacle of blooming cherry blossoms in April with their mobile phones (Figure 10.7). In a nation known for manufacturing high-quality still cameras, it was surprising to see so many mobile phones used as cameras. The inclusion of higher-quality digital cameras represents the convergence of media acquisition tools in the mobile phone.

    We found other digital technologies in unexpected places. In touring an Indian movie studio in Chennai (formerly known in colonial days as Madras), we were escorted into a large modern building filled with

Figure 10.7 Japanese tourists taking photos of springtime cherry blossoms in Kyoto with their mobile phones. Cameras in phones are rapidly improving in quality and features. *Photo*: Author.

computer workstations (Figure 10.8). Each station had two workers taking turns digitally retouching older films, many of them Hollywood classics. Using a retouching application similar to Adobe Photoshop, they painstakingly blotted out dirt and scratches on the film, frame by frame, in each film. At that rate, restoring a 90-minute film could take weeks, but it appeared that many of the workstations were working on the same film to speed up the process. The outsourcing and offshoring of this type of digital restoration is representative of the themes outlined by author Thomas Friedman in his book *The World Is Flat*.[23] In a world connected by undersea fiber-optic cables and Internet connections that function at the speed of light, digital work can be accomplished anywhere there is a skilled workforce. The digital universe includes the entire planet, thanks

Figure 10.8   Classic Hollywood films are being digitally re-mastered frame by frame by these workers in a film studio in Chennai, India. It is much less expensive to have this work done in India than in Hollywood, another example of outsourcing digital production work to Asia. *Photo*: John Scherr.

Figure 10.9   A tour guide in Vietnam uses her mobile phone in the Mekong Delta. Mobile phones can be found in all developing nations and may be a way to bridge the digital divide in these countries. *Photo*: Elise Gauvreau.

to the Internet and digital technologies which engage millions of digitally literate people who use these tools daily to make a living.

It is no secret that access to online information and media provides an advantage to individuals compared with those who don't have it. One example provided in the documentary film *A Mobile World* is instructive. Coffee growers in the West African nation of Ivory Coast formerly held a disadvantageous marketing position compared with coffee buyers when the producers sold their crop. The buyers knew the market rate for unroasted beans and would offer the grower a reduced price and then pocket the difference. With the advent of real-time online access to commodity markets in New York and London via the Internet, growers in producing nations can check the market rate for coffee traded that day and adjust their sale price accordingly. Knowledge *is* power, especially in a global economy.

notes

1. P. Elmer-DeWitt, "First Nation in Cyberspace," *Time International* (December 6, 1993). Retrieved February 20, 2010, from http://www. chemie.fu-berlin.de/outerspace/internet-article.html.
2. J. Goldsmith and T. Wu, *Who Controls the Internet?* (Oxford: Oxford University Press, 2006).
3. Ibid., 2. Note that the official corporate name of Yahoo is "Yahoo! Inc." The shorter version is used for clarity and to avoid the use of superfluous punctuation.
4. L. Davidowicz, *The War against the Jews: 1933–1945* (New York: Bantam, 1975). A poignant memorial to the victims of the Holocaust is located in Paris on the eastern end of the Île de la Cité near the Notre Dame cathedral, in addition to numerous memorials in the city's historic Père Lachaise cemetery.
5. Goldsmith and Wu, *Who Controls the Internet?*, 2–5.
6. Ibid., 8.
7. S. Olsen, "Yahoo Ads Closes in Visitors' Locale," *CNet News* (June 27, 2001). Retrieved November 25, 2010, from http://news.cnet.com/2100-1023-269155. html.
8. J. Leyne, "How Iran's Political Battle Is Fought in Cyberspace," BBC News (February 11, 2010). Retrieved February 20, 2010, from http://news.bbc.co. uk/2/hi/middle_east/8505645.stm.
9. N. Fathi, "In a Death Seen Around the World, a Symbol of Iranian Protests," *New York Times* (June 22, 2009). Retrieved November 24, 2010, from http:// www.nytimes.com/2009/06/23/world/middleeast/23neda.html.
10. N. Cohen, "Chinese Government Relaxes its Total Ban on Wikipedia," *New York Times* (October 10, 2006). Retrieved November 26, 2010, from http:// www.nytimes.com/2006/10/16/technology/16wikipedia.html?ex=1318651200& en=ff16408103d54a91&ei=5088&partner=rssnyt&emc=rss.

11. N. Kristof, "A Reassessment of How Many Died in the Military Crackdown in Beijing," *New York Times* (June 21, 1989). Retrieved November 26, 2010, from http://query.nytimes.com/gst/fullpage.html?res=950DE0DC143EF932 A15755C0A96F948260&sec=&spon=&pagewanted=all.

12. Wikipedia Language Editions. Retrieved January 22, 2011, from http://en. wikipedia.org/wiki/Wikipedia. The English subdomain in 2011 is 54 percent of the total number of articles online at the site, down from 100 percent in 2001.

13. Internet World Stats. Retrieved September 6, 2011, from http://www. internetworldstats.com/stats17.htm.

14. M. Wines, "China's Censors Misfire in Abuse-of-Power Case," *New York Times* (November 17, 2010). Retrieved November 22, 2010, from http:// www.nytimes.com/2010/11/18/world/asia/18li.html?scp=1&sq=my%20 father%20is%20li%20gang&st=cse.

15. Q. Lu, "Public Anger Over Hit-and-Run Case Reflects Call for Social Justice," *Xinhuanet.com* (October 27, 2010). Retrieved November 23, 2010, from http://news.xinhuanet.com/english2010/indepth/2010-10/27/c_13577445.htm.

16. Wines, "China's Censors Misfire."

17. US Supreme Court (1997). *ACLU v. Reno*. 521 US 844, 851.

18. US Supreme Court (2004). *Ashcroft v. ACLU*. 542 US 656. S. Nichols, "COPA Child-Porn Law Killed," *PC World* (January 22, 2009).

19. S. Shane and A. W. Lehrin, "Leaked Cables Offer Raw Look at U.S. Diplomacy," *New York Times* (November 29, 2010). Retrieved January 22, 2011, from http://www.nytimes.com/2010/11/29/world/29cables.html?_r=3&bl.

20. D. Murphy, "WikiLeaks Releases Video of US Forces Killing of Two Reuters Journalists in Iraq," *Christian Science Monitor* (April 10, 2010). Retrieved January 22, 2011, from http://www.csmonitor.com/World/Global-News/ 2010/0405/Wikileaks-releases-video-depicting-US-forces-killing-of-two-Reuters-journalists-in-Iraq.

21. WikiLeaks Mirror Website. Retrieved January 22, 2011, from http://mirror. wikileaks.info/.

22. "WikiLeaks Given Data on Swiss Bank Accounts," BBC News (January 17, 2011). Retrieved January 22, 2011, from http://www.bbc.co.uk/news/ business-12205690.

23. T. Friedman, *The World Is Flat: A Brief History of the 21st Century* (New York: Farrar, Straus & Giroux, 2005).

11

The Dark Side

"You have zero privacy anyway. Get over it."
(Scott McNealy, co-founder of Sun Microsystems, 1999)[1]

Privacy and the Digital Universe

Scott McNealy made the comment above to a group of market analysts and journalists at an event in 1999 sponsored by Sun to launch a new computer system. He was specifically commenting about privacy *online* with many well-publicized threats, but this point was lost in the commotion that followed. The flip comment attracted a significant amount of criticism from consumer groups at the time for its negative implications for the protection of personal privacy, but I doubt that it would do so today. Since McNealy made these remarks, increasing levels of surveillance and advances in data mining have made citizens cynical about privacy protection, both online and offline. Even the most carefully protected information – about one's medical history – can be compromised by those with password access. If you are careless about sharing your social security number in the US, the results can be unfortunate.

Todd Davis, chief executive of LifeLock, an Arizona company that protects users from identity theft, produced a series of television commercials in 2008 where he prominently displayed his personal

Digital Universe: The Global Telecommunication Revolution, First Edition. Peter B. Seel.
© 2012 Peter B. Seel. Published 2012 by Blackwell Publishing Ltd.

social security number (SSN) in the background (see Figure 11.1). He claimed that his company's software would protect his identity from theft even if criminals knew his SSN. He claimed that his company would similarly protect a client's identity from theft for a fee of only $15 a month and promised a guarantee of up to $1 million in compensation to any client whose identity was compromised or stolen. His challenge was obviously taken seriously by the criminal community, and there were 13 successful attempts to steal his identity, including a bogus $500 loan, $2,390 in AT&T phone bills, and hundreds of dollars in credit card losses, all in Davis' name and obtained with his SSN.[2] Hundreds of LifeLock clients whose identities were stolen filed class action lawsuits against the company claiming that their financial losses were not compensated. The company was also sued by the credit report firm Experian for false advertising and the Federal Trade Commission (FTC) agreed, slapping the company with a $12 million fine in 2010. FTC officials stated that eight million Americans had their identity stolen each year.[3]

The irony in the LifeLock case is that the financial burden for Mr. Davis' hubris must be absorbed by the companies who suffered the losses incurred by the theft of his identity. They provided the products and services stolen by others using his SSN. Ultimately,

Figure 11.1   The LifeLock challenge. Todd Davis, CEO of identity theft prevention company LifeLock, appears in a television commercial in 2008 with his social security number prominently displayed on a mobile billboard in the background. His identity was successfully stolen more than a dozen times after the commercials aired nationwide in the US.

all consumers end up paying for identify theft in the form of higher prices and credit card fees.

Privacy and Population

One of the classic definitions of privacy is "the right to be let alone," as defined by Warren and Brandeis in an 1890 article in the *Harvard Law Review*.[4] Co-author Louis Brandeis later became a Supreme Court justice who fought for personal privacy protections and individual free speech rights.[5] Their definition of privacy is still a rallying cry for privacy activists seeking to deter government, corporate, or even neighborly intrusions into our personal lives. Privacy was a much simpler concept in the early days of the American frontier when homes were located miles apart and one would typically only see a neighbor at church or at a general store in a nearby town. Personal privacy became more of an issue as citizens moved into cities and had to deal with increasingly crowded conditions. Newly arrived immigrants were packed into crowded urban tenements where privacy was a precious commodity. When they could finally escape to a private home, privacy was still a concern. As land costs increased with rising urban density, homes were built closer together and "privacy fences" were erected around backyards. Contemporary home lots are often so small (with only 10–15 feet of space between houses) that privacy fences are now included as part of the purchase price. Privacy fences take their ultimate shape in the form of the "gated community," where walls are erected around entire neighborhoods to provide increased security and privacy, at the expense of urban cohesion.

The world's population reached seven billion people in 2011 and will likely exceed nine billion by 2050, according to United Nations estimates.[6] On this crowded planet, and especially in megacities, personal privacy will become a valued (and often expensive) commodity. Urban areas where the bulk of humanity resides will become increasingly densely populated and the desire for greater privacy in this crowded world will have significant implications for privacy in our online lives. The press of humanity in urban areas will increase "media cocooning" as we navigate these crowded environments. This can be observed daily in New York, London, Moscow, Shanghai, or Tokyo. Older commuters on subways and buses burrow into their newspapers, while younger people read (or type into) their mobile phones. Eye contact with others is avoided at all costs while one is immersed in the media cocoon.

The use of media in these environments creates a virtual "privacy wall" that states that no trespassing (or unwanted conversation) is allowed. The use of alternative display devices such as semitransparent glasses or ultra-thin OLED screens (with wireless ear buds providing audio) will increase in future public life as we seek to create private spaces in dense urban settings.[7]

Changing Public Perceptions of Privacy

The concept of personal privacy is an elusive one to pin down since its meaning differs greatly between individuals and across cultures. In addition, I would argue that concerns about personal privacy vary widely between age groups in nations with universal Internet access. University students with social networking sites seem far less concerned about personal privacy than US citizens over age 50, who recall the "enemies list" and abuses by the Federal Bureau of Investigation (FBI) during the Nixon Administration in the 1970s. Perhaps many are not concerned

	Examples of Privacy Concern	Negative Consequences of Disclosure
Least restrictive	You provide an email address when signing up for a free online service. This address may then be sold to others.	Annoying. Additional spam messages clog your email in-box – additional time is needed to sort emails that get past spam filters.
	You provide your full name, email/postal addresses, and phone numbers to a person, organization, service, or company online.	Moderate. Much of this information is available in Internet and telecom white pages. Concern is linkage to other databases (even innocuous ones).
	An online company shares your personal account information, including product purchase preferences, with another company – perhaps as a result of a buy-out.	Potentially serious. What you buy online reveals a great deal about you and your lifestyle (and has great value to commercial interests). Do you care who knows what books you read or what you view online?
	You post amusing photos of yourself acting crazy at a party on a social networking site. These are then downloaded by others and saved on their computers. Once duplicated, nothing online is ever completely erasable.	Potentially serious consequences when seeking employment. You discover that once an image is posted online and copied by others, attempts to delete it are virtually impossible
	You respond to a bogus emailed message from your bank (which is actually a phishing scheme by criminals) with your personal financial information – bank account numbers, credit card data, and your password or pin.	Potentially severe. With account numbers and your password your bank accounts can be looted. Credit card data (with the security code) allows thieves to charge expenses to your card. Possible exposure to scams such as the "Nigerian letter."
Most restrictive	Your personal health and medical information is made public through an error of omission or commission. See UCLA Medical Center case discussed in the chapter.	Possible severe consequences beyond personal embarrassment. If your medical history is publicly accessible, you could be denied health or life insurance when you need it most.

Figure 11.2   The Privacy Continuum. *Source:* Author.

about privacy until some information that they would prefer to keep private is disclosed or compromised. There may be two types of netizens: those who are not concerned about online privacy, and those who have suffered a financial loss or individual embarrassment due to identity theft, compromised personal data, or maliciously posted photos/videos. Not only are many contemporary netizens unconcerned about their privacy online, they are busy posting increasing numbers of photos, videos, and tweets about themselves and their daily activities. Traditional concepts of privacy need to be redefined in an environment where citizens are devoting a significant part of each day interacting and communicating with others online. Between texting, e-mailing, and uploading content, the connected netizen is spending more time with ICT devices than ever before.

The Online Privacy Continuum

We negotiate with online privacy almost every day, and some decisions are easy. When asked, we agree to provide our name and e-mail address to subscribe to an online edition of a newspaper. It seems a fair *quid pro quo* for access to free news online. A common occurrence is the sale of this data by these companies to others without our knowledge. The tidal wave of spam is the result of the exchange of this basic information, which ends up on lists with thousands or millions of e-mail addresses. Some of these lists are built by spambots that surf the Internet looking for letters connected by an @ symbol. When posting your e-mail address online in a website, it may be advisable to list it as "firstname [dot] lastname [at] siteaddress [dot] domain" to frustrate the spambots.

We are willing to provide additional information to Internet companies such as iTunes, Amazon, or eBay that provide products and services. This includes home addresses for shipping, home and business telephone numbers, and in some cases our credit card numbers, security codes, and expiration dates for one-click ordering. We make an assumption that the transmission of these critical numbers is protected by our ISPs and that the client companies will house them securely. It is a source of great distress to customers to hear periodically that a company's database has been hacked by criminals and thousands of credit card numbers have been stolen. In May of 2011, 360,000 customers of Citigroup bank were sobered to find out that their names, e-mail addresses, and account numbers had been compromised in a data breach.[8] Citigroup later announced that $2.7 million had been stolen from 3,400 of the compromised accounts, and the company assumed responsibility for these losses.[9] Sony had servers for its Playstation and Entertainment divisions hacked by unknown sources with the potential loss of data for millions of customer accounts, including 12,700 credit and debit card numbers.[10] The Identity Theft Resource Center states that there have been 288 data breaches affecting 83 million customer records at US financial services companies in the past six years.[11]

Companies are aware of the trust placed in them by their clients to secure this key financial information, but have been lax in taking the needed steps – such as data encryption for transmitting and storing account information – to protect these records.

Criminals have become very skilled at creating fraudulent "phishing" schemes where customers receive what looks like an authentic e-mail from their bank. The e-mails look very realistic, with the company's logo and other familiar types of graphic design. The message claims that there has been a security lapse and some client account information may have been compromised. To ascertain if their account has been affected they are asked to provide their debit card number and PIN. While their account data has not been stolen, it soon may be if they respond. A bank or other financial institution will never ask for this information in an unsolicited e-mail – if in doubt customers should call the bank. Millions of dollars, pounds, euros, and yen are stolen each year in these phishing schemes.

As the 800 million users of Facebook (and other social networking sites) happily post images online to share with friends and family, they may be unaware that, once posted and copied by others, these images may be virtually impossible to delete. The primary problem is that the poster may be unaware that copies of the images are being made by friends of friends tagged in the photos. Images that may have supposedly been "deleted" may come back long afterward to haunt individuals as they seek employment or a security clearance. "Tagging" photos online is a common practice with Facebook and similar sites. 100 million photos are uploaded daily to Facebook, and another 100 million tags are applied daily to photos already posted on the site. Late in 2010, Facebook announced a new tagging technology that uses facial recognition to identify friends in photos posted on personal pages and then apply identifying tags to them.[12] Facebook executive Chris Cox stated that tagging is a key feature on the site and "is actually very important for control. Because every time a tag is created it means that there is a photo of you on the Internet that you didn't know about. Once you know that, you can remove the tag, or you can promote it with friends, or you can write the person and say, 'I'm not psyched about this photo.'"[13] This statement is a bit disingenuous as the tagging process itself may lead to compromised identities and a loss of personal privacy. Once your face is tagged and linked with your name, the tag and your identity might be used in an unscrupulous way by unethical individuals or companies.

The area of greatest privacy concern should be an individual's personal medical history and records. The US Congress passed the Health Insurance Portability and Accountability Act (HIPAA) in 1996.[14] The HIPAA Privacy Rule provides severe penalties for the unauthorized disclosure of private medical records and files. The rule defines what constitutes personal Protected Health Information (PHI) and how it can be securely shared between health providers.[15] The present concern is that a renewed emphasis on the creation and distribution of electronic medical records to reduce health-care costs may lead to more opportunities for leaked or compromised information. The consequences may be severe, as patients may be denied health insurance coverage or employment if their health status is revealed. For celebrity patients, information about their health has substantial financial value to medical staff willing to leak it to the media.

The *Los Angeles Times* reported that staff at the University of California Los Angeles (UCLA) Medical Center had improperly accessed the confidential medical records of singer Britney Spears, actress Farah Fawcett, and television personality Maria Shriver.[16] Each of them had an expectation of the protection of their medical records and each patient could have been harmed by the improper release of that information. The Medical Center was accountable for the security of these records under federal law, but it pointed out that the automation of medical records makes it possible for many people in a hospital to have password-"protected" access to them. This trend is a growing privacy concern in this century as federal officials have indicated that one key tool in containing exploding heath-care costs in the US is the digitization and transmission of medical records. As more records are digitized and transmitted electronically, the opportunity to copy and illegally divert them will increase. The Tao of technology will come into play again as the benefits of medical record digitization are offset by their replicability and possible diversion.

The Surveillance Society

Between 1972 and 2001, the Provisional wing of the Irish Republican Army (the IRA) conducted a series of bombings in England to protest British governance in Northern Ireland. Of the 2,100 dead on all sides during the war, more than 125 soldiers, civilians, and police were killed and 2,100 were injured in England over a 29-year period.[17] A series of lethal bombings in the heart of London in 1993 lead to the creation of a defensive "ring of steel" comprised of roadblocks and heavy police presence in the center of the city. During "The Troubles," London became one of the most surveilled cities in the world. Thousands of closed-circuit television (CCTV) cameras (Figure 11.3) were placed on buildings and tall poles aimed at key streets, subway exits, train stations, and other public transport facilities as means of identifying suspicious activity that might be terrorism-related. Not only have the CCTV cameras remained in place since the 2009 ceasefire with the IRA, they have proliferated in urban areas throughout the UK. It is a rare place in central London where one's image is not being captured by at least one CCTV camera. Since the ceasefire, London has been peaceful save for a multi-bomb attack on public transport by four terrorists that killed 56 commuters on July 7, 2005. The irony concerning the use of CCTV cameras to prevent terrorist acts and other crimes is that they are often used *after* an attack to identify the assailants. In the case of the four suicide bombers in the 2005 attacks,

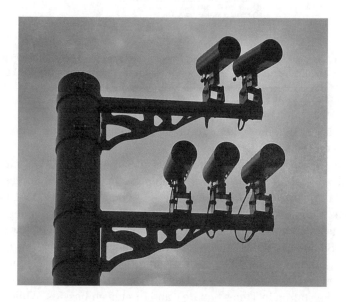

Figure 11.3   Surveillance television cameras on a tower aimed at the entrance to Pimlico tube (subway) station in London. There are few places in central London that are not covered by CCTV cameras. *Photo*: Creative Commons.

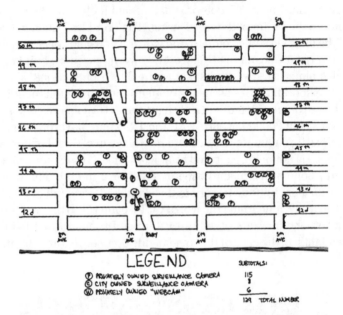

"Map of Surveillance Cameras in Times Square"

A Public Service Announcement by
The Surveillance Camera Players
http://www.notbored.org/the-scp.html

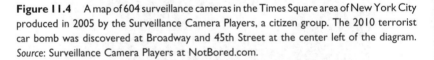

Figure 11.4   A map of 604 surveillance cameras in the Times Square area of New York City produced in 2005 by the Surveillance Camera Players, a citizen group. The 2010 terrorist car bomb was discovered at Broadway and 45th Street at the center left of the diagram. *Source*: Surveillance Camera Players at NotBored.com.

police later identified them from CCTV images entering Luton train station on their way to London.[18]

New York City also has thousands of surveillance CCTV cameras aimed at key intersections and buildings. In 2001, the Surveillance Camera Players (SCP) began a process of documenting CCTV cameras in areas of Manhattan Island.[19] By 2005, they were able to produce a map with the locations of 604 cameras on a 30-block area around New York's Times Square district (Figure 11.4). While many of the locations include cameras mounted in ATM cash machines, other CCTV cameras are operated by New York Police, the US Department of Defense (for a recruiting station in Times Square), and foreign embassies. While Times Square may be one of the most surveilled locations in the US, the hundreds of cameras did not identify a terrorist activating a large car bomb in the area on May 1, 2010. Police were notified by an alert T-shirt vendor at Broadway and 45th Street that smoke was coming from a car parked nearby.[20] When police investigated more closely, they found that the car was packed with highly explosive materials that might have killed hundreds of people in the area if they had been detonated.

Perhaps CCTV cameras do reduce crime in areas where they are conspicuously placed with signs indicating their presence. Studies support this hypothesis, but if they are intended to reduce terrorism, they fail at this task. As the London and New York cases illustrate, the cameras are typically used by police after a terrorist attack to deconstruct the terrifying events. Cities packed with surveillance cameras capturing every aspect of citizen's lives seemed an unlikely Orwellian prospect when George Orwell wrote his novel *Nineteen Eighty-Four* in 1949. Yet the public seems largely unconcerned about this growing phenomenon since the advent of terrorist attacks in London after 1970 and in New York after the first World Trade Center bombing in 1993.

The Invisible Databases

CCTV cameras are one of the most visible threats to personal privacy – others are perhaps more insidious because they are largely invisible. The personal information of netizens in wired nations is stored in thousands of databases that facilitate e-commerce, social networks, and government record keeping. Many are unaware of how pervasive these databases have become since the advent of the Internet. The classic work in this area is Simson Garfinkel's *Database Nation* (2000), in which he outlines the potential and actual threats to privacy posed by the massive collection and aggregation of personal data. For Garfinkel:

> Privacy isn't about hiding things. It's about self-possession, autonomy and integrity. As we move into the computerized world of the 21st century, privacy will be one of our most important civil rights. But this right of privacy isn't the right of people to close their doors and pull down their window shades – perhaps because they want to engage in some sort of illicit or illegal activity. It's about the right of people to control what details about their lives stay inside their own houses and what leaks to the outside.[21]

This concept is central to concerns about privacy in the present era: that we have lost the ability to maintain control of personal information that we might wish to keep private. So much of our personal information is circulating in corporate and governmental databases, not to mention in social media and personal websites, that we simply cannot keep track of it all. When some of that information is incorrect or aspects of our identity have been stolen or compromised, finding and fixing the cascading chain of data can take months or years. Correcting a damaged reputation is so vital in this digital age that it has become a growth industry. Reputation.com is one of many new companies dedicated to repairing and rehabilitating the online image of its fee-paying clients. It accomplishes this by deleting negative posts and publishing a blizzard of new complimentary information and personal images that push unflattering or outdated online content (e.g., photos of a past marriage or stories about legal problems) to the back pages of search inquiries.[22] For large corporations and celebrities this online task has been handled by their public relations firms for the past 20 years. However, this is a new service for individuals and it reflects the dramatic effects on personal privacy engendered by the Internet. Reputation.com CEO Michael Fertik stated, "Social networks, online comments and oversharing online have created a threat to everyone's reputation and privacy. Now people are trying to figure out how to put that toothpaste back in the bottle."[23]

The key privacy problem is that all that personal information still exists in multiple databases, and a determined investigator or reporter can quickly locate it. Garfinkel identified several related areas that he sees as significant threats to our personal privacy. Among them are:

The systematic capture of everyday events. The daily electronic trail we leave behind as we use credit cards, tablets, and mobile phones.

The bugging of the outside world. The systematic use of CCTV cameras and similar remote sensing devices in high-technology nations to track citizens in public places.

The misuse of medical records. The case illustrated by information leaks about celebrities at the UCLA Medical Center cited above.

Personal information as a commodity. The collection and sale of personal information for commercial purposes.

Intelligent computing. The merger of artificial intelligence with vast databases of personal information.[24]

The last item is the area that Garfinkel viewed as the "ultimate threat to privacy."[25] At the turn of the century in 2000, he looked ahead to the evolution of surveillance technology, remote sensing, facial identification, artificial intelligence, and massive expansions in computing power and saw a dystopian future from the perspective of protecting personal privacy. Perhaps we should throw up our collective hands in the face of these technologies and just "get over it," as Scott McNealy suggested in 1999. However, the recent trends in identify theft, online reputation damage, and the unauthorized release of private health information suggest otherwise. Protecting one's privacy online is going to increase in importance as more netizens realize the need to define which personal information is available in public fora such as social networks and which information must be kept private. We'll have to make these decisions daily as we post tweets and photos of personal activities and participate in e-commerce. Personal privacy online will become one of the central issues for telecommunication in the 21st century.

Global Threats to the Internet

In addition to the examination of actual and potential threats to personal privacy engendered in the Internet, it is instructive to analyze potential "dark side" threats to the Internet as the world's primary communication medium. The two key threats to the health and utility of the Internet are related: malware and cyber war. Examples of malware include digital viruses, Trojan horses, worms, adware, and spyware (Figure 11.5). A cyber war would involve the use of these tools to attack an enemy and disable their ability to use their information and communication technology networks.

The Trojan horse is the most common type of malware encountered worldwide, as shown in Figure 11.5. Much like its classical namesake, it masquerades as a useful type of software, but contains malicious code that can turn a user's computer into a bot (short for ro*bot* clone) used to attack other systems. Trojan horses do not self-replicate like worms or viruses, but can still be very harmful. Investigators believe that the Conficker worm was used in 2008 to infect millions of computers worldwide. Its creators then sent the owners of the computers an e-mailed notice that they should purchase special software (at $129 a copy) to remove the worm (that they had infected it with). It was a brilliant, if evil, strategy to infect systems with the worm of their creation, then sell unsuspecting users a Trojan horse that not only would not delete the worm, but turn their computer into a bot under their control.[26] Once part of a botnet, they could be used for massive denial-of-service attacks on Web hosts or to send out spam anti-virus messages. Such a Trojan horse is known as "scareware."[27]

A computer virus spreads like a biological virus, infecting a system and then infecting others that communicate with the host. A digital virus, once attached to an infected program or file, then requires the user to activate it.[28] Viruses have been plaguing computer systems since the

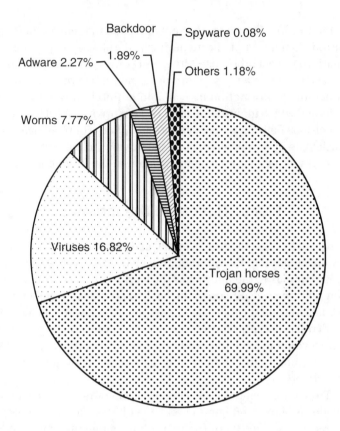

Figure 11.5   Global malware categories as of March 2011. *Source:* Kizar: Creative Commons License.

"Creeper" virus was first found on the early ARPANET in the 1970s. Some early viruses were created by computer scientists to test if a self-replicating system could be spread across connected computer networks. Over the four decades since Creeper first appeared, digital viruses have improved exponentially in their virulence and harmfulness. The spread of computer viruses and the economic damage they cause have created a booming industry in anti-viral software. New computer owners are now routinely urged to install anti-viral software on their systems prior to connecting to the Internet. Bots from infected computers are actively trolling the Internet looking for unprotected computers to attack.

Worms are the most insidious type of malware as they can spread without any overt action by the computer user. Conficker is one of the most malicious and threatening worms ever created, and it first began to infect PCs in November of 2008 by exploiting a vulnerability in the Windows operating system. Ironically, this vulnerability in its OS was highlighted in a message from Microsoft to Windows users three weeks prior to the first appearance of Conficker. Microsoft introduced a patch specifically to block Conficker, but it was not universally applied by computer owners, many of whom may have been using pirated copies of Windows and did not receive the urgent patch notice.[29]

As the worm infected millions of computers worldwide, it burrowed into their operating systems, blocking all attempts to delete or remove it, and awaited orders from its creator. A global team of computer security experts was mobilized to study Conficker and suggest ways that it could be destroyed or deactivated. The more they learned about the worm, the more concerned they became. It used a state-of-the-art SHA-2 encryption scheme to communicate with its creators and it appeared that April 1, 2009 was the date set for its update and activation on the estimated 6.2 million systems it inhabited.[30] Much like the year 2000 scare (that predicted the end of life as we know it at midnight on December 31, 1999), there were doomsday predictions that the activated Conficker worm would shut down the Internet on April 1. What did occur on that April Fool's Day was the distribution of malware called Maledec that sent out e-mails notifying users that their computers were infected (which they were) and offering a bogus virus removal program to eliminate it. Enough computer users responded to the e-mail to generate $72 million for a group of cybercriminals based in the Ukraine and Latvia in eastern Europe. The ringleaders were finally arrested in Latvia in June 2011, and will be tried in the United States for creating and disseminating the Conficker worm and selling the bogus anti-virus software.[31] It's a plot worthy of a movie script, and would be entertaining except for the fact that the worm could have crashed the Internet if the botnet had been designed to attack Internet infrastructure instead of selling phony anti-virus software. Certainly the story caught the attention of cyber warriors around the globe, who viewed Conficker-like worms as potential weapons in future international conflicts.

Cyber Warfare

For those who think that a cyber war is a concept out of a futuristic science fiction plot, think again. Cyberspace is an emerging domain for international conflict, a new venue compared to past wars fought on land, sea, and air. The first large-scale international cyber attack occurred in Estonia in 2007 after the removal of a statue in the capital city of Tallinn that commemorated a heroic Soviet World War II soldier. A massive distributed denial-of-service (DDoS) attack disrupted the websites of Estonian government agencies, banks, newspapers, and large corporations.[32] Estonia, formerly part of the USSR, had developed one of the most advanced digital networks in eastern Europe and was a pioneer in the diffusion of e-government services. Russia was implicated in the attacks by NATO cyber-terrorism experts, who viewed the hostile actions as retribution for the removal of the Russian statue.[33] NATO cyber war experts were put on notice that the Russians had developed technologies that could be used to effectively disable a nation's Internet connectivity – which in the present era is a game-stopper in terms of essential communication and e-commerce capabilities.

A similar distributed denial-of-service attack occurred in the nation of Georgia in 2008 when citizens in the Russian region of South Ossetia sought to break away and become part of Georgia.[34] Russia was again blamed for the DDoS disruption of vital Web services, as they were coordinated with their military ground attacks on Georgia. When analyzed, the DDoS attacks were first traced to Russian cyber criminals, who in turn had utilized botnets of thousands of infected US computers, much like those later mobilized by the Conficker worm in 2009. The actual source of a cyber attack may be difficult to discern, as a well-designed campaign should not appear to come from its true source. A hostile nation would have what is known as "plausible deniability" if the attack appeared to originate from criminals such as the Ukrainian-Latvian creators of the Conficker worm, or from amateur hackers seeking notoriety.

The irony of computers owned by Americans being used as bots in the relatively crude DDoS attacks in Estonia and Georgia was not lost on US and NATO cyber warfare experts. It is possible that future cyber attacks on American defense and corporate networks might be directed by overseas agencies using botnet computers actually owned by US citizens. This scenario was one reason for the great concern over the Conficker worm as it created botnets comprised of millions of computers worldwide. As Walt Kelly's cartoon character Pogo once famously said, "we have met the enemy, and he is us."

The United States finds itself in a difficult position regarding cyber warfare. US policy has been to promote an unfettered global Internet with few nationally imposed restrictions on international communication. However, the DDoS attacks in Europe in 2007–8 and recent cyber attacks on secret US military and intelligence databases led to a reappraisal of the need for defensive and offensive cyber war capabilities. In May 2010, the United States formally created its first Cyber Command as part of the US Strategic Command. It is based at Fort Meade, Maryland and commanded by General Keith Alexander of the National Security Agency (NSA), the super-secretive US intelligence-gathering agency (also based at Fort Meade). Its mission statement:

> USCYBERCOM plans, coordinates, integrates, synchronizes, and conducts activities to: direct the operations and defense of specified Department of Defense information networks and; prepare to, and when directed, conduct full-spectrum military cyberspace operations in order to enable actions in all domains, ensure US/Allied freedom of action in cyberspace and deny the same to our adversaries.[35]

Other nations with active cyber warfare operations include Iran, China, Great Britain, Israel, and North Korea. China has a very ambitious program suspected of attempting to infiltrate US security and corporate databases, and the Chinese government has not been shy in stating that its goal is to win any future cyber war in which it is engaged.[36]

Some have suggested that it is time for the nations of the world to develop cyber weapons control protocols for the Internet similar to those created to deal with the creation and proliferation of nuclear weapons.[37] The Internet has become so crucial for global telecommunication and e-commerce that its disruption would be catastrophic for all nations of the world. It would be in the best interest of all global citizens if their governments could agree on protocols inhibiting the use of cyber weapons. There has been enough damage to computers and global networks in the past two decades caused by viruses, worms, and digital Trojan horses created by hackers and cyber criminals without adding the new threat of nationally sponsored cyber terrorism.

Notes

1. P. Sprenger, "Sun on Privacy: 'Get Over It,'" *Wired* (January 26, 1999). Retrieved January 14, 2011, from http://www.wired.com/politics/law/news/1999/01/17538.
2. S. Stern, "Cracking LifeLock: Even after a $12 Million Penalty for Deceptive Advertising, the Tempe Company Can't Be Honest about Its Identity-Theft-Protection Service," *Phoenix New Times News* (May 13, 2010). Retrieved November 27, 2010, from http://www.phoenixnewtimes.com/2010-05-13/news/cracking-life-lock-even-after-a-12-million-penalty-for-deceptive-ad-vertising-the-tempe-company-can-t-be-honest-about-its-identity-theft-pro-tection-service/. Many consumers are not aware that to prevent identity theft they can request a lock on the release of their credit reports from the top three reporting companies for free. The lock can be lifted case-by-case for large purchases or loans requiring a credit check.

3. E. Wyatt, "LifeLock Settles with F.T.C. Over Charges of Deception," *New York Times* (March 9, 2010). Retrieved November 26, 2010, from http://www.nytimes.com/2010/03/10/business/10ftc.html?_r=1&scp=1&sq=LifeLock&st=cse.
4. S. D. Warren and L. D. Brandeis, "The Right to Privacy," *Harvard Law Review*, 4/5 (1890). Retrieved January 14, 2011, from http://groups.csail.mit.edu/mac/classes/6.805/articles/privacy/Privacy_brand_warr2.html.
5. P. Strum, *Louis D. Brandeis: Justice for the People* (Cambridge, MA: Harvard University Press, 1988). Justice Brandeis served on the US Supreme Court from 1916 to 1939.
6. *World Population Prospects: The 2008 Revision* (New York: United Nations, 2008). Retrieved January 14, 2011, from http://www.un.org/esa/population/publications/popnews/Newsltr_87.pdf.
7. OLED is an acronym for Organic Light-Emitting Diode display technology. It is presently used for mobile phone screens and some very expensive televisions. It can be used to make very thin displays – about the thickness of three credit cards.
8. E. Dash, "Citi Says Many More Customers Had Data Stolen by Hackers," *New York Times* (June 16, 2011). Retrieved June 23, 2011, from http://www.nytimes.com/2011/06/16/technology/16citi.html?scp=2&sq=credit%20card%20data%20&st=cse.
9. A. Smith, "Millions Stolen in May Hack Attack," *CNN Money* (June 27, 2011). Retrieved June 27, 2011, from http://money.cnn.com/2011/06/27/technology/citi_credit_card/.
10. N. Bilton, "New Questions as Sony Is Hacked Again," *New York Times* (June 8, 2011). Retrieved June 23, 2011, from http://bits.blogs.nytimes.com/2011/06/08/new-questions-as-sony-is-hacked-again/?scp=1&sq=New%20questions%20as%20Sony%20is%20hacked%20again&st=cse.
11. E. Dash, "Citi Data Theft Points Up a Nagging Problem," *New York Times* (June 9, 2011). Retrieved June 23, 2011, from http://www.nytimes.com/2011/06/10/business/10citi.html?scp=3&sq=credit%20card%20data%20&st=cse.
12. C. McCarthy, "Facial Recognition Comes to Facebook Photo Tags," *CNet News* (December 15, 2010). Retrieved May 14, 2011, from http://news.cnet.com/8301-13577_3-20025818-36.html.
13. Ibid.
14. 42 USC § 1320, 1395.
15. 45 CFR 164.501.
16. R. Lin, "More UCLA Patient Records Accessed," *Los Angles Times* (October 30, 2008). Retrieved January 14, 2011, from http://articles.latimes.com/2008/oct/30/local/me-ucla30.
17. "The IRA Campaigns in England," BBC News World Edition (March 4, 2001). Retrieved February 20, 2011, from http://news.bbc.co.uk/2/hi/uk_news/1201738.stm. See also the *Sutton Index of Deaths* on all sides of "The Troubles," as they are called, at: http://cain.ulst.ac.uk/sutton/.

18. "Image of Bombers' Deadly Journey," BBC News (July 17, 2005). Retrieved February 20, 2011, from http://news.bbc.co.uk/2/hi/uk_news/politics/4689739.stm#.

19. *Surveillance Camera Players: Ten-Year Report* (December 10, 2006). Retrieved February 20, 2011, from http://www.notbored.org/10-year-report.html.

20. M. S. Schmidt, "T-Shirt Vendor Takes On New Persona: Reluctant Hero of Times Square," *New York Times* (May 2, 2010). Retrieved February 2011, from http://cityroom.blogs.nytimes.com/2010/05/02/t-shirt-vendor-takes-on-new-persona-reluctant-hero-of-times-square/?partner=rss&emc=rss.

21. S. Garfinkel, *Database Nation: The Death of Privacy in the 21st Century* (Sebastopol, CA: O'Reilly, 2000), 4.

22. N. Bilton, "Erasing the Digital Past," *New York Times* (April 1, 2011). Retrieved June 23, 2011, from http://www.nytimes.com/2011/04/03/fashion/03reputation.html?scp=1&sq=Erasing%20the%20digital%20past&st=cse.

23. Ibid.

24. Garfinkel, *Database Nation*, 10–12.

25. Ibid., 12.

26. M. Bowden, "The Enemy Within," *Atlantic Monthly* (June 2010). Retrieved February 22, 2011, from http://www.theatlantic.com/magazine/archive/2010/06/the-enemy-within/8098/.

27. V. G. Kopytoff, "Latvians Arrested in Scareware Scam," *New York Times* (June 23, 2011). Retrieved June 23, 2011, from http://bits.blogs.nytimes.com/2011/06/23/latvians-arrested-in-scareware-scam/?scp=1&sq=Latvians%20arrested%20in%20scareware%20scam&st=cse.

28. Bowden, "The Enemy Within."

29. Ibid.

30. Ibid.

31. Kopytoff, "Latvians Arrested in Scareware Scam."

32. I. Traynor, "Russia Accused of Unleashing Cyberwar to Disable Estonia," *The Guardian* (May 17, 2007). Retrieved June 23, 2011, from http://www.guardian.co.uk/world/2007/may/17/topstories3.russia.

33. Ibid.

34. T. Espiner, "Georgia Accuses Russia of Coordinated Cyberattack," *CNet News* (August 11, 2008). Retrieved June 23, 2011, from http://news.cnet.com/8301-1009_3-10014150-83.html.

35. *U.S. Cyber Command Mission Statement* (2011). Retrieved June 23, 2011, from http://www.stratcom.mil/factsheets/Cyber_Command/.

36. "It Is Time for Countries to Start Talking about Arms Control on the Internet," *The Economist* (July 1, 2010). Retrieved June 23, 2011, from http://www.economist.com/node/16481504.

37. Ibid.

Part V

New Communication Technologies and the Future

12

Wired and Wireless Technologies

"What is in the air will go into the ground and what is in the ground will go into the air."
(Nicholas Negroponte, former director of MIT's Media Lab, 1995)[1]

This phenomenon is known today as the *Negroponte Switch*: what was once wired is now wireless, and vice versa.[2] The transition began with the development of cable television in the 1970s, picked up speed with the diffusion of the Internet between 1970 and 2000, and became ubiquitous with the rapid growth of mobile phone networks worldwide after 1990. Television evolved as an over-the-air broadcast system between 1930 and 1970, but is increasingly a wired service provided by cable systems (and now over the Internet as IPTV). Telephony was a hard-wired service from its creation in the late 1800s until mobile radio phones were developed after World War II. The switch is not universal as there are still outliers to the model such as direct broadcast satellite (DBS) television services and telephone conversations using wired Voice over Internet Protocol (VoIP) technologies such as Skype and Vonage. The point is that once voice or media content is digitized, it can be transmitted either through wires or

Digital Universe: The Global Telecommunication Revolution, First Edition. Peter B. Seel.
© 2012 Peter B. Seel. Published 2012 by Blackwell Publishing Ltd.

through the air. Most non-satellite digital wireless transmissions are 60 miles or less (and less than ten miles for mobile phones) and almost all transcontinental Internet traffic uses undersea fiber-optic cable. Terrestrial "wireless" mobile phone calls travel via cables for most of the length of their connection.

Wired is not Tired

As we've seen in Chapter 7, electrical telecommunication began in the mid-1900s with the advent of telegraphy as the first instantaneous (speed of light) communication medium, and co-evolved with telephony after 1876. While telegraphy was a medium for experts trained in encoding and decoding Morse dots and dashes at rapid rates, telephones were a medium anyone could use.[3] They democratized electrical communication beyond the Morse-knowledgeable minority, and the telephone's early adopters were professionals and business executives who could justify the significant expense of setting up a telephone line. Early phone lines were set up as pairs, typically from an office to an office, and the caller signaled that they wished to speak by whistling into the

Figure 12.1   In the first fifty years of telephone adoption in the US, each new telephone required the addition of a separate line from the subscriber to the central office. Urban areas such as New York City had masses of telephone lines suspended over city streets. *Photo*: Metropolitan Postcard Club of New York City.

Figure 12.2   A 1960s-style portable television designed to receive over-the-air signals included a built-in "rabbit-ears" antenna for wireless reception. *Photo*: Creative Commons.

mouthpiece, as the line was live at all times.[4] All early telephone systems were hard-wired, and each telephone in a local network had a dedicated line to the central office. Until the development of automated switching systems, human operators sat at large switchboards and literally completed each connection by plugging an extensible wire into a socket. Cities with large numbers of telephones had forests of telephone poles festooned with hundreds of lines running from homes and offices to a local central office where the operators worked (Figure 12.1).

   Wires at present are typically invisible when laid under streets and alongside railroad tracks (unlike the New York photo in Figure 12.1), and there is still significant global investment in telecommunication cables

Figure 12.3   Wired to wireless: a woman uses a laptop while talking on her mobile phone. Wireless telecommunication and battery technology facilitates using communication devices everywhere. *Photo*: Author.

buried in the ground and laid under the sea. The available over-the-air spectrum is finite, but the ability to add global wired capacity is infinite, constrained only by available capital. The present transition on land mirrors what took place in the world's oceans in the 1980s: the conversion from copper wires to fiber-optic cables. As Thomas Friedman pointed out, the global dot-com financial bust in 2000–1 had a silver lining in that enormous capacity in fiber-optic cable was installed in anticipation of the growth of broadband services after 2000.[5] When the market for items such as online dog food delivery proved to be unsustainable, many dot-com businesses folded, but by then the global installed fiber network had expanded exponentially. While much of the installed fiber was unused or "dark" initially, worldwide demand for broadband online services such as streamed video had eventually filled that capacity by 2010. Not only were there more miles of fiber installed across continents and under the oceans, new technology made more

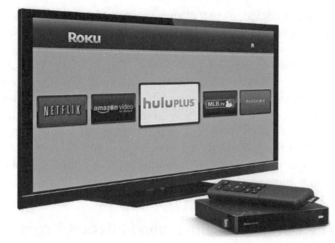

Figure 12.4 Wireless to wired: a Roku box routes Facebook and other online content to a digital television set that can display both cable and Internet content – the "telecomputer" predicted by futurists for the past three decades. *Photo*: Copyright Roku Inc.

efficient use of the already installed fiber-optic lines. In recent decades, scientists and engineers have perfected wavelength division multiplex (WDM) fiber-optic technology that uses multi-color laser light to expand fiber capacity by up to 160 times that of single-color laser systems. Thus a Skype VoIP phone call from Australia to Sweden is traveling under the world's oceans via a rainbow of light – voice by light.

The role of the laser in this process is an ideal example of Jacques Ellul's thesis on the unforeseen effects of technology. The first working laser was created in 1960 by Theodore Maiman at Hughes Research Laboratories in California based on prior research by Gould, Townes, and Schawlow.[6] First used as a tool to study the physical properties of coherent light, it was later discovered to have many useful practical applications, including vision correction surgery, optical-media devices, and in telecommunications. Red laser light is used to read media data encoded in microscopic pits on CDs and DVDs, and blue lasers are used in newer Blu-ray disk players. When the laser was first created, its inventors had no idea how prevalent the technology would become in daily life.

The modern Internet could not function at anywhere near its present capacity without the high-speed connectivity provided by fiber-optic cables that utilize multicolor laser light. The additional global fiber capacity installed prior to the dot-com bust has been absorbed, and the worldwide demand for bandwidth is steadily increasing with the explosion in Internet video content and other telecommunication services. Allied Fiber announced in 2010 that it planned to construct an 11,500-mile nationwide ring of long-haul fiber to link US telecommunication companies with undersea cables along the coasts.[7] The company is anticipating that trans-Atlantic bandwidth demand will continue doubling every two years from 2010 to 2015.[8] The company planned to partner with US railroad companies to use their rights of way to bury the fiber lines. The US has come full circle from the first deployment of telegraphy lines along then-new railroads in the 1860s to their descendants negotiating access to their rail corridors for the placement of new Internet fiber-optic lines linking US telecommunication networks to transoceanic cables.

The Diffusion of Broadband Internet Access

Cable and telephone company providers have a significant advantage over wireless services in providing Internet access. As wired telecommunication has progressed from telegraph wires to telephone lines to coaxial wires to fiber-optic cables, signal-carrying capacity has increased dramatically with each improvement in technology. The coaxial conduit used by cable companies is a "fat pipe" compared with the thin "twisted pair" wiring used for telephone connection. However, telephone company engineers have performed great feats of technological legerdemain in squeezing additional carrying capacity out of telephone lines to provide Internet access to subscribers. The added ingredient is fiber-optic cable, and both telephone and cable companies have been racing to install fiber lines ever closer to subscribers' homes.

The design of the network matters in that the local loops of 200–500 homes used by cable "television" systems are much like a "party line" network of rural telephone networks with four or five homes sharing a line. With the hybrid fiber-coaxial design in a series of neighborhood loops, Internet access will noticeably slow down as more users are online at the same time. Ironically, modern telephone networks that provide subscribers with direct access to the central office are less susceptible to the "party line" problem faced by cable broadband subscribers. As cable systems convert to fiber-to-the-home technology, these bottlenecks will be less of a problem due to an overall increase in network bandwidth.

For cable companies the solution is called *hybrid fiber-coaxial*, and it involves converting as much of each local network from coaxial cable to fiber-optic lines as is economically feasible. As Figure 12.5 shows, most local cable systems in the US have converted their trunk lines to fiber and

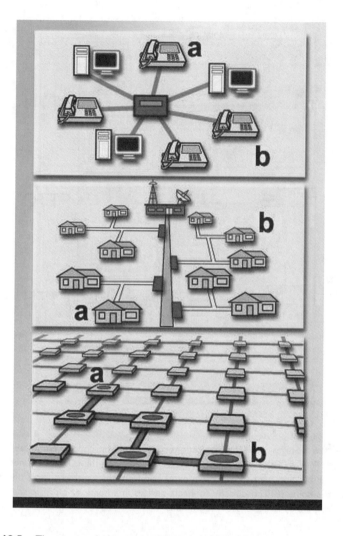

Figure 12.5   Three types of telecommunication system: a local telephone network at top, a local cable system at center with nodes along a central trunk line, and the web of the Internet at bottom. Making a phone call from point **a** to point **b** is routed through the switch at top and through the cable system's headend at center. A VoIP call on the Internet is sent through routers from IP address **a** to IP address **b**. *Source*: Diagram by Gary Atkins.

are now pushing out from nodes to install fiber closer to each subscriber's home. The process is proceeding in stages, as cable companies have the capital to pay for system upgrades (Figure 12.6). Fiber-to-the-node (FTTN) is the norm at present, with upgrades to convert to fiber-to-the-curb (FTTC)

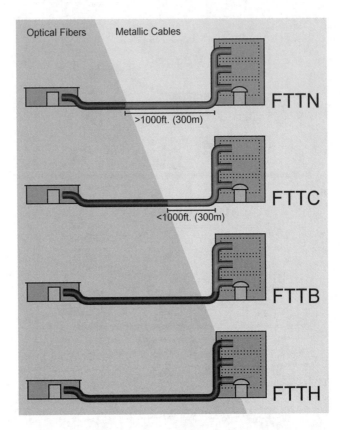

Figure 12.6   Stages of telecommunications conversion from copper coaxial cables to glass fiber-optic lines. FTTN is fiber-to-the-node, FTTC is fiber-to-the-curb (or cabinet), FTTB is fiber-to-the-building, with coaxial cable extending from the basement to all floors, while fiber-to-the-home (FTTH) directly connects devices in a home or office to the network. *Source*: Diagram by Riick. Creative Commons.

networks with fiber lines to the "drop" that extends to each home (the "last 100 feet" is typically coaxial cable). Fiber-to-the-home (FTTH) is the telecommunications "holy grail" that will enable very fast broadband connectivity for subscribers.

Fiber-to-the-home is found in over six million US households and the service is presently available to 18 percent of homes that are passed by FTTH cable.[9] FTTH systems typically offer 1 Gigabit/second connectivity, compared with 10–20 Megabit/second for hybrid fiber-coaxial systems. This level of bandwidth access has been described as drinking from a fire hose of data compared with sipping through a straw with

FTTN or FTTC connectivity. The demand for more bandwidth will rise as increasing numbers of Internet users access video and other multimedia online content. Can the Internet handle this level of demand? Netflix alone absorbs 20 percent of available prime-time Internet bandwidth as viewers stream movies online.[10] The real-time entertainment category (which includes Netflix) absorbs 46 percent of prime-time bandwidth according to Sandvine Research, and the US is not the only nation with this problem. In Canada, Sandvine found that Netflix streaming absorbed 95 percent of available prime-time Internet bandwidth.[11] This doesn't leave much bandwidth available for all other Internet users online at that time. These demands on the network not only affect the last mile in a cable loop, they are stressing carrying capacity on the Internet's fiber backbones.

This growth in demand for streamed film and television content is adding heat to the debate over network neutrality in the US and other countries with extensive broadband networks. To support network neutrality means that one advocates *no* restrictions by Internet Service Providers (ISPs such as Comcast and other telecommunication companies) on the amount of bandwidth a network customer can use. It also presumes that ISPs would be legally enjoined from restricting access to specific Internet content based on bandwidth. The ISPs make the claim that high bandwidth users should pay more for streamed and downloaded content. This contentious issue is being debated by both the US Congress and the Federal Communications Commission.

The Wireless Phone Revolution

While the rapid expansion in wiring the world was under way after 1990, a simultaneous revolution took place in telephony as subscribers shifted from landlines to mobile phones. In 2002 the number of global telephone landline subscribers was exceeded by the number of mobile customers. It appears in hindsight that the telephone should ideally have been mobile all along, but computer technology was not available to Alexander Graham Bell (or Elisha Gray, who filed his patent application for the telephone several hours after Bell).[12] Cellular telephone technology functions by using radio signals from mobile phones as they pass from cell to cell in a community. The signals are captured by towers spaced about every five miles, typically situated on hills or tall structures (Figure 12.7). The calls are forwarded via wired landlines to a Mobile Telephone Switching Office owned by the mobile phone company. The MTSO is where the electronic magic occurs. Despite processing the calls

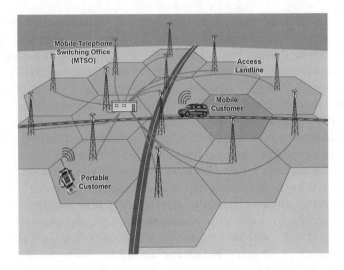

Figure 12.7   As a mobile phone customer drives from cell to cell, a computer in the Mobile Telephone Switching Office (MTSO) automatically switches their call from the tower in the cell they are departing from to the tower in the cell they are driving into. The towers are connected to the MTSO using landlines. From the MTSO the call is routed to the public switched telephone network (PSTN) and on to any phone in the world. Mobile telephone service is dependent on landlines that link the cells in a network to the MTSO and also on computers to automatically switch hundreds of calls at a time at each site. *Source*: Diagram by Gary Atkins.

being made by hundreds of subscribers at once, the computers in the MTSO sense when a call's signal is diminishing and then picks up the same call as the signal strengthens in the cell the caller is moving into. The handover process is so seamless that callers are unaware of it – unless they drive out of the cell grid and the call is "dropped." The process of simultaneously tracking and switching hundreds (or thousands) of mobile calls is beyond the realm of human competence and is thus handled by computer-based switching systems. Dr. Martin Cooper of Motorola made the first US cellular phone call in 1973 and the technology was dependent on computerized switching. The expansion of mobile cellular systems was also dependent on each company constructing a national network of cell towers and MTSOs. Only since 1990 have these companies offered a nationwide service in the US, and there are still extensive areas of the country that do not have a mobile phone service.

As mobile phones have advanced through successive iterations from 0G to 4G at present (Table 12.1), their size has steadily shrunk (Figure 12.8). Phones are getting a bit larger as more designs include a pull-out

Table 12.1   Mobile phone evolution in ten-year leaps, 1980–2020

Iteration	Time frame	Description and features	Examples
0G	1946 to 1980s in US	**Analog radio telephones** with small number of subscribers using limited spectrum.	Improved Mobile Telephone System (IMTS) and Radio Common Carrier (RCC) mobile technologies.
1G	1980s	**Analog voice-only cellular telephones.** Advanced Mobile Phone System (AMPS) introduced in US in 1983.	AMPS in US, C-NETZ in Germany, JTAGS in Japan, NMT in Scandinavia, Radiocom 2000 in France, and TACS in the UK.
2G	1990s	**Digital transmission** between phones and towers introduced. Data delivery using SMS, enhanced privacy, and improved spectrum efficiency.	TDMA-based (GSM) technology in Europe. CDMA-based transmission in North America and Asia.
3G	2000s	**IMT-2000** standard[a] features include Internet access and a still camera.	Optional features include a video camera, video conferencing, GPS location finder, and mobile TV.
4G	2009 – present	**IMT-Advanced** "smartphones" with $100+$ Mbit/s mobile and $1+$ Gbit/s pedestrian access.[b] Higher speeds enable improved multimedia broadband services.	Features include all-IP broadband, interactive gaming, "tethered" hotspot modems, improved video conferencing, and HDTV access via Apple iPhone and Android-enabled 4G phones.
5G	2020 or sooner? (would mirror prior 10-year jumps between generations)	**A global mobile standard** using smart-radio mobile broadband technology. Spectrum-efficient ubiquitous services on six continents.	5G phones may be wearable with voice-activated calling, HD-quality video conferencing in augmented-reality headsets, and optional location tracking.

[a] IMT - 2000 is an abbreviation of International Mobile Telecommunications-2000, a 3G international mobile phone standard.
[b] 1 Gbit/second download speeds for 4G IMT-Advanced mobile phones as defined by the International Telecommunications Union-Radiocommunication Sector (ITU-R).

Figure 12.8   The evolution of mobile phones, as they have shrunk from the first brick-sized Motorola model at upper left to smaller than a candy bar at lower right. Future voice-activated mobile phones will be built into eyeglass frames and watches. *Photo*: Anders. Creative Commons.

keyboard for sending texts and e-mail and larger screens for watching videos. The irony of the need to include a keyboard in a phone is being driven by the popularity of texting. For teenagers in wired nations, texting is the preferred mode of communication at home and school. In schools where the use of mobile phones is banned, texts can be sent from the back of a classroom where the sender is ostensibly reading a book. In fact, some teens have even acquired the thumb-typing skill needed to surreptitiously send a text while the phone is hidden in a pants pocket. Part of the appeal of texting for teens is that it is a private message channel that doesn't require speech. Teens also like the ability to send short bursts of text much like a 140-character tweet.[13] Texts can also serve as a sort of alert network much like the SAGE air defense system in the 1960s – I've seen students send an urgent text to a classmate that a surprise quiz is being given in a course, only to see the late student fly in the door a few minutes later.

Global Wireless Telephony

The International Telecommunications Union (ITU) estimated the number of cellular subscribers worldwide at 5.3 billion in 2010, and 940 million of these have 3G or better service.[14] With a global population of 6.8 billion at the end of 2010, the ITU wireless penetration figure indicates that 73 percent of the world's population subscribes to a wireless service and 90 percent of the population now has access to mobile services (but not necessarily a mobile phone).[15] In many developing countries a neighborhood vendor will supply mobile phone access for a fee. According to ITU statistics, rural resident access is lower than for the general population – 80 percent – but this level of service is a significant improvement on 2000. More subscribers are trading up from 2G to 3G services (with improved Internet access) with their availability in 143 countries in 2010 – up from 95 nations in 2007. Areas with 2G service are primarily in West Asia and North and Central Africa. India and China are nations with exploding mobile phone adoption: combined they added 300 million subscribers in 2010. If one solution to bridging the digital divide is the mobile phone, users in developing nations are rapidly catching up with residents of more developed ones.

The transition to 4G services is under way in the Scandinavian nations, led by Norway and Sweden, and in North America and the Ukraine.[16] However, the growth rate in developed nations is progressing slowly as mobile phone penetration now exceeds 100 percent. For example, the penetration rate in Luxembourg is 147 percent – which means that every resident owns an average of 1.5 mobile phones.[17] There are several key trends being driven by the rapid adoption of mobile phones worldwide. In the US and other developed nations, increasing numbers of user households are becoming CPO – cell phone only. They are discontinuing mobile service after observing that their 3G and 4G phones feature many applications that are not available with landline models. Why pay two phone bills each month when only one phone (the mobile one) is used on a regular basis? In the US, 18 percent of households are now solely wireless for telephone services (up from 6 percent in 2005) and have reduced their annual telecommunications costs by $400–$500.[18] This is not good news for landline telephone companies (if they do not have a wireless subsidiary) as their revenue falls each year as increasing numbers of US households go CPO.

In his 1995 book *The Road Ahead*, Bill Gates, then CEO of Microsoft, had this to say about the future of accessing information via the Internet:

> High-end telephones will have screens that display information, including yellow pages advertising. Various companies will promote terminals specifically for Web browsing. Cellular phones and pagers will get more powerful. Some of these special-purpose devices will find a place in the market for a few years, but in the long run almost all of them will give way to programmable, general purpose devices – "computers" – connected visibly or invisibly to the network.[19]

At the time, Bill Gates was an astute executive leading one of the world's largest ICT companies, but he was still fixated on the notion of Moore's law leading to ever smaller personal computers. One of Microsoft's primary markets was selling the Windows operating system for personal computers, large and small. What he apparently did not see was the emergence of the mobile phone as a "general purpose computer" connected invisibly to the network.

To be fair to Gates, in 1995 Moore's law had not driven IC miniaturization to the point that a mobile phone could be a small computer capable of multiple functions. The 2G phones of that era could display text data on tiny screens (see Table 12.1), but the notion of a phone browser was still being developed in labs at that point. In fact, it wasn't until Apple introduced the iPhone on January 9, 2007 that consumers understood that many useful and diverse applications could be loaded into a mobile phone. The first iPhone was introduced by Apple CEO Steve Jobs at the company's annual Macworld show in San Francisco and made an immediate splash as hundreds of potential purchasers lined up outside Apple stores to order one.[20] It was a radical departure in design from previous phones in that it had a bright, colorful touch-screen interface. It also had a unique display system for accessing features and content at the flick of a finger. Voicemail appeared as a scrollable list instead of having to listen to all messages in the order received as with other phones. The iPhone was the personal computer that Bill Gates had predicted in 1995.

It had its own unique OS and included a music player, a camera, Wi-Fi/USB/Bluetooth connectivity, and included quad-mode wireless phone capability. Apple sold over six million phones in the 15 months after they went on sale in mid-2007.[21]

More than 250,000 apps had been developed specifically for the iPhone by 2009, a key factor in its early success.[22] Apple tightly controlled the iPhone's technology and operating system, but it was a very bright move on their part to encourage third-party application development (each of which had to be approved by Apple to be sold in their stores and online). The success of the iPhone has led to many 4G copycat designs with touch screens and the option to create apps for them. Google entered the fray with its Android operating system for mobile phones, which has been adopted by many of Apple's competitors. This competition, combined with the ongoing effects of Moore's law, will push mobile phone innovation forward at a very rapid rate. The introduction of the iPhone proved that consumers will respond if products are well designed. They will also become very irritated if the supporting technology does not work as advertised. The success of the iPhone soon overwhelmed the bandwidth capacity of its initial carrier, AT&T, leading to many complaints about the service. The need to provide sufficient bandwidth for mobile customers will continue to be an issue for carriers as more users seek to watch movies and television shows on their phones. The convergence of television and telephone technology is advancing globally at a rapid pace.

The Social Effects of mobile Phone Use

The discussion concerning the social use of mobile phones is typically focused on distraction issues, but there are several pro-social points that are often overlooked in the debate. While there are many stories about lives being saved because the user had a mobile phone to summon aid, there has been less emphasis on their use in promoting a sense of safety while alone. A decade ago, I first noticed women talking on their mobile phones while they hiked alone in an expansive mountain park near our home. At first I thought this behavior was a bit odd, given that most people head to this park for the solitude and quiet that it offers. After observing this behavior multiple times, it slowly dawned on me that these women were sending a message to any would-be stalkers or assailants – "stay away from me, the person that I'm talking with can summon the park police if you threaten me." When I ask students in my classes how many of them carry a mobile phone for security, a majority of the women (and many of the honest men) indicate that this is commonplace. Carrying a mobile phone provides immediate access to assistance if one's car breaks down or if emergency services are required. In Colorado there are signs along the main highways encouraging drivers to report aggressive driving by others by simply calling *CSP (*277) on their phones. There are few statistics on how many accidents are caused by distracted drivers calling the highway patrol to report others, but the program does put aggressive drivers on notice that cutting off other drivers may lead to a ticket.

The issue of distracted driving is a real one and it appears to be a growing problem as drivers seek to multitask while operating a 2,000-pound vehicle at 50-plus miles per hour. In cars built before 2000 there were few front seat distractions other than operating the radio or cassette player. In modern cars there are myriad distractions: mobile phones, GPS mapping devices, radio/CD/digital music players, and now pop-up screens (Figure 12.9). Newer car models have voice recognition technologies for making mobile phone calls and sending text messages. Ford has designed its Sync technology to make all these systems responsive to voice commands, but research has shown that hands-free systems can be just as distracting as those that are not. In fact, mobile phone distraction can be equivalent to driving while intoxicated with .08 percent blood alcohol content.[23] In response, the US Department of Transportation has

Figure 12.9   The interior of a car with a pop-up LCD screen in the center of the dashboard that can display GPS map data and Internet-delivered content such as Google Earth satellite images of any location on earth. *Photo*: Author.

Figure 12.10   Texting while driving. This distracting behavior has been outlawed by several US states, including texting by teen drivers in Colorado. *Photo*: Author.

created a national campaign to fight distracted driving, which claims an estimated 5,400 lives in the United States each year.[24]

A tragic case occurred on November 25, 2008 when 9-year-old Erica Forney was struck by a car while riding her bike home from school in Fort Collins, Colorado. The driver of the car, a 35-year-old woman driving to pick up her own child at the same school, admitted that she had veered into the bike lane after being distracted by a mobile phone call.[25] While Erica's death was only one of the thousands of lives lost in 2008 due to distracted driving, it had a significant effect on legislation in the state and nation. Shelley Forney, her mother, became a national spokesperson for legislation banning the use of mobile phones while driving. Colorado legislators responded to Erica's death by passing a bill in 2009 banning texting while driving and the use of mobile phones by teen drivers in the state.[26]

Thomas Friedman's observation that this is the "Age of Interruption" was cited in Chapter 3. It seems that this has become such a problem in the United States that legislation has been proposed to ban using electronic devices while walking about in public. New York state senator Carl Kruger proposed making it a misdemeanor (with a possible $100 fine) to cross a public thoroughfare while using a distracting mobile phone or music device. This occurred after a young man listening to his iPod at high volume (with earbuds that blocked his hearing) was crushed to death in New York City in December 2010 after he failed to hear the back-up beeps of a large truck.[27] Users of these electronic devices are so fixated on music, text messages, or sports scores that they are oblivious to the world around them. A mall surveillance camera video posted on YouTube shows a woman so engrossed in her text messages that she falls into the center court fountain.[28]

Mobile devices are the "wearable" computers that we'll use in the future to access information while away from our homes and offices. The challenge for their designers will be to create appropriate technology that can be accessed in a heads-up manner so that we don't have to look away from the road or sidewalk in the process. The larger problem is that in attending to this added flow of visual and auditory stimuli, our human analog information-processing capabilities are being pushed beyond their limits by these increasingly powerful broadband communication devices. Perhaps the best advice for drivers who also text or call behind the wheel is to heed what the bumper stickers say – "hang up and drive."

Notes

1. N. Negroponte, *Being Digital* (New York: Alfred A. Knopf, 1995), 24. Negroponte states that he referred to this transition in a meeting at Northern Telecom as "trading places," but his colleague George Gilder insisted on naming it "the Negroponte Switch."
2. Ibid.
3. To be more specific, those who are mute or who have other speech impairments can use computers to translate text into voice to make "telephone" calls.
4. D. Mercer, *The Telephone: The Life Story of a Technology* (Westport, CT: Greenwood Press, 2006).
5. T. Friedman, *The World Is Flat: A Brief History of the 21st Century* (New York: Farrar, Straus & Giroux, 2005), 66.
6. N. Taylor, *LASER: The Inventor, the Nobel Laureate, and the Thirty-Year Patent War* (New York: Simon & Schuster, 2000).
7. "Allied Fiber Announces that the First Phase of its Long-Haul Dark Fiber Cable Across America Is Underway and Fully Funded," *Telecom News Now* (May 25, 2010). Retrieved January 10, 2011, from http://www.jaymiescotto. com/jsablog/2010/05/24/allied-fiber-announces-that-the-first-phase-of-its-long-haul-dark-fiber-cable-across-america-is-underway-and-fully-funded/.
8. Ibid.
9. Fiber-to-the-Home Council, *Next Generation Bandwidth Is Here Now* (2011). Retrieved January 10, 2011, from http://www.ftthcouncil.org/en/content/next-generation-broadband-is-here-and-now.

10. S. J. Vaughan-Nichols, "The Internet Belongs to Netflix," *ZDNet* (October 22, 2010). Retrieved January 10, 2011, from http://www.zdnet.com/blog/networking/the-internet-belongs-to-netflix/265#.
11. Ibid.
12. Mercer, *The Telephone.*
13. P. J. Seel, personal communication, January 25, 2011.
14. International Telecommunications Union, *The World in 2010: ICT Facts and Figures* (2010). Retrieved January 9, 2011, from http://www.itu.int/ITU-D/ict/material/FactsFigures2010.pdf.
15. Ibid.
16. All mobile statistics from the ITU, ibid.
17. Luxembourg for ICT, *ICT Development Index* (2010). Retrieved January 29, 2011, from http://www.luxembourgforict.lu/en/international-scoreboard/ict/index.html.
18. S. A. Bonser, "Getting Rid of the Landline Phone," *Examiner.com* (April 18, 2009). Retrieved January 29, 2011, from http://www.examiner.com/gadgets-in-philadelphia/getting-rid-of-the-landline-telephone.
19. W. H. Gates, *The Road Ahead* (New York: Penguin, 1995), 77.
20. F. Vogelstein, "The Untold Story: How the iPhone Blew Up the Wireless Industry," *Wired* (January 9, 2008). Retrieved January 24, 2011, from http://www.wired.com/gadgets/wireless/magazine/16-02/ff_iphone?currentPage=all#.
21. Ibid.
22. Ibid.
23. D. Strayer, F. A. Drews, and D. J. Crouch, "A Comparison of the Cell Phone Driver and the Drunk Driver," *Human Factors* 48 (January 1, 2006), 381–91. See also June 29, 2006 news release from the University of Utah at http://www.unews.utah.edu/p/?r=062206-1.
24. J. Hobson, "Automakers Will Be Asked to Curb Distracted Driving," *Marketplace* (January 24, 2011). American Public Radio. Retrieved January 30, 2011, from http://marketplace.publicradio.org/display/web/2011/01/24/am-automakers-will-be-asked-to-curb-distracted-driving/.
25. M. Whaley, "Driver Admits use of Cell Likely Led to Girl's Death," *The Denver Post* (May 7, 2009). Retrieved January 30, 2011, from http://www.denverpost.com/search/ci_12312532.
26. Ibid.
27. "Rise in Pedestrian Deaths Renews Call for iPod Bill," *International Business Times* (January 26, 2011). Retrieved January 30, 2011, from http://www.ibtimes.com/articles/105153/20110126/rise-in-pedestrian-deaths-renews-call-for-ipod-bill.htm#.
28. See "Girl Falls into Mall Fountain while Texting," YouTube. Retrieved January 30, 2011, from http://www.youtube.com/watch?v=umRXAkZ8Xo0.

13

Virtual and Augmented Worlds

A display connected to a digital computer gives us a chance to gain familiarity with concepts not realizable in the physical world … If the task of the display is to serve as a looking-glass into the mathematical wonderland constructed in computer memory, *it should serve as many senses as possible.* So far as I know, no one seriously proposes computer displays of smell, or taste. Excellent audio displays exist, but unfortunately we have little ability to have the computer produce meaningful sounds.

(Ivan Sutherland, 1965)[1]

The Sensorama and Morton Heilig

The first multimedia virtual reality system in the US was developed in the late 1950s (and patented in 1962) by Morton Heilig (1925–97) with his Sensorama system (Figure 13.1).[2] It was not computer-based, but rather a completely analog system that included the provision of sight, sound, and smell to its riders. The seated rider held onto handlebars in the enclosed kiosk and watched a projected 3-D film through a binocular-type viewer while the chair vibrated to replicate movement

Digital Universe: The Global Telecommunication Revolution, First Edition. Peter B. Seel.
© 2012 Peter B. Seel. Published 2012 by Blackwell Publishing Ltd.

Figure 13.1   Morton Heilig's Sensorama "ride" in use in the 1960s. He patented the 4-D technology that replicated multimedia rides through New York City and Los Angeles filmed using his 3-D camera. Similar 2-D systems are now in use in amusement arcades worldwide, but they lack the multi-sensory stimulation of Heilig's technology. *Photo*: Courtesy of Marianne and Katalin Heilig.

in a motorcycle or car. The 3-D films were shot using a special hand-held 35 mm movie camera of Heilig's own design (Figure 13.2). Other 4-D multisensory elements in the kiosk included sound fed through speakers on the sides of the viewer's head, a fan that pushed air into

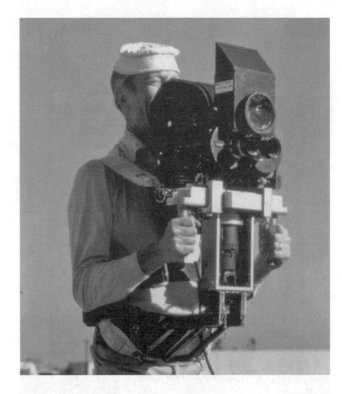

Figure 13.2   Cinematographer and virtual reality pioneer Morton Heilig demonstrates the Sensorama 3-D camera system he invented in the late 1950s that has a large periscope-type viewing lens positioned above two smaller lenses for the pair of 35 mm film cameras mounted side by side below. *Photo*: Courtesy of Marianne and Katalin Heilig.

their face, and even a nose piece that wafted representations of the smells encountered along the way.[3] The Sensorama system simultaneously engaged four of the five Aristotelian human senses: vision, hearing, touch, and smell – only taste was omitted.

Howard Rheingold visited Morton Heilig in 1990 at his Los Angeles home and discovered that he kept a (mostly) functional Sensorama booth out on the covered patio. Despite the fact that the 3-D film had yellowed and the fan and scent systems were broken, Rheingold reported that the system was remarkably realistic in its 3-D depictions of a dune buggy and motorcycle ride in New York, and helicopter, bicycle, and convertible rides in Los Angeles.[4] The ride in a convertible with a young woman named Sabina ended with a scene with another woman, a belly dancer who danced provocatively in front of the camera with her finger cymbals ringing in alternate speakers. Heilig explained to Rheingold that some of his investors especially enjoyed that scene since it was accompanied in the original Sensorama booth with the scent of perfume.[5] The Sensorama's technical complexity was part of the reason it was not widely adopted. The first system was installed in a game arcade at 52nd and Broadway in New York and promptly broke down the same day. Efforts were made to improve the robustness of the kiosk, but it seemed that the multi-sensory technology was too complicated for that era.[6]

A documentary film producer and cinematographer, Heilig was inspired to create the Sensorama after viewing the widescreen spectacle of Cinerama when it debuted in New York in 1953.[7] As a child I recall watching the same film in Ohio, *This is Cinerama*, that inspired Heilig in New York. It was displayed in a special Cinerama theater in Columbus on a giant three-section screen using three synchronized projectors housed in separate booths. It opened with a thrilling point-of-view sequence with the camera mounted in the front of a roller coaster that made some audience members scream, including my younger sister. I did not know the terms "telepresence" or "immersion" at the time, but wide-screen Cinerama films that filled our peripheral vision made us feel like we were actually riding the roller coaster. The sense of immersion in the places depicted in Cinerama films was a revelation to Heilig, and was the motivation for his subsequent work with 3-D filmmaking and multimedia presentation. Cinerama and Sensorama were early forms of virtual reality, but more profound immersive applications awaited the development of digital simulations.

The State of Digital Reality

The boundary between actual (non-mediated) and mediated human experience is blurred and becoming more so with recent technological developments, especially with augmented reality. Digital game expert Edward Castronova prefers to call virtual and augmented mediated experiences "digital realities," and I will also use this overarching term.[8] Castronova also makes a distinction between "scientific" virtual reality (see Figure 13.5, of researcher Ivan Sutherland in 1965) and "practical" virtual reality, as experienced by online players of games such as *World of Warcraft* and *Second Life*.[9] I would expand the universe of practical virtual realities to include high-definition conferencing technologies such

Figure 13.3   *Escaping Criticism* is an 1874 *trompe-l'œil* painting by Spanish artist Pere Borrell del Caso, whose intention was to add the illusion of a third dimension (depth) to a two-dimensional image. *Source:* Courtesy of Banco de España, Madrid.

as Cisco's *TelePresence®* system, shown in Figure 13.4. Note that Cisco's teleconferencing system uses a *trompe-l'œil* conference room table that seamlessly blends with similar tables in the monitors of those participating at a distance. The high-definition monitors are sized and framed against an illuminated background to enhance the illusion of telepresence. Ogden and Jackson define telepresence as "a series of technologies that allow for face-to-face meetings between [those] separated geographically," especially with large-screen high-definition technologies.[10] The concept of *trompe-l'œil* (French for "deceive the eye") is a visual technique first used by Greek and Roman artists to create the illusion of a larger space or 3-D objects rendered in two dimensions.

Figure 13.4 Cisco's *TelePresence*® video conferencing system uses high-definition moni-tors and an extension of the conference room table to create the illusion that distant meeting participants in the background are in the same room as those in the foreground. Each HDTV-equipped room costs $300,000 and requires significant transmission bandwidth. *Photo*: Copyright Cisco Systems.

The technique has been used by artists for more than 20 centuries for murals, domes, and stage sets that create the illusion of depth in a two-dimensional frame (see Figure 13.3). Humans enjoy seeing images that fool the eye, and this may be part of the appeal of watching videos and films in 3-D at present.

Another key concept in the differentiation of telepresence from traditional video conferencing is the notion of "immersion."[11] The de-signers of Cisco's conferencing system went to great lengths to design the table and place and size the monitors to enhance the illusion of immer-sion in this mediated environment.[12] Such an environment with multiple high-definition displays and high-quality audio exemplifies the concept of media "richness."[13] This involves the use of high-definition display systems to facilitate more complex messages that allow for the obser-vation of minute non-verbal cues with real-time feedback. In essence, the life-size high-definition monitors provide a level of visual detail that mimics the direct observation of behavior (and the minute cues that can indicate truthfulness or evasiveness) that we seek in daily face-to-face encounters.

While corporations and large organizations can afford teleconfer-encing rooms that cost hundreds of thousands of dollars, most netizens will encounter this technology using small webcams mounted on their desktop displays or built into their laptops or mobile phones. I would argue that the concept of telepresence should be expanded to include these lower-definition technologies, despite their comparative lack of the media richness found in high-definition systems. What they may lack in immersive image and sound quality is compensated by the *emotional* telepresence in communicating with friends and loved ones. We can imagine the emotional reaction of a soldier on a distant battlefield at seeing and hearing their children laugh or smile thousands of miles away via a webcam call. The concept of media richness needs to be expanded to include emotional richness using low-definition technologies typical of contemporary webcams and mobile phones.

Teleconferencing using high-definition technologies such as Cisco's *TelePresence*® or lower-definition desktop systems such as HP's *Skyroom*® or Skype are the types of digital reality most likely to be encountered in the near future by non-gamers. The escalating expense of air travel due to high fuel costs will lead to the increased use of video conferencing technology for professional and personal purposes. With increased bandwidth and the utilization of twin HD cameras, the future development of 3-D high-definition conferencing will provide startling images with remarkable realism for the viewer. However, even low-cost video conferencing technologies such as Skype will offer enhanced realism due to improved webcams and mobile phone cameras.

Sketchpad and Computer Graphics

The development of computer-based virtual reality technologies in the 1970s and 1980s was dependent on the creation of computer graphic technologies in the 1960s. They were led by then graduate student (and subsequently university professor) Ivan Sutherland. His career involves collaborative work with two generations of computer scientists and graphic artists, and his work in the field continues to this day. As a professor, he was a demanding mentor to many graduate students who went on to productive careers in computer graphics and science. Sutherland taught himself to write mathematics programs for the early Simon computer while a high school student in Hastings, Nebraska in the early 1950s. He was a programming prodigy considering that electronic computers had just been created in the late 1940s. He received a B.S. in Electrical Engineering from Carnegie Tech in 1959 and an M.S. degree from the California Institute of Technology in 1960, with full scholarships for both.

He started his doctoral studies at MIT in 1960 at its top-secret Lincoln Lab as it continued development of the Semi-Automatic Ground Environment (SAGE) US air defense system outlined in Chapter 4. The large round cathode ray tube (CRT) screen and light gun shown in Figure 4.3 were used by air defense officers during the Cold War to track incoming Russian planes, and were a key HCI element of the SAGE system. Using the light guns (later renamed "pens" as their shape changed), US Air Force officers would click on a radar blip onscreen that represented a potential target to be tracked. As the target moved, a second click on the blip with the light gun would establish its course as a white "target trail" on screen and would also calculate its speed. Interceptor aircraft would then be vectored to meet and identify the target (most likely a Russian bomber testing US air defenses).[14] The vector drawing process led to the name "vector graphics."[15] Controlled by IBM's massive AN/FSQ-7 mainframe system, the screens were an early example of the power of computers to process and visually display vast amounts of incoming information in a format that humans could see and quickly respond to.[16] Sutherland's pioneering work in computer graphics and virtual reality was supported by prior work accomplished at MIT's Lincoln Lab in tracking and intercepting aircraft using massive computer power, round CRT screens, and light guns to create vectors. Not only did the US Defense Department fund the creation of the Internet through ARPANET, DoD funding for the SAGE air defense system helped create the new fields of computer graphics and virtual reality in the 1960s and 1970s.

MIT professor Claude Shannon was Sutherland's Ph.D. advisor. Shannon had worked on Vannevar Bush's analog Differential Analyzer computer as a graduate student in 1936, and was the pioneering developer of Information Theory derived from the related Shannon–Weaver Communication Model.[17] It was a testament to Sutherland's prior academic record, as Shannon was an introvert who was very selective about picking his doctoral advisees.[18]

Sketchpad was Sutherland's Ph.D. dissertation topic, and it was the forerunner of all computer graphic systems used today. Its spinoffs include computer-generated imagery (CGI) used in films and videos and widely used software such as Adobe Photoshop and Illustrator.[19] The process of computer-aided design is familiar to anyone who has ever used a draw program to make a diagram in a document. In the Sketchpad program, users clicked on a point on the CRT with a light pen, then dragged the line to another point – the operator used a toggle switch on

Figure 13.5   Doctoral student Ivan Sutherland demonstrates his Sketchpad program using the TX-2 computer at MIT's Lincoln Lab in 1965. He used a point-and-click light pen to mark points on the screen and then connected them with lines. *Photo*: Massachusetts Institute of Technology.

the Lincoln Lab TX-2 computer to mark the points (Figure 13.5).[20] Once a drawing was created the operator could use computer geometric algorithms to make equalized angles (say at 30 or 90 degrees) and make lines similar lengths or parallel.

One key aspect of Sketchpad was its ability to use a clipping tool to resize a drawing. This technique will also be familiar to any computer user who pulls the corner of an image or diagram to make it resize larger or smaller in perfect scale. Sketchpad created quite a stir in the computer world at the time of its creation. Observers (many of them graduate students) had an epiphany when they saw a user interacting with a computer in real time. Recall that in that era most human–computer interaction consisted of the creation of batches of punch cards to be run on a large mainframe system overnight. Not only was Sketchpad a revelation in terms of graphic design, it marked a watershed moment in human skills augmentation. It led to the development of computer-aided design (CAD) tools used universally by engineers, planners, and

Figure 13.6   Dr. Claude Shannon was Ivan Sutherland's dissertation advisor at MIT. He defined Information Theory in a 1948 paper, and coined the term "bit" from "binary digit." He is shown here in 1950 with his electromechanical mouse Theseus that he programmed to navigate a maze and learn while doing so. It was one of his early experiments with artificial intelligence. *Photo*: Copyright AT&T Shannon Lab.

architects. Anyone who ever studied mechanical drawing in junior high school before 1980 (as I did) and struggled with T-squares, plastic triangles, pencil sharpeners, and technical drawing pens appreciates computer-aided design for its speed of use and the relative ease of fixing errors.

Virtual Reality

While an engineering professor at Harvard in 1968, Sutherland developed (with graduate student Robert Sproull) the first virtual reality system with a head-mounted display (HMD). The HMD was so heavy it had to be stored on a pipe suspended from the ceiling and then detached for use – it later became known as the Sword of Damocles for its tracking frame hanging above the user (Figure 13.7). The X-shaped frame contained sensors that tracked the user's head movements in space and then

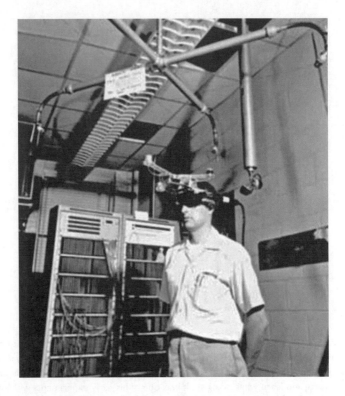

Figure 13.7   Computer graphics and VR pioneer Ivan Sutherland tests an early head-mounted display (HMD) at MIT in 1968. The X-shaped sensor attached to the ceiling captures the direction of the viewer's gaze by tracking the position of the subject's head in space. *Photo*: Massachusetts Institute of Technology.

correspondingly altered the visual image seen by the user. It was the first application of a digitally created world (although just a wireframe sketch at first) that could be experienced by the user as they physically moved about.

While the first computer-generated visualizations were very crude by present video game standards, they progressed from wireframe outlines to elaborate 3D objects comprised of visible polygons. The HMDs evolved into helmets that covered the top of the head and provided vivid color images with improved resolution. To enhance the sense of realism experienced by the user, VR pioneers Thomas Zimmerman and Jaron Lanier created a "data glove" that could be used to grab and manipulate virtual objects.[21] The goal was to create multi-sensory interfaces where

Figure 13.8   In the 2002 futuristic film *Minority Report* pre-crime detective John Anderton, played by actor Tom Cruise, dons data gloves to extract information using a virtual 3-D display from a database about suspects about to commit a crime. In the future the use of such visual databases may be verbally or thought-directed, but the visual effect of this virtual reality scene was memorable. *Photo*: Twentieth Century Fox Film Corporation and Dreamworks SKG.

humans could interact in computer-created 3-D environments with HMDs and data gloves that provided sound, vision, and touch interfaces.

From ArchMac to Google Earth

The pioneering work in computer visualization at MIT led to the founding of the Architecture Machine Group by professors Richard Bolt and Nicholas Negroponte. Better known today as the MIT Media Lab, it was then known colloquially as the ArchMac, and it influenced a new generation of computer graphics specialists. They advanced the concept of a cave-like media rooms where users could interact with computer-generated images projected on the walls and ceiling of the enclosed space. The multimedia environment included experimental technologies for voice recognition, eye-tracking, and "put that there" gesture recognition for the type of human–computer interaction that Licklider had first conceptualized in 1960.

Negroponte excelled at obtaining government and private funding for the innovative projects developed at ArchMac. The US Department of Defense (through ARPA) sponsored an ArchMac project that was personally memorable. It was called the Aspen Movie Map project, and the demonstration I viewed was a keynote session at a communication technology conference in the early 1980s. The presentation featured a large screen display using two of the then new optical videodisc players controlled by a small computer. It started with a map of the Colorado ski town of Aspen, and the operator indicated starting and destination points on the interactive map of the city. The program would then plot an ideal route between them. While this is a commonplace feature in online map programs at present, at the time it was quite an innovative concept. When the operator hit the start button we observed a driver's level point of view as we left the starting point along the route. Using on-screen touch controls, the operator could shift from the frontal view to either side or even behind our moving vehicle. To this point the Movie Map replicated Disney's Circle-Vision 360-degree movie experience that featured the images taken from nine 35 mm film cameras mounted on the top of an automobile and then projected in a large Disneyland theater on a 360-degree circular screen.

The first hint that this was not going to be another Circle-Vision movie was when we approached an intersection on screen and could proceed any one of three ways. The movie skipped for a millisecond as we turned the corner and continued down the next street. The next surprise was in a side view as the operator clicked a building and we saw a similar view in a still photo from the 1880s. He clicked again and the movie cut to a brief documentary about that location. We were observing seamless interactive hypermedia for the first time, and the effect on the audience was audible as gasps and exclamations. The map's designers had created a multilayered, multimedia profile of Aspen that included the filmed streets (using four car-mounted 16 mm motion picture cameras), each intersection filmed from multiple directions, 3-D diagrams and archival photos of key buildings such as the Wheeler Opera House, and the navigation map overlay. The *pièce de résistance* that drew applause from the audience was the operator switching between fall and winter views as the audience progressed down a street. The ArchLab group, led by principal investigator Andrew Lippman, had filmed each street and intersection in fall and then again covered in snow in midwinter. The key technology involved the use of computer-controlled dual videodisc players to quickly cue between scenes as the viewer progressed through the streets of Aspen.[22]

What excited the communication technology experts in the audience was the vivid demonstration of the use of multiple layers of media to augment human understanding of a place and its history. The layers of informative material added to the movie enhanced the viewer's appreciation for Aspen's history as a mining town in the 1880s and as a ski town in

1979. It was also a preview of the *telecomputer* of the future – the merging of film, video, and computing to access multiple layers of related multimedia information. At present, online netizens can experience a similar multimedia environment using Google Earth's Street View technology accessed via the Internet. Although the images are still and not animated, an online user can see in 360 degrees from each photo point and can virtually jump down a selected street from point to point. This is actually more useful than motion media in that the user can look around and see detailed views at each point. Users in Google Earth are also replicating 2-D satellite images of buildings with 3-D versions that pop up when that mode is turned on. Google Earth has always rendered the planet's landscapes in 3-D; now the man-made structures are emerging in 3-D as well.

Video Games as Virtual Worlds

Electronic games are almost as old as digital computing. Students at MIT, led by Steven Russell, Wayne Wittanen, and J. M. Graetz, created *Spacewar!* in 1961, one of the first computer-based "video" games. It involved using very basic controls running on MIT's first DEC PDP-1 minicomputer to aim 2-D space ships to navigate through space while shooting at approaching targets.[23] By present-day standards it looks extremely primitive, but hundreds of computer science students played the game or its descendants on computers and consoles. A complete history of computer and video game evolution would fill several books, so a brief summary is included in the context of the evolution of electronic games as virtual environments.[24]

There are many types of electronic games, ranging in scale from those installed on a mobile phone to games displayed on a wall-mounted 52-inch plasma screen. Early games such as *Spacewar!* ran on mainframes and minicomputers. Arcade electronic games made their debut in the 1970s and were among the first in the 1990s to include touch-sensitive haptic interfaces as the players sat on a mock snowmobile or jet ski. With the development of stand-alone game consoles that were designed to connect to television displays, a series of games was produced in Japan and the US that should be familiar with most netizens born between 1960 and 1990: *Pac-Man, Donkey Kong, Super Mario Brothers, Oregon Trail, Myst, The Sims, Dungeons & Dragons, Gran Turismo, Legend of Zelda, Grand Theft Auto,* and *Halo* (Table 13.1). Images from childhood during these years are often colored by vivid memories of electronic games played with friends and family.

Table 13.1 Electronic game evolution

Era	Platforms and types	Systems	Games
Infancy: 1961–72	Mainframe and mini-computers	EDSAC, Brookhaven, DEC PDP-1 (MIT)	Noughts and Crosses, Tennis for Two, Spacewar!
First boom: 1972–83	Early console and arcade games	Magnavox, Atari, Commodore, Sega	Pong, Space Invaders, Asteroids, Pac-Man, Donkey Kong, Super Mario Brothers
PC games: 1980s–present	Personal computers	Atari, Commodore, Apple, all PCs	Oregon Trail, Myst, Sim City, Dungeons & Dragons
The big bust: 1984	Console games	Atari	E.T.: The Extra-Terrestrial was released prematurely
Golden age: 1984–present	Higher-performance consoles	Nintendo NES-SNES-64-GC, Sony PlayStation 1-2-3, Microsoft Xbox 360	Gran Turismo, Legend of Zelda, Grand Theft Auto, Halo, Call of Duty, Guitar Hero
Portable: 1980s–present	Hand-held and in mobile phones	Nintendo DS – Game Boy, Sega Gamegear	New Super Mario Brothers, Tetris, Angry Birds
MMORPGs: 2000–present	Massively multiplayer online role-playing games	Personal computers: desktops, laptops, netbooks, and tablets	EverQuest, World of Warcraft, Second Life, FarmVille (Facebook)
Kinetic games: 2006–present	Interactive motion-sensing games	Nintendo's Wii (2006), Kinect (Xbox 360) (2010)	Wii Play, Dance Central, Kinect Sports, Wii Fit

Table 13.1   *(continued)*

Era	Platforms and types	Systems	Games
2015 and beyond	Collaborative, motion-sensing, immersive, 3-D, high-definition games	Nintendo, Sony, Blizzard, Microsoft, Apple (iPhone and iPad)	In development. . . .

Sources: E. Castronova, *Exodus to the Virtual World* (New York: Palgrave Macmillan, 2007); S. E. Nielsen, J. H. Smith, and S. P. Tosca, *Understanding Video Games* (New York: Routledge, 2008); B. Guillory, "Video Games," in A. E. Grant and J. H. Meadows (eds.), *Communication Technology Update and Fundamentals*, 12th edn. (Boston: Focal Press, 2010).

Video games have been through a boom and bust and boom cycle, with an initial boom cycle from 1972 to 1983 as consumers purchased early versions of home console games. In 1984, console game sales collapsed due to over-production and Atari had to haul truckloads of unsold game consoles and cartridges into the New Mexico desert and bury them.[25] The arrival of the home computer, with its improved graphics cards, proved to be a better game platform than the consoles of that era. It wasn't until higher-performance video game consoles arrived after 1990 that these systems made a comeback against computer games.

A golden age of electronic games started with the introduction of more powerful consoles such as the Nintendo Entertainment System in 1985, and the evolution has continued in ten-year jumps over 20 years with the introduction of Sony's PlayStation in 1995, and Microsoft's Xbox 360 in 2005. While some consoles became larger, miniaturization pushed by Moore's law led to the creation of hand-held systems such as Nintendo's Game Boy (1989) and DS. Nintendo also created the first interactive motion-sensing game with the introduction of the Wii console and remote in 2006.

Two Virtual Worlds: *Second Life* and *World of Warcraft*

Both *Second Life* and *World of Warcraft* are known as Massively Multiplayer Online Role Playing Games (MMORPGs). Both games went live at about the same time, *Second Life* in 2003 and *World of Warcraft* (*WoW*) in 2004.[26] They make for an interesting comparison, as the former is shrinking in terms of subscribers while the latter continues to expand, with over 12 million *Warcraft* subscribers in 2010. *Second Life* was created by Phillip Rosedale in 1999 after an epiphany at the annual Burning Man celebration held in the Northern Nevada desert.[27] He founded Linden Lab and hired a core group of technologists to create an online world where users could interact with others as avatars and explore the sights and sounds in user-created 3-D environments. It was an early Web 2.0 technology in that Linden Lab created the land and sea areas in the virtual world and subsequently the world's user community built almost everything else in it. The creation of user-generated content is a hallmark of Web 2.0 and will be so for subsequent iterations of the Web.

The ability of *Second Life* (*SL*) residents (as users are called) to create and then modify objects, structures, landscapes, and even their own appearance led to the development of a remarkable multi-faceted world that can be navigated by walking, flying, or using virtual vehicles created by residents. It gained national publicity between 2006 and 2008 as the number of residents (a mix of paying and nonpaying subscribers) climbed past 10 million. Large corporations such as Adidas, Toyota, Sony, IBM, and Major League Baseball became part of a land rush to create virtual spaces in *Second Life* where they could market their products to residents. Linden Lab claims that 23 million participants are presently enrolled as residents; however, in 2010 the number of active participants was estimated at 680,000, who spend at least an hour in-world per month.[28] Visitors can become residents for free (owning land and buildings still requires a subscription) and readers are encouraged to take a look at the many fascinating spaces in *Second Life* built by its participants. *Second Life* fulfills a dream held by many pioneers in virtual reality and writers of science fiction – the creation of virtual worlds known as *metaverses*. William Gibson's cyberpunk novel *Neuromancer* (1984) and Neal Stephenson's *Snow Crash* (1992) predicted the development of virtual worlds inhabited by human-directed avatars. *Second Life* is the first widely adopted metaverse, and it will certainly not be the last, as they will be used in the future for educational, teleconferencing, and entertainment purposes.

When the staff at Linden Lab were planning the roll-out of the game, they sought a new and innovative name for it. Staffer Hunter Walk thought of the name "Life Two" based on Milton Bradley's *Game of Life* and then suggested *Second Life* as a catchier title.[29] The staff objected, saying that critics would say that players "needed to get a first life" – which was exactly what several pundits said about the game. The irony is that another game developed at about the same time turned out to be the one that consumed the free time of many devotees.

Figure 13.9   The author's avatar in *Second Life* strolls through a 3-D weather map of the United States. Note the virtual rain falling in the state of Kansas in the center of the map. Weather in the virtual map is updated in real time with data supplied by the US National Oceanic and Atmospheric Administration (NOAA). *Source*: Author.

World of Warcraft is presently the world's most successful MMORP game. It has over 12 million subscribers and the third expansion of the game, *Cataclysm*, sold over three million copies at $30 each on the first day of sale in December 2010.[30] A one-month subscription to the game costs $15 (or $78 for six months), and the parent company Activision Blizzard Entertainment earned revenue of $4.28 billion in 2009. The company enjoyed prior success with games such as *Diablo* and *Starcraft*, but nothing compared with the adoption rate of *World of Warcraft*. The game takes place in an elaborately rendered fantasy world where players can choose to role-play as avatars against others or to play against the environment. They also choose to be either orcs or trolls as part of the Horde faction, or to be humans or dwarves in the Alliance. Players amass rewards in the game, including virtual "gold," which much like Linden dollars, has value in the non-game world. Game play in *World of Warcraft* is psychologically compelling, so much so that players can spend hours or even days immersed in this virtual world. This may come at the expense of eating, sleeping, attending class, or maintaining real-world relationships. Women whose husbands become highly involved in the game are known as *widows of Warcraft*.

The definition of "immersive" needs to be expanded beyond experiences that engage the viewer's senses of sight, sound, and touch to include game experiences that are emotionally involving. Game developers over the past 20 years have developed innovative methods of making them even more immersive. Vivid, realistic graphics, combined with surround audio (with original music in some cases), and emotionally compelling interactions with hundreds of online gamers creates a virtual environment that is so immersive that players are reluctant to leave. The city-planning game *Sim City* is relatively ancient history compared with MMORPGs such as *World of Warcraft*, but I cannot possibly explain why I spent literally hundreds of hours building virtual cities, subjecting them to earthquakes and alien attacks, and then repairing the damage. Along with fellow faculty members, I routinely have students in new media technology courses meet virtually in immersive environments such as *Second Life* so that they can experience human interaction as an avatar (yet with their own voice).

Lest any reader think that I'm addressing these comments to those under the age of 30, please reconsider. Twenty-five percent of active gamers are over the age of 50 and increasing numbers are female, a major shift in the demographics of game play over the past decade. The online game *FarmVille* has been very successful with Facebook (and now iPhone) subscribers. Developed by Silicon Valley-based Zynga, the game has 80 million active players, who grow virtual crops on their fantasy farms. The typical player of online social games such as *FarmVille* is a 43-year-old woman.[31]

The immersive appeal of a well-designed electronic game is not rational – even the ancient arcade game *Donkey Kong* has its compulsive players.[32] Newer games such as *World of Warcraft* are so seductive in terms of fantasy role-play interaction and the opportunity to amass rewards that they can affect behavior in the non-game world. Note that I do not use the term "real" world for the non-game one, as most serious game players would not describe their immersive game experiences as "unreal." Video game addiction is a serious issue, as many high school and university students worldwide will attest. A committee of the American Medical Association (AMA) recommended in 2007 that video game addiction be added to the index of psychological disorders, stating that up to 15 percent of US players were addicted to them in a way that negatively affected their daily lives. However, the group deferred the issue until 2012, stating that not enough peer-reviewed research had been conducted on video game addiction.[33]

As games become even more immersive in the coming decades with 3-D and holographic imagery combined with multi-sensory feedback systems and telepresence (driven by advances in digital technology enhanced by Moore's law), online games are going to become even more compelling. While there is increasing evidence that electronic games are highly addictive at present, I would argue that we haven't seen anything yet – and the Kinect system for Xbox 360 may provide a preview. The Kinect is a $150 add-on to the Xbox that uses a camera and infrared beams to "read" player movements, which are then folded into the on-screen game being played. It wasn't long until innovative computer scientists such as Oliver Kreylos "hacked" the Kinect sensor to create quasi-holographic 3-D images of himself on screen.[34] Scientists and artists are using the Kinect sensor to explore the merger of real-time video images of human players with game virtual worlds.

Electronic games have become an entertainment phenomenon, with sales of hardware and software estimated at $18.6 billion in 2010. Game revenues dropped from a high of $21.4 billion in 2008 due to the global recession, but Xbox 360 sales increased in 2010 due to the introduction of the Kinect system.[35] The future of electronic games is also closely tied to Moore's law. As game chips, graphics cards, and consoles have become more powerful over the past 30 years, game images and features have improved dramatically. Comparing the relatively coarse imagery of early 2-D versions of Mario Brothers with the detailed landscapes in any contemporary video game will illustrate this point.

Augmented Reality

Visualize standing at the actual stone wall on Cemetery Ridge at the Gettysburg National Battlefield Park in southeastern Pennsylvania. It is a hot summer afternoon in 2025, much like the one on July 3, 1863 when the crucial battle in the US Civil War occurred at this site. Confederate General Robert E. Lee ordered the army of northern Virginia under the command of General James Longstreet to launch a frontal assault again Union positions taking cover at the stone wall. General George Pickett, in command of a division from Virginia, considered the order a suicide mission, as his forces had to travel one mile across open fields against the heavily fortified Union line on the ridge.[36] Over 12,500 confederate soldiers set off from Seminary Ridge toward the east amidst the smoke and flame from cannons firing from both positions. By the time Long-street's men reached the stone wall, over 50 percent had been killed by intense Union fire from the front and both flanks. The attack faltered at the wall and the survivors withdrew. The defeat of Lee's forces at this crucial juncture in the war became known as "the high water mark of the Confederacy." Visitors to the site have had to reconcile the tranquil vista of green meadows with grasses swaying in the breeze and birds singing in the nearby copse of trees with the disconcerting knowledge of the unimaginable violence of the Confederate assault on Cemetery Ridge in 1863.

Imagine donning a special pair of lightweight 3-D glasses that allow you to see through them at the site of the battle. As you turn your head to look at the open fields west of the wall, a GPS sensor in the glasses notes your direction of view. You gradually begin to hear the sounds of echoing rifle and cannon fire through earpieces attached to the glasses. Dense white smoke drifts across your field of view, but you realize that the moving images are being projected on the lenses of the glasses when you lift them slightly. The hair on the back of your neck stands up when you begin to see the faint outlines of soldiers dressed in gray Confederate uniforms approaching though the dense smoke. You resist the urge to duck as they get closer and begin to fire their rifles directly toward you; the sound of gunfire is almost deafening. As you look to your right and left, ranks of virtual Union soldiers in blue fire back, and some fall under the fusillade from the Confederates. The ghostlike images and reverberating sounds of the battle are surreal as you can see through the movie of the smoky battlefield to the sunny fields of the present-day meadows. This is the potential of augmented reality. While such augmented audiovisual technologies are laboratory experiments at present, your children may be able to witness historic virtual re-enactments when they visit sites such as Gettysburg in the future.

Many innovative applications of augmented reality (AR) are being developed and applied in real-world environments. Luxury car maker BMW is using AR technology to teach new repair techniques to their technicians. They don special eyewear (with ear pieces and a microphone) that displays animations of routine maintenance tasks over the actual parts on which they are working. The worker advances to each step in the process by simply saying the word "next" while a female voice narrates the maintenance process.[37] The use of AR technology in a head-mounted overlay display allows the technician to use both hands in making the needed repairs. The repair "manual" is a series of 3-D animations that illustrates all facets of auto maintenance from the technician's point of view. Similar augmented reality technologies are being developed for virtual guides to national parks, for robotic surgery, and for video game play that combines virtual worlds with the real world.

Replicating the World in 4-D

The hubris associated with 4-D technology is that it assumes that providing sufficient visual and auditory information (and perhaps additional tactile stimulation) could at present substitute for the multifaceted ways that humans experience the world. During a recent visit to Yosemite National Park in California, I stood below the majestic Vernal Falls on a warm sunny summer day, immersed in a chilling spray as the water of the Merced River crashed into the rocks in front of me (Figure 13.10). The roar of the falls was tangible not only to my ears: I could viscerally feel the shock waves from the river crashing into the boulders that line the river bed. I sensed others in their rain ponchos (the prepared ones) moving past me in the dense mist and heard the shrieks of others (without a jacket or raincoat) as the ice-cold spray drenched them. A vivid rainbow appeared in the mist at the base as I climbed the narrow Mist Trail to the top of the falls.

I could attempt to reproduce this experience with a very large screen, a $200,000 IMAX digital video projector (or with 3-D glasses), water spray guns, and huge fans to blow it in my face, but it would always be a mediated replica of the actual experience. The Disney Company tried to replicate an aerial tour of the state with the five-minute "Soarin' Over California" multimedia ride in their Anaheim, California park.[38] Disney used a high-resolution 70 mm IMAX camera mounted looking forward on a helicopter to shoot low-altitude images of scenic areas of California. They filmed Yosemite Falls, surfers off the coast, skiers in the mountains, rafters on a river, and a golfer hitting a 3-D ball at the audience. Disney enhanced the effect of flying by lifting the entire audience seated in a large metal gantry so that their feet were dangling as if in a giant swing. As the helicopter tilts and banks, the gantry mimics the same movements to convince the viewer's brain that the visual stimuli are being experienced suspended in midair. The Disney Imagineers (as they call their creative ride designers) added other touches to make this a 4-D multisensory experience. Flying over southern California orange groves, the audience can smell the scent of oranges, over forests the smell of pine trees wafts toward them, and zooming low over the coast a light, salt-scented mist sprays their faces. 4-D technology is the next step beyond 3-D: the addition of tactile and scented stimuli to add to the illusion of a mediated 3-D visual experience.

Will filmmakers, ride engineers, and game designers eventually be able to replicate multisensory human experiences to completely immerse the viewer in an imaginary world? Could humans take a virtual vacation much as Douglas Quaid (Arnold Schwarzenegger's lead character) does

Figure 13.10   The 70-meter-high Vernal Falls on the Merced River in California's Yosemite National Park. The spray at the base drenches anyone who ventures up the adjacent Mist Trail to the top of the falls. *Photo*: Creative Commons.

to Mars in the 1990 film *Total Recall*? (Ideally without the "bad trip" experienced by Quaid in that scene.) The answers to both these questions in the future will be an unequivocal yes – and Disney's Soarin' experience is just one of the steps in that direction. Netizens can presently take a virtual visual tour of almost any place in the developed world using Google Earth's Street View, combined with Panoramio photos uploaded by travelers to that site, and view related YouTube videos.[39] We can only imagine how this technology might evolve in the next two to three decades as designers find new ways to provide information to netizens and game players that extend beyond visual and auditory stimuli. In the meantime, we will still seek out vivid experiences, such as the hike past

Vernal Falls, that engage all of our senses without the need for virtual technologies to replicate what is in front of us. Perhaps one day soon VR and AR technologies can match the realism of a good meal with friends, a ski run down a mountainside bowl full of fresh powder snow, or slipping into a soothing hot tub, but for now reality will have to suffice.

Notes

1. I. E. Sutherland, *The Ultimate Display* (Washington: Information Processing Techniques Office, ARPA, US Department of Defense, 1965). As cited by B. Sterling in "Augmented Reality: 'The Ultimate Display' by Ivan Sutherland," *Wired* (September 2009). Emphasis added in the quote. Sterling has parenthetically inserted into the essay the digital technologies in use at present that were predicted by Sutherland in his essay. Retrieved December 30, 2010, from http://www.wired.com/beyond_the_beyond/2009/09/augmented-reality-the-ultimate-display-by-ivan-sutherland-1965/. Much like Licklider's "Man–Computer Symbiosis" essay, Sutherland's then outlandish predictions of now commonplace multimedia technologies are fascinating to read.
2. H. Rheingold, *Virtual Reality* (New York: Summit/Simon & Schuster, 1991).
3. Ibid. The diagrams for Heilig's 1962 US patent No. 3,050,870 for the "Sensorama Simulator" are online at the Morton Heilig.com website: http://www.mortonheilig.com/SensoramaPatent.pdf. The site also includes the 1969 patent diagrams for an "Experience Theater" with an IMAX-like spherical screen and steeply banked seats that are prescient of Disney's "Soarin' Over California" VR attraction. Much like Paul Otlet and the Mundaneum, Heilig was clearly ahead of his time with innovative ideas that preceded the technical means of accomplishing them.
4. Ibid., 53.
5. Ibid. The aroma function was not working for Rheingold's trial ride in 1990.
6. Ibid., 59.
7. Ibid., 54–5.
8. E. Castronova, *Exodus to the Virtual World* (New York: Palgrave Macmillan, 2007).
9. Ibid., p. xiv.
10. M. R. Ogden and S. Jackson, "Telepresence," in A. E. Grant and J. H. Meadows (eds.), *Communication Technology Update and Fundamentals*, 12th edn. (Boston: Focal Press, 2010), 322–41.
11. Ibid., 323.
12. This is likely why Cisco registered the name *TelePresence*® as a trademark.
13. R. L. Daft, R. H. Lengel, and L. K. Trevino, "Message Equivocality, Media Selection, and Manager Performance: Implications for Information Systems," *MIS Quarterly* (1987), 355–66.

14. K. C. Redmond and T. M. Smith, *From Whirlwind to MITRE: The R&D Story of the SAGE Air Defense System* (Cambridge, MA: MIT Press, 2000), 81–2. Credit for the invention of the light gun is attributed to SAGE engineer Bob Everitt. Later modified by Lincoln Lab engineers as a light pen, it was a key design element in Ivan Sutherland's Sketchpad project.

15. Vector graphics differ from the raster graphics used for television in that the electronic beam in the CRT display oscillates between the indicated points of a line, rather than scanning from top to bottom in raster mode.

16. Redmond and Smith, *From Whirlwind to MITRE*.

17. The Shannon–Weaver Communication Model formalized the process as "information source (sender), message, transmitter, channel, signal, noise, and receiver" with a feedback loop in the cybernetic circuit. If messages were encoded using a binary system of zeroes and ones, any message (be it coded text, images, or sound) could be transmitted as digital code. This was the source of Negroponte's observation that content in the digital universe exists as "bits are bits," the Internet does not make distinctions. Shannon coined the portmanteau "bit" from "**bi**nary digi**t**" in his original 1948 paper on this topic. See W. Weaver and C. E. Shannon, *The Mathematical Theory of Communication* (Champaign, IL: University of Illinois Press, 1963).

18. Rheingold, *Virtual Reality*, 89.

19. Sutherland and Licklider were colleagues at MIT, and in 1964 Sutherland became the director of ARPA's Information Processing Technology Office (IPTO) when Licklider returned to MIT. As a key computer scientist at Utah, he was influential in securing ARPA grants, and the university was one of the first four nodes on the ARPANET in 1969.

20. This was the same TX-2 computer at Lincoln Lab that J. C. R. Licklider had used to learn programming and that led to his "conversion experience," as Rheingold calls it.

21. US Patent 4988981 was awarded to Thomas Zimmerman and Jaron Lanier in 1989 for a "data glove" that could track hand movements.

22. S. Brand, *The Media Lab: Inventing the Future at MIT* (New York: Penguin Books, 1985), 141. ARPA funded the ArchLab Movie Map project as a test of creating virtual environments that could be used to train special forces conducting military operations in unfamiliar locations. Video of the Aspen Movie Map is no longer available at the MIT Media Lab website; however, project designer Michael Naimark has a brief clip on his personal website at http://www.naimark.net/projects/aspen.html.

23. S. E. Nielsen, J. H. Smith, and S. P. Tosca, *Understanding Video Games* (New York: Routledge, 2008), 50–1.

24. There is a remarkable video game history timeline produced by Mauricio Giraldo Arteaga online: http://www.mauriciogiraldo.com/vgline/beta/#/145.

25. Neilsen et al., *Understanding Video Games*, 60.

26. W. J. Au, *The Making of Second Life* (New York: HarperCollins, 2008).

27. Ibid., 20.
28. M. Wagner, "Second Life Seeks Mainstream Adoption," *Computer World* (February 23, 2010). Retrieved January 22, 2011, from http://blogs.computer world.com/15638/second_life. The estimate of 680,000 active residents is from Linden Lab chief product officer Tom Hale.
29. Au, *The Making of Second Life*, 33–4.
30. Blizzard Entertainment. "'World of Warcraft'® Subscriber Base Reaches Over 12 Million Worldwide" (October 7, 2010). Retrieved January 22, 2011, from http://us.blizzard.com/en-us/company/press/pressreleases.html?101007.
31. T. Walker, "Welcome to FarmVille: Population 80 Million," *The Independent* (February 22, 2010). Retrieved January 22, 2011, from http://www.indepen dent.co.uk/life-style/gadgets-and-tech/features/welcome-to-farmville-pop ulation-80-million-1906260.html.
32. Readers with an interest in electronic games should see the feature-length documentary *King of Kong: A Fistful of Quarters* (2007) about two men who compete to see who can get the highest possible score in the arcade version of *Donkey Kong*.
33. L. Tanner, "Is Video Game Addiction a Mental Disorder?", MSNBC.com (Associated Press report) (June 22, 2007). Retrieved January 23, 2011, from http://www.msnbc.msn.com/id/19354827/#.
34. J. Wortham, "With Kinect Controller, Hackers Take Liberties," *New York Times* (November 21, 2010). Retrieved January 23, 2011, from http://www. nytimes.com/2010/11/22/technology/22hack.html?_r=1#. The YouTube video with two million views of Oliver Kreylos' 3-D Kinect experiments is at http:// www.youtube.com/user/okreylos#p/u/4/7QrnwoO1-8A.
35. J. Newman, "2010 Game Sales: It's Now Microsoft's Game to Lose," *Tech-nologizer* (January 14, 2011). Retrieved January 23, 2011, from http:// technologizer.com/2011/01/14/2010-game-sales-microsoft/.
36. E. C. Bearss, *Fields of Honor: Pivotal Battles of the Civil War* (Washington, DC: National Geographic Society, 2006).
37. See the BMW augmented-reality YouTube video at http://www.youtube. com/watch?v=P9KPJlA5yds.
38. The Soarin' Over California ride debuted with the 2001 opening of Disney's California Adventure park next to Disneyland in Anaheim, California. There is an identical ride (Soarin') at Disney's Epcot Park in Orlando, Florida that opened in 2005. To view a low-resolution 2D version of the film (without the sense of 3D depth or added 4D sensory effects) see http://www.youtube. com/watch?v=p6YISwoNrgE.
39. Note that each of these services is now owned by Google Inc. Panoramio was created in 2005 by two Spanish entrepreneurs, Joaquín Cuenca Abela and Eduardo Manchón Aguilar, as a means of inserting photos in Google Earth placed where they were taken. There is also a mechanism to correct the location of photos if the viewer thinks they are misplaced. I added a

photo in Panoramio of the palm tree on the island of Mauritius that was actually a cell tower (see Figure 10.6). A year later I received an e-mail from Panoramio that a viewer thought that the photo was misplaced and suggested an alternative location. They were correct, and I agreed to move its location, another example of the self-correcting nature of crowd-sourced online content. Google purchased YouTube in November 2006 and Panoramio in July 2007.

14

The Future of the Digital Universe

I like to think
      (right now, please!)
of a cybernetic forest
filled with pines and electronics
where deer stroll peacefully
past computers
as if they were flowers
with spinning blossoms.
      (Richard Brautigan, 1967)[1]

When I was a university student in San Francisco in the 1970s, local writer and iconoclast Richard Brautigan (1935–84) was one of my favorite poets.[2] As with many others excited by the promise of how digital technologies might augment human intelligence, I enjoyed the imagery in Brautigan's poem. Not only could humans peacefully coexist with computer technology, there might even be a symbiosis there, much as Licklider had described in 1960. Could Henry David Thoreau have gotten it wrong? Perhaps we were meant to live side by side with our machines, our computers, in virtual cybernetic forests (and not in literal ones such as Thoreau's Walden Woods), "watched over by machines of

Digital Universe: The Global Telecommunication Revolution, First Edition. Peter B. Seel.
© 2012 Peter B. Seel. Published 2012 by Blackwell Publishing Ltd.

loving grace." As I observe students stream out of classroom buildings on our campus and immediately turn on their mobile phones, I'm struck by the symbiosis we've developed recently with our portable computers. Ironically, their use in classrooms on our campus is largely prohibited due to disruption from ringing phones. When their phones are turned off in class, students now use their tablet or notebook computers to take notes or even confirm lecture content in real time.[3] More than a few professors (including myself) have had the somewhat disconcerting experience of having a student raise their hand to add real-time updates on a topic being discussed or even, gasp, correct a factual error in a lecture.

Visionaries are often depicted as walking around with their "head in the clouds." In the near future this will literally be true as the person on the street (and hopefully not sitting next to you in a movie theater) makes online search requests verbally into their Bluetooth headset (or wrist watch or eyeglasses). As wearable access devices with Internet connectivity are more widely adopted, their use will transform almost every aspect of human life in all nations, not just the more developed ones. Will our future coexistence with these portable personal computers be as idyllic as that described by Brautigan in his poem? This is, I think, one of the essential existential questions of the 21st century.

The technological trends driving the evolution of telecommunication and human – computer symbiosis have been addressed in earlier chapters of this book; however, a brief recap at this point may be helpful. Most of the world's computers are now linked through the global Internet, and net-connected mobile phones are the fastest-growing part of this network of networks. The minds and the personal creativity of their users should be considered part of the global network in a wired world where online participation will be the norm. The human – computer symbiosis predicted by Licklider is exactly that: a mutually beneficial relationship (at present) between human intellect and machine information processing and storage. Human participation is immediately visible in the form of websites, e-mails, shareware, social networks, tweets, and posted multimedia. It is largely invisible as search algorithms, Internet governance policies, corporate bandwidth restrictions, user tracking, and varied national network censorship policies. The planet's natural systems are also increasingly wired into the network in the form of remote sensing systems in space, in the oceans, and embedded in the Earth itself as seismic sensors. All of the world's radio and television broadcast networks are tied in through their Web linkages such as IPTV. The global network is a blend of fiber-optic and copper cables laid in the ground and under the world's oceans linked with a vast number of local wireless cellular, Wi-Fi, and WiMAX networks. It is what Nicholas Carr calls *the* "World Wide Computer" – in the singular.[4]

Wired editor Kevin Kelly wrote a widely cited 2005 essay about the implications of the growth of user-generated online content as the hallmark of Web 2.0.[5] Written before the explosive growth of social networking sites such as Facebook, the essay examined the "gift economy" of Web 2.0 sites such as Flickr, Wikipedia, and YouTube and described it as an "accretion of tiny marvels" that numb netizens to the "arrival of the stupendous." In the aggregate, for Kelly the billions of contributors to the new Web provided multiple views of the world that were "spookily godlike." He went on to famously conclude "we will live inside this thing."[6] For any netizen who has recently spent hours online playing a game or interacting in a social networking site, this view of the digital universe does not appear to be far from the mark.

If an individual is a back-to-nature neo-Thoreau or a technology rejectionist neo-Luddite, do they have the option of going "off the grid" in terms of disconnecting from the network? Of course this is an option, and one highly recommended for those on vacation or on a sabbatical from work, but for most information and high-technology workers disconnecting is typically an impossible task, even for brief periods of time. While the need to be connected to the network is typically based at present on interpersonal communication, access to its collective intelligence will be essential from a competitive perspective in the future. If personal, corporate, and national competitors have access to networked information that you do not, then the disadvantage will likely be yours. Young people understand this dependence on phone and data networks today (they look aghast at losing digital phone contacts if their mobiles are lost or stolen, as the numbers are no longer memorized). They may not realize that in the near future carrying their phone everywhere may not be a personal choice, but rather one dictated by their employer, their career choice, or the desire to succeed in a connected world.

In terms of specific technologies enabling this convergence of networks (recall that "Internet" is a contraction of "interconnected networks") artificial intelligence (AI), ubiquitous computing, intelligence amplification (IA), and cloud computing are central. The latter term may not be familiar to non-computer scientists, but if a netizen uses online search engines, seeks information at Wikipedia, or uploads photos in Facebook or similar social networking sites, they are working in "the cloud."

Figure 14.1   Google's massive data center in The Dalles, Oregon, which began operation in 2006. Each of the two data centers is the size of a football field; they consume enormous amounts of electricity in operating thousands of aggregated computers, and use prodigious amounts of Columbia River water in keeping them cool. *Photo:* Gary MacFadden.

The Future of the Cloud

In 2005, Google Inc. purchased 30 acres of land alongside the Columbia River in The Dalles, Oregon.[7] At first, locals only knew that an entity named Design LLC was negotiating for the riverfront site, which was near that of a defunct Martin Marietta aluminum smelter. However, it soon leaked out that Google was behind the purchase and planned to build one of the world's largest data centers on the site. It was selected partially because it was just downriver from the US Army Corps of Engineers 1,780 Megawatt hydro-electric Dalles power-generating station. By the time the center opened in 2006 it was estimated that Google had installed hundreds of thousands of networked computers in the two main buildings – so many servers that cold water from the river was needed for air-conditioning to cool the massive array. Journalist Robin Harris estimates that the two data centers contain a total of 1.25 million processor cores. Compare that with four in a typical personal computer and this explains how a Google search for text or multimedia can be completed in a fraction of a second from almost any location on earth.[8]

Google's 15-plus US data centers (with an additional 16 located outside the US) are just one example of the growth of cloud computing since 2000.[9] Microsoft has invested an additional $2 billion in its efforts to match Google's success at providing cloud-based services.[10] Amazon Web Services (a division of Amazon.com) is also a leading provider of cloud-based services to a long list of corporate clients that include Netflix, Twitter, and the online editions of the *New York Times*. Merrill Lynch estimates that annual revenues for cloud-based computing services will reach $160 billion in 2011.[11] Carr sees the growth of cloud computing as part of the evolution of computing from mainframes, to personal computers, to Internet-linked computers, and presently to Net-connected devices such as mobile phones and tablets. He draws a parallel between the historic development of electric utilities in the US by Thomas Edison and Samuel Insull to the evolution of computing from in-house corporate IT services to the development of cloud-based information utilities since 2000.

Augmented Human Intelligence

The aggregated human knowledge and creativity of the ages is available to all netizens – all one has to do is request it. Apple's iPhone has a voice-activated search application that responds to verbal queries. This was Licklider's dream in 1960: that artificial intelligence could be combined with speech recognition as an interface to augment the information-processing capability of humans. A mobile phone user voices a search question such as "Who is the author of 'Water for Elephants'?" into their Bluetooth headset and gets an almost immediate response ("Sara Gruen") from Google or Bing on their handset or headset. In seconds they have fulfilled a century of the collective information-augmentation dreams of not only Licklider, but also Paul Otlet, Vannevar Bush, Douglas Engelbart, Ted Nelson, and Tim Berners-Lee. For all but Berners-Lee, the speed and accuracy of the response would have exceeded their wildest dreams of information search and delivery.

For Paul Otlet in Belgium the goal of the Mundaneum project was an electronically accessible bibliography of all human creative work, including text and works of art and music (Chapter 6). Using the search tool (an enormous card catalog) and communication devices (telephone and telegraph) of the early 20th century, the process took at least a day to complete and return the response to the requester. His ideas predated by 50 years the development of digital networks that would automate the search process. Vannevar Bush's dream for his Memex system was to facilitate the creation of "associative trails" linking related information together. The information was stored on microfilm, and a series of electronic switches recorded the links produced by the viewer. It was never constructed, but the publication in 1945 of his ideas about searching and linking information galvanized a generation of computer scientists, including Douglas Engelbart and Ted Nelson. Engelbart created the Augmentation Lab at Stanford and trained a new generation of scientists who subsequently developed the first personal computers at Xerox PARC. Ted Nelson advanced the concepts of linked information beyond Vannevar Bush's "associative trails" and named them hypertext and hypermedia. Tim Berners-Lee melded hypertext with the burgeoning Internet and a simple HTML coding system to create the World Wide Web, which provides the mechanism to instantly route search requests from information client to information server. Larry Page and Sergei Brin devised an innovative system to rank search results based on prior hits and called their new company Google. Total elapsed time from Mundaneum staff providing telegraphed search results in 1930 to Google doing the same thing online in 1998 – less than one human generation, 68 years. The result is, I think, a watershed event in human evolution – the creation of a real-time, intelligence-augmentation network available to all global citizens with Internet access.

Artificial intelligence emerged as a distinct field of study in computer science in the US in the mid-1950s led by legendary researchers Marvin Minsky of MIT, Claude Shannon of Bell Labs, and John McCarthy of Dartmouth University.[12] The latter scientist coined the term which he defined as the "science and engineering of making intelligent machines, especially intelligent computer programs."[13] *Wired* writer Steven Levy notes that the early promise of AI was unfulfilled as computer scientists attempted to replicate logic-based human reasoning in the 1950s and 1960s. These attempts were not successful as they were trying to copy thought processes in the human brain that are still largely a mystery. Ironically, the breakthroughs in artificial intelligence involved what Levy called the creation of "new technologies that were decidedly not modeled on human intelligence."[14] Researchers developed algorithms that could mimic how humans made meaning out of large amounts of data – this is the pattern-recognition process at which humans excel, as Licklider noted. Scientists instructed computers to mimic this process in an automated trial-and-error process that utilized code that worked more effectively and rejected code that did not. The result is a machine-based iterative process that mimics how humans learn a new task and then master it. This is how IBM scientists programmed the company's "Watson" supercomputer to win the television game *Jeopardy* in 2011, beating two human champions in the process. The computer scientists had to teach Watson how to make sense of context in interpreting the puns embedded in the game. Watson was powered by 2,880 processor cores and 16 Terabytes of RAM in playing the game.[15] Massively parallel computer systems (such as Watson's and in the racks of Google's data centers) enable these algorithms to be performed at breathtaking speeds, which can create problems for us relatively slow-witted humans.

The Flash Crash and Other Dystopian Tales

In the spring of 2010, the Dow Jones company created Lexicon, an Internet-based service that scanned thousands of business news sources a day and forwarded the results to its clients. This type of news aggregation is familiar to anyone who uses RSS feeds to screen and forward articles of interest to them. What is unusual about Lexicon is that many of its clients are other computers which quickly filter the thousands of scanned articles for keywords and phrases programmed into *their* search algorithms.[16] The computers of these Wall Street firms would then search for patterns in the millions of bits of news data that might provide useful trading information. These computers would then execute buy and sell orders at a pace far beyond the ability of humans. While this type of automated trading has existed for years on Wall Street, news-scanning services such as Lexicon have ramped up the amount of data that can be scanned in making trading decisions based on successful algorithms. It is estimated that high-frequency, computer-assisted trading now comprises approximately 70 percent of total Wall Street trade volume.[17]

In the process of ceding a majority of trading decisions to high-speed computers, a few odd glitches occurred along the way. On May 6, 2010, one of these "glitches" led to US Congressional hearings and a Securities and Exchange Commission (SEC) investigation. The Dow Jones Indus-trial Average (the DJIA, which tracks the daily movement of 30 key stocks in the New York market) had already dropped 300 points that day due to concerns over the financial stability of Greece. At 2:42 p.m. the DJIA fell off a cliff, plunging 573 points in five minutes. Financial experts all over the world were shocked by the speed of the market crash and the lack of an obvious rationale for its magnitude. However, the market quickly rebounded in the 78 minutes left in the trading day and the DJIA regained the 600 points almost as quickly as it had fallen. After an intense, months-long investigation by the SEC, it was discovered that at 2:32 p.m. (New York time), a mutual fund company in Kansas City had executed a sell order for $4.1 billion in futures contracts using an automated trading program.[18] The size of the sale and the speed at which it was executed triggered other automated programs in hundreds of Wall Street computers and a massive sell-off stampede ensued. A single computer executing a rapid sale of significant size in a marketplace of automated programs had caused the "flash crash." Later in 2010, other smaller, but equally random, glitches occurred. In September, a US utility company saw its shares plunge 90 percent out of the blue before quickly recovering, and that same month saw Apple shares drop almost 4 percent without any rational justification. The SEC has taken steps to curtail these random glitches which undermine investor confidence in stock markets that utilize automated trading. The fundamental problem is that key buy-sell decisions are being made by computer programs that utilize complex AI algorithms. Humans cannot possibly keep up – until they have to clean up an automated melt-down in the markets. This is the dark side of ceding control to systems that use artificial intelligence in networks where an unanticipated event such as the May quick-sale can trigger an unpredictable concatenation of events. Just as Ellul predicted in his essays on *La Technique*, the seeming solution to this problem induced by technology is itself a technical one with its own flaws.

While the flash crash may have caused losses to some investors in the brief interval before normal values returned, the consequences of ceding control to algorithmic decision-making may be far more serious in utility and defense systems. This was basically the plot of the science fiction film *War Games* in 1983. In that film a North American Defense Command (NORAD) super-computer nicknamed Joshua controls the US nuclear defense arsenal. It engages in what it thinks is a playful game of *Global Thermonuclear War* with a teenage hacker (played by a young Matthew Broderick) as it leads the world on a path to accidental Armageddon. It was a cautionary fictional tale of how humans must be exceedingly careful in how they write crucial computer algorithms that are designed to run on autopilot, especially ones that have life-or-death implications for many species on Earth. While the film *War Games* was a work of imagination, nations worldwide are becoming increasingly dependent on automated systems to provide electrical power and to operate the international ICT grid that includes communication satellites. A primary concern of defense planners is that the first act of a hot cyber war will be attempts to take out the digital command-and-control capabilities of an opponent. This could be accomplished by hacking an opponent's computer systems that control key functions such as their power grid, launching massive denial of service (DoS) attacks on their networked systems, and, as some have theorized, aggressively taking out their satellites that provide real-time global intelligence.[19]

Most cyber war attacks are hidden from view and only belatedly revealed to the public. Computers that controlled centrifuges refining uranium for Iran's nuclear bomb-making program were infected in 2009 by a mysterious digital "worm" named Stuxnet.[20] Introduced into their computer network by an infected flash drive, it spread to 984 networked Siemens controllers and caused the centrifuges to spin at such a high rate that they self-destructed. The worm even included software that sent "all systems OK" data from the crashing centrifuges to the control systems to foil their self-regulation mechanisms. It was later revealed that the Stuxnet worm had been engineered by US and Israeli intelligence agencies to delay Iran's bomb-making program. Beyond the tale of foiling Iranian nuclear ambitions, the Stuxnet story should be a cautionary tale for any nation that uses computer controls for vital systems such as power generation and defense. Citizens of vulnerable nations built of proverbial networked "glass houses" should be very careful in throwing digital viral "stones" at others.

Predictions of Superhuman Intelligence

"The Singularity" is a term coined in 1993 by mathematics professor and science fiction novelist Vernor Vinge.[21] He was building on an idea first proposed by mathematician I. J. Good in 1965, where he predicted that the evolution of human – computer symbiosis would lead to an "intelligence explosion" by machines that would far exceed human intellect.[22] Vinge's Singularity describes the "imminent creation by technology of entities with greater-than-human intelligence" typified by:

- The development of computers that are "awake" and superhumanly intelligent.
- Large computer networks may "wake up" as a superhumanly intelligent entity.
- Computer – human interfaces may become so intimate that *users* may reasonably be considered superhumanly intelligent. (*emphasis added*)

- Biological science may find ways to improve upon the natural human intellect.[23]

Vinge predicted in 1993 that the Singularity would not occur "before 2005 and not later than 2030."[24] At the time of the Singularity the rate of technological change would become exponential and AI developments that might have taken centuries prior to its inception would take place in months or years, assisted by superhuman intelligence. His AI-focused vision of the future is inherently dystopian and describes a world where technological development linked to human competitive advantage leads to the possible extinction of humanity by the super-intelligent machines we have created. An algorithm designed to promote the self-perpetuation of *the* machine and the continual expansion of its intellect might lead to its perception (recall that by definition it would be sentient) that humans would view this expansion as a threat, and it would take drastic action against human life. If this sounds like the theme from the *Terminator* films, that is not coincidental. Another dystopian scenario is that millions of remote sensing devices placed around the earth provide data to the sentient Web, which may logically interpret that humans are causing irreversible environmental harm to the planet and then use its control over vital systems to rapidly reduce the human population as a form of mitigation.

Are these seemingly far-fetched future scenarios solely the product of the fertile imaginations of science fiction novelists and Hollywood screenwriters? It appears not.[25]

At a 2009 meeting of the Association for the Advancement of Artificial Intelligence (AAAI), a group of AI researchers discussed whether there should be self-imposed limits on the design and creation of autonomous systems that use artificial intelligence.[26] They agreed that the era of a sentient Internet is not likely to arrive any time soon, but were concerned about the creation of robots with the capability of killing humans. The US is operating drone aircraft in Iran, Afghanistan, and Yemen that have attacked opposition forces, but these are directed by human pilots in Nevada and are not autonomous.[27] Criminals or foreign powers might create rogue robots that would ignore Asimov's Three Laws of Robotics to not harm a human. AAAI president Dr. Eric Horvitz of Harvard University stated that, "Something new has taken place in the past five to eight years. Technologists are replacing religion, and their ideas are resonating in some ways with the same idea of the Rapture."[28] Such a critique of technology as religion would be expected of Jacques Ellul or Neil Postman, but it is a shock to hear such a statement from a leading AI researcher.

However, Vinge claimed in 1993 that there were two possible paths to the Singularity. While the AI path might lead to negative outcomes for humans, the path of intelligence amplification (IA) might be more positive and he termed it a "much easier road to the achievement of super-humanity than pure AI."[29] He called for the development of projects that would combine the power of human intuition with machine intelligence and that of human artistic creativity with computer graphics programs. The latter exists in all digitally animated films made since the first CGI-generated movie, *Toy Story*, in 1995. Much like J. C. R. Licklider and augmentation pioneer Douglas Engelbart, Vinge sees IA as a promising technology that builds on the human skills of pattern recognition and creativity in finding innovative solutions to global problems.

Inventor Raymond Kurzweil has amplified Vinge's thesis on the Singularity by extrapolating an extension of Moore's law past 2010 and incorporating recent developments in AI and IA.[30] His vision of the Singularity is more sanguine and less dystopian than Vinge's. Kurzweil's utopian vision states that:

> The Singularity will represent the culmination of the merger of our biological thinking and existence with our technology, resulting in a world that is still human but that transcends our biological roots. There will be no distinction, post-Singularity, between human and machine or between physical and virtual reality.

Given recent developments in extending Moore's law, Kurzweil predicts that the Singularity will occur in about the year 2045. He says that at that point individuals can load their consciousness into the machine and theoretically have eternal life. The good news is that for people alive in 2045 their consciousness may live forever – the bad news is that their new "body" might resemble that of C3pio from *Star Wars*, or that they will be "living in" chip 248 of machine 16 in rack 572 of Google's Dalles data center. Kurzweil's perspectives on the nature and timing of the Singularity have been criticized as implausible by many computer technology experts, including Gordon Moore, John Holland, and Jaron Lanier.[31]

Critical Perspectives

Jaron Lanier, well known in computing circles as a pioneer in the development of virtual reality, thinks the concept of the Singularity is possible in a cosmic time scale, but unlikely in the near term. His more

recent critical concern is the evolution of Web 2.0 participatory technologies such as Wikipedia as negatively exemplifying "hive mind," a
positive attribute for Kevin Kelly in his 1995 *Wired* essay. Lanier's
concern is that, as we pump personal information into the cloud in the
form of photos, videos, and personal data, we increasingly view "the
machine" as a living, breathing creature. As the information-processing
ability of machines increases rapidly in this century (as predicted by AI
scientists) and they acquire the ability to learn from all the data we've
uploaded into them, humans may cede godlike status to the network of
networks that they've come to depend on for edification, communication,
and entertainment. In his critique Lanier laments the loss of the contrib-
utory spirit of the early Web and its replacement by "a different faith in the
centrality of imaginary entities epitomized by the idea that the internet as
a whole is coming alive and turning into a superhuman creature."[32] Lanier
draws a comparison between the Singularity and the theology of the
Rapture – the end of days when only saved souls ascend into heaven – and
notes sardonically that they both have "one thing in common: they can
never be verified by the living."[33]

This critical perspective is not a new one and dates from Ellul's
concern that the development of powerful new technologies would lead
to their worshipful deification by humans dependent on them. Neil
Postman amplified this theme in his description of *technopoly* outlined
in Chapter 3 – a self-perpetuating system where "deified technology is
granted sovereignty over social institutions and national life."[34] Postman
elaborated that technology "does not invite a close examination of its
own consequences," a key point in that new information and communication technologies are marketed to society by emphasizing their positive attributes. Only after adoption by significant numbers of the population do the harmful effects become apparent, as with the use of
automated trading programs by large financial companies.

In the second half of the 20th century, one essential life-and-death
technology question emerged for the nations of the world – could a
planetary civilization survive the discovery of thermonuclear weapons?
The answer to date is, mercifully, a qualified yes, but there are still
thousands of nuclear warheads on missiles in underground silos and
beneath the world's seas, managed without mishap so far by vast
command-and-control computerized networks. The new survival question is whether human society can co-evolve with its increasingly
intelligent machines in a benign way. The concern extends beyond the
gradual replacement of human labor and creativity by machines. The
danger is that the decisions that cede control of our lives to digital

systems will not be made democratically – they will be made in the form of hundreds of thousands of small decisions that incrementally give control to autonomous systems governed by AI algorithms that affect human life.

My hope is that as humans we can utilize our collective augmented intellects to design artificial intelligences that are benevolent and protective of all forms of organic life. I am optimistic that we can achieve this world in conjunction with "machines of loving grace" as described by Richard Brautigan. If we become as wise as we are smart, we'll design intelligent systems that support the long-term health of all life on the planet. There are key *ethical* decisions to be made along the path ahead, and my hope is that we'll have the collective wisdom as a global society to make enlightened ones. The Web will be a key mechanism for communicating globally about the design of these systems and making intelligent decisions about their implementation – the medium will ideally be the mediator, to paraphrase McLuhan.

A Humanistic Perspective

Our greatest challenge in the future, as we come to increasingly rely upon augmented intelligence, will be to maintain the unique qualities that define us as humans. Some are admirable, such as charity and compassion for others; others are less so: innate human aggression and hunter-killer instincts that have led to the survival of our species over millennia. Lest you think that these have been sublimated by civilization and socialization, watch a teenager play a first-person shooter game such as *Halo* on a computer game console.

Humans are creatures with narrow bandwidth input and output capabilities compared to networked computers. We each have magical intellectual abilities to creatively process information, but we'll need to learn to deal with multiple distractions in a world increasingly filled with screens, noise, and the siren songs of entertainment. Humans will consciously need to avoid overstimulation in a multimedia-saturated future that we can barely imagine by squaring the noise of contemporary cacophonous environments. We will have to adapt by consciously training ourselves to selectively disconnect: by seeking time to reflect by meditation, conversing with family and friends, playing music, and seeking peace in quiet places. In fact, recent research shows that daily meditation may enhance the functioning of the human brain in ways that are complementary to augmented intelligence.[35] The search for improved quality of life in the age of information saturation may be typified by spending an hour laughing with friends over a meal. To take a mobile call in the middle of this experience should become the epitome of rudeness. We will spend so much of each workday jacked into the network, we may need to schedule time each day to be offline. We may need to write employment contracts that expressly identify how much time each week we're expected to be connected for work purposes (as some individuals working in information and communication technology professions are doing now).

In a wired world where netizens sit at computer and television screens for eight – ten – twelve – fifteen hours each day, we will have to find ways to interact with information without becoming sedentary. Recent studies have demonstrated that this aspect of immersion in the mediated world may be more lethal to society far sooner than any dystopian Singularity. A group of UK researchers published a report in 2011 that found that middle-aged men who spend more than four hours a day sitting in front of a screen were 50 percent more likely to die prematurely of cardiovascular disease than those in a control group.[36] A sobering discovery was that being somewhat physically active for the sedentary group did not significantly improve their health. This four-year study of 4,512 men was just the latest in a series of reports establishing a direct correlation between sedentary screen time and deleterious health effects. We need exercise each day to stay mentally sharp and physically fit considering the increasing amount of time that we spend online. Perhaps more future human – computer interfaces will need to be Wii-enabled to require physical activity during our hours of daily screen time.

Humans must be vigilant about monitoring the negative social effects of ever more pervasive information and communication technologies. The term *informed ambivalence* describes how I hope you will view these technologies in the future. By *informed*, readers should understand not only the capabilities of what technology can accomplish at present, but also the need to know technological history (one purpose of this book) and to consider what the future applications of ICT might be. *Ambivalence* provides the perspective to think critically about the present and future effects of the adoption of these technologies. New technologies are always marketed with the "blue sky" perspective of beneficial social effects – only after adoption do we understand their negative effects. My hope is that each reader of this book will view the future of our species with excitement about our augmented powers of observation and communication. We have examined the progress accomplished in the past 50 years in terms of enhancing human intelligence and can only imagine how IA will advance in the next 50. This view will be tempered by the need to critically examine the implications of the coming symbiosis of human and machine intelligence and seek to mitigate their pathological effects as we co-evolve in this century.

notes

1. R. Brautigan, *All Watched Over by Machines of Loving Grace* (San Francisco: The Communication Company, 1967). This was first published in a limited edition of hand-distributed copies. The poem was reprinted in *Richard Brautigan's Trout Fishing in America; The Pill Versus the Spring Hill Mine Disaster; and, In Watermelon Sugar* anthology (Boston: Houghton Mifflin/Seymour Lawrence, 1968). Excerpt copyright 1968 by Richard Brautigan, reprinted by permission of Houghton Mifflin Harcourt. All rights reserved.
2. I enrolled in the fall of 1972 as a photography student at the San Francisco Art Institute on Russian Hill near North Beach.
3. There is a mordant joke circulating online that states that a college education is now a process of transferring information (via PowerPoint) from the professor's laptop computer to the student's notebook PC, without passing through the mind of either person.
4. N. Carr, *The Big Switch: Rewiring the World from Edison to Google* (New York. W. W. Norton, 2008), 113.
5. K. Kelly, "We Are the Web," *Wired* (August 2005). Retrieved January 15, 2011, from http://www.wired.com/wired/archive/13.08/tech.html. This is a very interesting article about the evolution of Web 2.0 as the era began.
6. Ibid.
7. Carr, *The Big Switch*, 64.
8. R. Harris, "Google's 650,000-Core Warehouse-Size Computer," *ZDNet* (October 23, 2007). Retrieved December 22, 2010, from http://www.zdnet.com/blog/storage/googles-650000-core-warehouse-size-computer/213#.
9. R. Miller, "Google Data Center FAQ," *DataCenter Knowledge* (March 23, 2008). Retrieved December 24, 2010, from http://www.datacenterknowledge.com/archives/2008/03/27/google-data-center-faq/. These figures are estimates by Miller as Google keeps the actual number of its worldwide data centers confidential as a trade secret.
10. Carr, *The Big Switch*, 82.
11. M. Harris, "You Can Fire Us on a Minute's Notice," *The Guardian* (March 26, 2009). Retrieved January 15, 2011, from http://www.guardian.co.uk/technology/2009/mar/26/amazon-adam-selipsky#.
12. J. Skillings, "Getting Machines to Think Like Us," *CNet News* (July 3, 2006). Retrieved December 23, 2010, from http://news.cnet.com/Getting-machines-to-think-like-us/2008-11394_3-6090207.html.

13. J. McCarthy, *What Is Artificial Intelligence?* (November 12, 2007). Retrieved December 23, 2010, from http://www-formal.stanford.edu/jmc/whatisai/whatisai.html. This website is a useful primer on AI for the interested layperson.

14. S. Levy, "The A.I. Revolution," *Wired* (January 2011). Retrieved August 30, 2011, from http://www.wired.com/magazine/2010/12/ff_ai_essay_airevolution/.

15. M. P. Mills, "IBM's Watson Jeopardy Stunt Unleashes a Third Great Cycle in Computing," *Forbes* (February 21, 2011). Retrieved February 21, 2011, from http://blogs.forbes.com/markpmills/2011/02/21/ibms-watson-jeopardy-stunt-unleashes-a-third-great-cycle-in-computing/.

16. F. Salmon and J. Stokes, "Algorithms Take Control of Wall Street," *Wired* (January 2011). Retrieved August 30, 2011, from http://www.wired.com/magazine/2010/12/ff_ai_flashtrading/all/1.

17. Ibid.

18. G. Bowley, "Lone $4.1 Billion Sale Led to 'Flash Crash' in May," *New York Times* (October 1, 2010). Retrieved December 26, 2010, from http://www.nytimes.com/2010/10/02/business/02flash.html?_r=2&scp=1&sq=flash+crash&st=nyt.

19. W. Scott, M. Coumatos, W. Birns, and G. Noory, *Space Wars: The First Six Hours of World War III* (New York: Forge Books, 2007).

20. W. J. Broad, J. Markoff, and D. E. Sanger, "Israel Tests on Worm Called Crucial in Iran Nuclear Delay," *New York Times* (January 15, 2011). Retrieved January 16, 2011, from http://www.nytimes.com/2011/01/16/world/middleeast/16stuxnet.html?hp.

21. V. Vinge, *The Coming Technological Singularity: How to Survive in the Post-Human Era.* Paper presented to the VISION-21 Symposium, NASA Lewis Research Center and the Ohio Aerospace Institute (1993). Retrieved December 22, 2010, from http://www-rohan.sdsu.edu/faculty/vinge/misc/singularity.html. An interesting annotated version is online at http://www-rohan.sdsu.edu/faculty/vinge/misc/WER2.html.

22. I. J. Good, "Speculations Concerning the First Ultra-Intelligent Machine," in F. L. Alt and M. Rubinoff (eds.), *Advances in Computers*, 6 (1965), 31–88.

23. Vinge, *The Coming Technological Singularity.*

24. Ibid.

25. G. Zorpette, "Waiting for the Rapture," *IEEE Spectrum* (June 2008). Retrieved January 15, 2011, from http://spectrum.ieee.org/biomedical/ethics/waiting-for-the-rapture/2. The complete June 2008 *IEEE Spectrum* issue on Singularity: http://spectrum.ieee.org/static/singularity.

26. J. Markoff, "Scientists Worry Machines May Outsmart Man," *New York Times* (July 26, 2009). Retrieved January 12, 2011, from http://www.nytimes.com/2009/07/26/science/26robot.html.

27. In fact, after a series of drone missions that killed non-combatant civilians in Afghanistan, the rules of engagement now require that a soldier on the ground confirm the target as hostile prior to an air attack.
28. Zorpette, "Waiting for the Rapture."
29. Vinge, *The Coming Technological Singularity*.
30. R. Kurzweil, *The Singularity Is Near* (New York: Viking, 2005).
31. "Tech Luminaries Address Singularity," *IEEE Spectrum* (June 2008). Retrieved January 15, 2011, from http://spectrum.ieee.org/computing/hardware/tech-luminaries-address-singularity. This is an enlightening pro and con survey of ten informed experts on the subject, including Gordon Moore.
32. J. Lanier, *You Are Not a Gadget* (New York: Knopf, 2010), 14. Lanier also makes a convincing case that one of the fundamental flaws of the Internet is the ability to post content anonymously – which has promoted harmful online behavior such as cyber-bullying.
33. Ibid., 26.
34. N. Postman, *Technopoly: The Surrender of Culture to Technology* (New York: Vintage, 1992), 71.
35. S. N. Bahnoo, "How Meditation May Change the Brain," *New York Times* (January 28, 2011). Retrieved January 30, 2011, from http://well.blogs.nytimes.com/2011/01/28/how-meditation-may-change-the-brain/?src=me&ref=general#.
36. E. Stamatakis, M. Hamer, and D. W. Dunstan, "Screen-Based Entertainment Time, All-Cause Mortality, and Cardiovascular Events," *Journal of the American College of Cardiology* 57 (2011), 292–9. Retrieved January 16, 2011, from http://content.onlinejacc.org/cgi/content/abstract/57/3/292.

Index

Digital Universe: The Global Telecommunication Revolution, First Edition. Peter B. Seel.
© 2012 Peter B. Seel. Published 2012 by Blackwell Publishing Ltd.